*Calvin and the Foundations
of Modern Politics*

CALVIN *and the* FOUNDATIONS *of* MODERN POLITICS

Ralph C. Hancock

Cornell University Press

ITHACA AND LONDON

First published 1989 by Cornell University Press.

International Standard Book Number 0-8014-2118-7
Library of Congress Catalog Card Number 88-47931
Printed in the United States of America
Librarians: Library of Congress cataloging information
appears on the last page of the book.

The paper in this book is acid-free and meets the guidelines for
permanence and durability of the Committee on Production Guidelines
for Book Longevity of the Council on Library Resources.

To Julie

Contents

Preface

I first became aware of the problem of the relationship between Calvinism and modern political thought in reflecting on the Puritan background of American political idealism, on what Tocqueville calls the "marvelous combination" in America of the "spirit of religion" and the "spirit of freedom." I found this combination to be a puzzle as well as a marvel, since American liberalism obviously owes much to a distinctly rationalistic and secular theory of natural rights founded by Hobbes and refined by Locke in direct opposition to the political claims of religion. How could a religious worldview provide a motive for the pursuit of distinctly secular ends?

It may be that this American mingling of religion and rationalism, this fusion of Calvin and Locke, was no more than a confusion, as most scholars now seem to assume. I was not sure. Is it not possible that a certain understanding of reason and a certain interpretation of revelation jointly inspire a single project?

If the activity of natural reason itself is understood as the essence of the best way of life, as in the classical Socratic tradition, then our answer would be no. But modern rationalism cannot be identified with openness to reason as an end in itself. Rather, it implies a definite, programmatic hostility to any nonrational authority and a commitment to an antispeculative method as a means to the indefinite expansion of human freedom. Rationalism represents not the freedom of the intellect to articulate or contemplate the distinctive goodness of ideas but the demand that the mind be deployed methodically against all limitations on the power of humanity as a whole. Since defining the end of human action and articulating its goodness would set limits on human beings and subordinate them to something beyond their power, rationalists give a much fuller and more definite account of the obstacles (prejudices, traditions, institutions) standing between them and their "ideal" than of the nature of the ideal itself (e.g., freedom, progress, liberation). Modern rationalism is a method and a means, not a way of life; secularism is not so much an end as a process. Thus the project of *rationalism* is not only distinct from but directly opposed to classical *reason* as the pursuit of the best way of life by nature.

I claim no originality for this statement of the opposition between classical reason and modern rationalism, and my main purpose is not to demonstrate or expand this insight. Rather, I rely on the contrast between reason and rationalism to question the contrast between rationalism and revelation. I attempt to show that beneath the obvious and direct opposition between modern rationalism and Christianity lies the potential of a profound convergence, a potential that can be most clearly discerned not in the possibly confused rhetoric of Calvinist Lockeans but in John Calvin's rigorous reading of Christianity.

To defend this view I must show that Calvin not only attacks the classical, teleogical conception of reason but is fundamentally open to the authority of reason with respect to method and means. But the deepest ground of the convergence of the spirit of modern rationalism with that of Calvinism comes to light only in looking beyond the instrumentality of reason to consider how both enjoin absolute commitment to a practical program whose end cannot be grasped; both crown with the finality of salvation the project of liberating the innocent needs of humanity from reason's perverse claim to rule for its own sake.

Instead of allowing rationalism's attack on its immediate enemy, the political power of Christianity, to stand as its defining characteristic, I thus seek to elucidate a curious kinship between these two rivals. I argue that the opposition between the claims of rationalism and those of revelation may be less profound theoretically and less consequential practically than that between both of these on the one hand and "reason" as classically conceived on the other.

Within the framework of these fundamental questions (which can be fully articulated only gradually and sometimes indirectly as my argument develops) I intend to reopen, or to open in a new way, the historical question of the contribution of Christianity, in particular the Protestant Reformation, to the emergence of a distinctively modern view of human beings and their relation to the nonhuman world. I say *reopen* because the idea that the Reformation was an essentially modern movement is in itself far from original. As I indicate in the introduction, this idea has been espoused, in quite different forms, by Hegel, by the Whig historians, and by generations of liberal Protestants. An example more familiar to many contemporary scholars is Max Weber's justly famous argument that Calvinism tended to dispose its adherents to modern capitalist enterprise. In general, however, the view that Protestant teaching itself made an essential contribution to the modern world has been on the defensive since modern liberalism began to lose confidence that it owned the future.

Many scholars consider the survival of the modernist interpretation of the Reformation and particularly of Calvinism a testimony more to human credulity than to the plausibility of the thesis itself. For, they point out, whereas it is obvious that Calvin acted out of or at least in the name of an extreme religious or otherworldly zeal, it seems equally clear that modern rationalism implies a concentration on the goods of this world, on the "secular" realm. The central purpose of my introduction is to prepare a fresh reflection on Calvinism by beginning to render questionable this simple dichotomy between the secular and rationalistic and the religious and otherworldly. In this chapter I begin to articulate the philosophical problem Calvin posed by investigating the historical question of the influence of Calvinism. I proceed by briefly considering certain representative modern scholars whose ultimate rejection of the modernity of Calvinism depends on the quite reasonable premise that the categories of secular and religious are simply opposed. This discussion allows me to demonstrate that, to come to grips with Calvin, one must be ready to reconsider the meaning of the "secularism" or "worldliness" we so readily associate with the modern and thus to question the modern dichotomy between rationalism and religion. The view of "this world" involved in this dichotomy is not a self-evident and eternal truth but part of the distinctive background of the modern mind.

After this critique of a set of categories whose unquestioned authority would have prevented us from coming to terms with the fundamental significance of Calvinism, I turn, in the body of the book, to a discussion of original Calvinism. This discussion focuses almost exclusively on the Reformer's most authoritative work, *The Institutes of the Christian Religion,* and generally takes the form of a rather close-to-the-text commentary. I am convinced that this sometimes indirect approach to my central themes is the only way to defend a rather surprising view of Calvin's thought and fully to reveal the depth and intricacy, as well as the blind spots, of his argument.

I explore Calvin's system by beginning with his most directly political and ethical teachings and tracing these to their theological foundations (part 1), and then by examining the foundations themselves in order to locate a central, generating idea or intention (part 2). I show that Calvin explodes the simple dichotomy between secular and religious concerns; he distinguishes radically between them, to be sure, but precisely in order to join them fast together. God is elevated so far above human beings that the divine can serve no longer as a standard for ranking human concerns as higher or lower but only as a sanction for the manifest and universal interests of humanity.

Since this view of Calvin's thought is likely to surprise and risks offending, let me emphasize at the outset that I have concentrated on what I regard as the most profound and original thrust of Calvin's thought as it is exhibited in his most systematic work. I do not claim to give an account of or to account for all his teachings, only to uncover a philosophically significant underlying structure. Clearly Calvin did not always draw the ultimate conclusions of his own radical premises; clearly he remained on many points within the horizon of a traditional Christian piety. Though such traditional piety is not the subject of this book, the understanding reader will see that my argument implies no disrespect to this less distinctive and truly humane part of Calvin's legacy.

Most surprising, as I suggest in chapter 5 and elaborate more fully in the conclusion, is that Calvin's interpretation of Christianity essentially mirrors the deep structure of modern "rationalism." This argument implies that we may ignore the full background and implications of our own distinctively modern assumptions. The secular is not a self-evident theoretical category or a self-sustaining domain of practical activity; the theoretical and practical concentration on "this world," this allegedly "rational" world, is part of a broader intentional context. In other words, our concentration on the secular and rational cannot be understood without reference to a standpoint beyond (if not "above") this world. Whether this standpoint claims religious authority or not, the intention that constitutes this world does not itself fall within this world; the modern world thus cannot be *simply* "worldly" or "secular" or "rationalistic."

My reading of Calvin implies that Max Weber was more correct than he knew in suggesting an affinity between the Protestant ethic and the spirit of capitalism. At one level, therefore, one might say that I intend to rehabilitate the modernist interpretation of Calvinism. But a full reflection on this affinity must work in both directions; it challenges our view of modernity as well our view of Calvinism. It is thus not my intention simply to resituate Calvinism with respect to a ready-made definition of modernity or to nominate Calvin for inclusion within some established pantheon of modern founders. Rather (and this is where I depart from Leo Strauss), I mean precisely to question whether modernity is susceptible of a fundamentally consistent definition on its own terms and thus whether it has founders or a foundation. I wish to hold up Calvin's spiritual secularism as a mirror to the idealistic materialism of the modern age in order to ask whether, any more than Calvinism, with its explicit reliance on a power beyond reason, modern rationalism can give a full and fully rational account of itself.

If not, then Tocqueville was right to judge that to defend civilization in the modern world requires more than the defense of modern civilization.

This book is based on research I first began, if memory serves, in 1979. Given limitations of space and my lack both of strong memory and of restraint in imposing my often inchoate thoughts and incomplete manuscripts on vulnerable friends and colleagues, it is impossible to give fair credit here to all who have given valuable advice and encouragement as this project developed. Indeed, I seem to have spared so few of my scholarly friends that it is a minimal courtesy to take this occasion to thank them all. I venture to mention the names of just a few who have been especially generous with their time and insight.

For more than ten years I have benefited much from stimulating conversations with Peter Minowitz and James Stoner, first as fellow graduate students and now—less frequently, alas—as professional colleagues at distant institutions. In my first faculty position, I was extremely fortunate, in my work on the present book and in many other respects, to have ready access to the intelligence and judgment of Thomas F. Payne, Rodler Morris, and Kendall Brown. Robert Eden and Jeremy Rabkin also gave valuable advice and encouragement to this project. I am indebted to the anonymous readers for Cornell University Press, for many indispensable criticisms and suggestions, and particularly to my editor, John Ackerman, for his skillful and amiable handling of a process we both hoped would be shorter.

It is impossible to calculate my debt to various teachers over the years; without them I would have been unable not only to execute but even to conceive of the present project. Beyond this, they have made it possible for me to develop interests and faculties without which my life would be immeasurably poorer. I must mention in particular three of my teachers at Brigham Young University, from whom, now as colleagues, I continue to learn: Don Sorensen, Louis Midgley, and Noel Reynolds. Stephen Holmes was intellectually helpful and personally accommodating as a reader of an earlier version of this work. Finally, I acknowledge my immense good fortune in discovering Harvey Mansfield in my first year of graduate study. It was at an opening lecture of his on ancient political philosophy that I was first seized by the possibility that great texts of the past could shed light on the deepest contemporary concerns. He also called my attention to the paradoxical idealism of modern materialism, as well as the materialism of modern idealism, a far-reaching insight without which this book would not have been possible. Mr. Mansfield later credited my belief that I was on to something in my study of Calvin long before I could prove it and provided prompt and indispensable criticisms and encouragement. I continue to value his advice and his example most highly.

For financial support during the writing of an earlier version, I thank the Mrs. Giles Whiting Foundation; the Earhart Foundation of Ann Arbor, Michigan; and the Higginson and Hancock families. For assistance in preparing the manuscript at various stages, I single out for thanks Susan Nelson, Jeanne McCaskey, and Gina Reid. The MIT Press kindly allowed me to consult their manuscript translation of Hans Blumenberg's *The Legitimacy of the Modern Age* as they were preparing it for publication.

Finally, it is a pleasure to thank my parents, who taught me to honor both rectitude and reflection; my wife, Julie, who has supported me in every way throughout this project; our sons, John, Nathaniel, and Jared, whose birth and development coincided approximately with that of this work but who outshine it by far; and Anne Marie, who came into the world as the last of these pages were being written, just in time to remind us how infinitely that which is given to us surpasses anything we can make.

RALPH C. HANCOCK

Provo, Utah

Note on References

I have kept notes to a minimum by referring in the text itself to author and, where appropriate, to title or publication date. Page numbers and volume numbers (where applicable) are enclosed within parentheses. *"Comm."* refers to John Calvin's biblical *Commentaries.* Works cited are listed in the bibliography.

Unless otherwise indicated, references to Calvin embedded in the text refer to the final (1559) Latin edition of the *Institutes of the Christian Religion,* translated by Ford Lewis Battles and edited by John T. McNeill. References are indicated by book, chapter, section, and (following a semicolon) page number. Thus (II.i.2; 243) refers to book 2 of the 1559 *Institutes,* chapter 1, section 2, page 243 of the McNeill edition. The reference is often abbreviated when part of the citation repeats a reference already indicated in the immediate context (e.g., 3; 244).

I have also consulted Calvin's own French translation of the final edition of the *Institutes* (1560), edited by J.-D. Bénoit.

Introduction

The Protestant Reformation and
the Origins of Modern Politics

"It is from the bosom of the Protestant Church that Christianity, restored at once to its ancient purity and to its progressive advancement, is now presented as a doctrine contemporaneous with every age, because it keeps pace with every age; open to every access of light, because it accepts it from every quarter; enriching itself with every discovery, because it contends against none; placing itself on a level with every epoch, and thus laying aside every notion which is behind the progress that is daily made by the human mind." Such was the view of Benjamin Constant,[1] against which John Calvin—arguably a superior authority on the essence of Protestantism—would surely have contended vehemently. Even a superficial acquaintance with Calvin's life and teachings is sufficient to dismiss the suggestion that the founder of Reformed Protestantism could personally have approved the ideal of tolerant progressivism reflected in Constant's characterization of "pure" Christianity. To take only the most notorious example: the man who urged the execution of the Spanish heretic Michael Servetus for the blasphemy of denying the Trinity would not seem to measure up to Constant's standard of openness to "every access of light."

Yet, despite such sensible and rather obvious objections, the notion that the Protestant Reformation, particularly in its Calvinist form, was an essentially modern movement, that it in some sense laid the foundations for our modern openness to new accesses of light, has enjoyed currency at least since the early nineteenth century. The Whig historians were of course fond of demonstrating the contributions of Calvinism to the progress of liberty.[2] But perhaps the most famous and influential version of the thesis associating Protestantism and progress was offered by Hegel, who observes, in his *Philosophy of History*, that "in Germany the eclaircissement was conducted in the interest of theology; in France it immediately took up a position of hostility to the Church." This was possible in part because "the Protestant world itself . . . advanced so far in thought as to realize the absolute culmination of self-consciousness" (444). "This is the essence of the Reformation," Hegel writes: "Man is in his very nature destined to be free" (417).

The idea of a kinship between Protestantism and political and social progress became a commonplace among liberal Protestants. The boldest and most prolific representative of this view among Calvin scholars was certainly Emil Doumergue, whose monumental seven-volume study, *Jean Calvin: Les hommes et les choses de son temps*, appeared from 1899 to 1927. Doumergue's position on the relationship between Calvinism and modernity is clear: he argues straightforwardly that Calvin deserves the title "founder of the modern world" (V.212).

Even as Doumergue wrote, however, the tide of Protestant opinion was turning against the fathering of modernity on the Reformation. The Great War helped to bring many religious thinkers to distrust the mingling of religious commitment with faith in social progress. Most eminent among these thinkers was Karl Barth, whose "dialectical theology" or "theology of crisis" emphasized the infinite distance between a radically transcendent God and sinful man, in effect constituting a repudiation of the link between Protestantism and modernity. Meanwhile, modern historical scholarship since Ranke (who insisted that history must be written *wie es gewesen ist*) had been eroding the grandiose edifice of Hegel's philosophy of history and reminding philosophers and liberal Protestants alike of the quite obvious differences between original Protestantism and more recent political and social ideas. To take a ready example: the apparently vast difference between the idea that "man is in his very nature destined to be free" and the doctrine, common to Luther and Calvin, of the radical depravity of man.

Thus many twentieth-century treatments of Calvin and Calvinism appear preoccupied with refuting over and over again a thesis that seems not even to deserve a hearing. Marc-Edouard Chenevière introduces his study of *La pensée politique de Calvin* (1937) by insisting that "there is no spiritual kinship between the Reformation and modern democracy" (9); and J. W. Allen, in *A History of Political Thought in the Sixteenth Century*, first published in 1928, observes, "If the essence of Protestantism is a claim to liberty for the individual," then "certainly Calvin was not a Protestant" (3).

Allen's point is hard to deny. And yet the idea that some inner connection exists between Protestantism and modernity or some aspect of modernity seems to grow new heads faster than rigorously empirical historians and no-nonsense neo-orthodox theologians can cut them off. Many of these heads cluster around the justly famous argument of Max Weber, whose *Protestant Ethic and the Spirit of Capitalism* continues after eighty years to generate scholarly controversy. To Weber's argument that Calvinist religion tended to dispose its adherents to capitalist enterprise, many have objected that Calvin himself quite obviously opposed much that appears to be essential to modern capitalism and therefore that Calvinists, in order to become capitalists, had to depart from the authentic Calvinist teaching on important points. Yet Weber's argument remains impressive and continues to attract serious attention from many disciplines. The resilience of the notion of the essential modernity of the Reformation in the face of commonsense objections often based on undisputed historical fact in itself suggests that this notion may deserve more careful attention and that the facts evident to our modern historical sense may not be sufficient to inform this attention.

The historiography of the Reformation of course exhibits much more complexity and many subtler shades of opinion than is suggested by simply opposing what one might call "modernist" interpretations to "nonmodernist" ones.[3] Contemporary scholars, in particular, seem to have learned to avoid sectarianism, or the appearance of sectarianism, by carefully balancing their judgments on the relationship between the Reformation and modern civilization. Thus Harold Grimm, in *The Reformation Era, 1500–1650*, argues that in this period many secular or humanist elements coexisted with much that remained medieval; the Protestant reformers themselves rejected "the humanist belief in man's ability to solve his own problems" but anticipated a modern view in their emphasis on man's individuality (467, 468). Such an apparently sober balancing and mixing of views is seductive. But it finally does not demonstrate but merely presupposes that either Protestantism or modernity or both are not in themselves ordered wholes with ascertainable meanings but incoherent jumbles of discrete "elements"; it assumes what Hegelian philosophy argues; namely, that these elements are intelligible only from the standpoint of a theoretical wholeness accessible to the mind of a more enlightened age. The real question is whether, despite obvious differences, Protestant and secular individualism have something fundamental, and fundamentally modern, in common. But to answer this question requires reflection on the various meanings of *individualism* and on the meaning of *modern.* To shun this reflection is, in effect, to assume that human beings cannot deliberately mix their own ideas by forming the elements at their disposal, that their thinking and choosing is determined by accidental circumstances or by the mixing powers of some impersonal force such as "secularization."

J. W. Allen

To avoid such difficulties the student of Calvinism might perhaps simply address Calvin on his own terms, relieving a sixteenth-century writer of the burden of addressing contemporary preoccupations with the nature and origins of modernity. Thus J. W. Allen, in his classic *History of Political Thought in the Sixteenth Century,* warns of the dangers of endeavoring to "exhibit ideas of the past in relation to something vaguely called 'modern thought,'" since, in the first place, there are no such entities as "modern thought" or "medieval thought" and, furthermore, any thought of the twentieth century is irrelevant to that of the sixteenth (xix).

In order to see how a study of Calvin's theology might contribute to a reinterpretation of the history of political thought, it will prove useful to point out certain theoretical difficulties and troubling practical implications in Allen's apparently quite sensible position. Despite his own warnings, Allen soon begins referring to "medieval thought" as a single entity, a whole constituted by certain "basic assumptions" that continued to prevail in the sixteenth century, namely, the assumptions that "the Scriptures were the very Word of God" and that there exists a " 'natural' moral law, recognized by all men alike and binding absolutely, world without end" (xiv). The very fact that we, like Allen, tend to distinguish our thought from an age we designate as medieval— the fact that, as Allen says, there exists a general "temptation to dub one's own thought as modern" (xix)—itself suggests that some common basic assumption underlies postmedieval thought as well.

It is not Allen's purpose to bring such an assumption to light. Still, in order to show that Calvin is medieval, he must at least suggest what *postmedieval* or *modern* means. Thus Allen sometimes suggests that in opposing the use of modern concepts in the interpretation of the sixteenth century, he has in mind mainly the opinion that Calvin was somehow a forerunner of contemporary notions of liberty, individualism, or democracy (3, 66). But Allen himself does not finally accept these notions as representative of the basic assumptions of modernity. Instead, for him, the political history of the sixteenth century becomes intelligible when seen as a chapter in the rise of the purely or "frankly" secular state that merely "tolerates" religion; the modern state was founded by men who "did not wish to think . . . of any world other than this" (13; cf. 516). It appears that for him the modern state has no positive foundations but is merely an accident of thoughtlessness and forgetting (13).

No surprise, then, that Allen is not very sanguine about the prospects for modernity. The forgetting of belief that once undermined popes, then kings, he expects to lead to a "skepticism of all values." "If that be so, faith in democracy will fade as completely as faith in the divine right of kings." If such a trend were to continue, then "complete skepticism must needs destroy the bases of even the crudest utilitarianism." And if the course of modern politics is so understood, it goes without saying that

"there can hardly be any question of 'progress.'" Rather, the
terminus of modernity is likely to be nihilism: "in the long run,
even desire will fail" (516).

This disparagement of the progressive interpretation of the history of modern political thought brings to mind Allen's impa-
tience with those who succumb to the "temptation to dub one's
own thought 'modern'" (xix). But to disparage this belief in progress, this faith that newer is better, is to recognize that it exists and
thus to suggest that modern political thought rests on something
more than sheer forgetfulness or shallowness. For belief in progress does not necessarily follow from unbelief in God—indeed, it
might seem likely to be discouraged by such unbelief. Moderns, as
the "temptation" deplored by Allen suggests, are (or claim to be)
quite aware of their difference with previous ages. Indeed, they
insist upon it. It is hard to see how one might account for this self-
consciousness on the assumption that the age of unbelief is simply
what was left over from the age of belief, once belief was forgotten.
A new belief seems to have arisen, but Allen's interpretation
cannot show a reason for it.[4]

To discover such reasons it may not be sufficient to follow Allen
in attending more to "the writings of obscure or anonymous persons than [to] the work of writers whose real distinction and
originality makes them untypical" (xviii). Such an approach is not
likely to bring to light the basic beliefs of an age, for surely the
typical assumptions are best understood *as assumptions*—and
this is not how typical writers understand them; these writers
tend rather to assume what others have understood. If, for example, as Allen writes, the basic assumption of the Middle Ages was
that a natural moral law existed which was also a divine law, then
certainly one can learn something more fundamental about medieval thought by reading authors who first articulated the notions
of nature, moral law, and divine law, and authors who first made it
possible to mingle the realm of nature with the realm of law and
the realm of the natural with the realm of the divine, than by
reading authors who took all this for granted.

More to the point, if Allen fails to bring to light the typical
assumptions of modernity, it may be because he reads atypical
authors in too typical a fashion. Allen sees Calvin, for example, as

simply assuming what all medievals assume: that the purpose of this life is salvation in the next. But is it fair to brand a priori as a typical assumption a view of this world and the next that understands itself as radically opposed to prevailing views and that is articulated, explained, and defined systematically in four lengthy volumes, the fruit of a quarter-century's spiritual and intellectual labor? Before attributing typical assumptions to Calvin, it is fair to ask whether he examined and understood what others, particularly his followers, may have assumed. If in the end we conclude that certain assumptions lie at the bottom of Calvin's teaching, a careful consideration of his ideas is likely to afford a better understanding of these assumptions and of their place in the history of political assumptions.

I attempt in this book to illuminate the essential character of Calvin's thought and to situate Calvinism in relation to the most fundamental difference between medieval and modern ideas. It doubtless appears foolhardy to encumber a study of Calvin with such a vast and controversial question. But I believe, as Allen's effort illustrates, that it is impossible to disengage the problem of the significance of Calvinism from an inquiry into the fundamental assumptions of the modern age, for the reason—quite simple, but hard to grasp—that we cannot know whether the problem has been disengaged until we know what the assumptions are. We cannot rise above the horizons of our age simply by wishing to do so; we must first know what these horizons are. We can only hope to understand past ages if we are ready to allow thinkers of the past to help us understand ourselves.

The question of the historical role of Calvinism in the emergence of modern political thought is thus inseparable from and indeed logically posterior to that of the meaning of Calvinism on the one hand and modernity on the other. In order to see how a study of Calvin's own thought might advance the latter inquiry along with the former, let us now briefly examine the arguments of two eminent students of the history of political thought, Quentin Skinner and Michael Walzer. Both these authors seem to give a large place to Calvinism in their interpretations of the rise of modern political ideas; both, however, conclude finally that religious belief cannot have contributed directly to the formation of a nonreligious body of thought. This is because Skinner and Walzer simply assume that the basic philosophical or theological premises of Calvinism and those of modernity are absolutely incompatible. However, in juxtaposing Skinner's argument with Walzer's, we can begin to put this assumption in question, and thus we can begin to see how a reflection on the foundations of Calvinism might reopen the questions not only of the historical influence of Reformation theology but of the meaning of modernity itself.

Quentin Skinner

A glance at the organization of Quentin Skinner's highly praised *Foundations of Modern Political Thought* certainly suggests that he considers the contribution of Calvinism to those foundations to be important. The second of his two volumes is entitled *The Age of Reformation,* and its third part bears the name "Calvinism and the Theory of Revolution." Here Skinner argues that "the modern theory [of a right of resistance] was first fully articulated by the Huguenots during the French religious wars in the second half of the sixteenth century" (II.240). It would be a mistake, however, to infer from this that Skinner credits Calvin or his followers with making any decisive *theoretical* contribution to this process, for he argues that the "modern theory" the Huguenots first used at this time was in fact borrowed from much earlier writers. Indeed, the main burden of Skinner's study of Calvinism is to disprove the widespread opinion that in its political dimension Calvin's teaching was somehow intrinsically more revolutionary than Lutheranism or Catholicism. Although he notes the apparent development of a bold "private law" theory of resistance in certain of Calvin's biblical commentaries and in the final edition of the *Institutes* (II.219–20), and although he concedes that Calvin's reference to the right of popularly elected inferior magistrates to resist tyranny contributed a "secular and constitutional element" to the development of "radical political ideas" (II.232), Skinner insists that Calvinist revolutionaries really depended upon Lutheran theories of resistance, since "Calvin's discussion of the right of resistance appears at first to have exercised singularly little influence" (II.233). Rather, the practically effective aspect of the Genevan's teachings continued for some time to be his repeated insistence that "it is absolutely forbidden to any private individuals to take up arms" (II.219–21).[5]

For evidence of effective progress beyond the Lutheran justification of resistance in this period, Skinner thinks that we must look to the English Calvinists John Ponet and Christopher Goodman, who went far beyond Calvin in their political radicalism. Skinner explains that they first took the critical step of abandoning "the cardinal Augustininan assumption that, even if our rulers failed to discharge the duties of their offices, they must still be regarded as powers ordained of God" (II.227). Again, it is Ponet and Goodman who break decisively with the assumption that the right of resistance is limited to ordained magistrates (II.235). But even these relatively advanced theories remain, according to Skinner, at the level of a "religious duty to resist," which yet awaits transformation into "the modern and strictly political concept of a moral right of resistance" (II.240). This most decisive transformation, he argues, was first effective among the French Calvinists, or Huguenots, following the St. Bartholomew's day massacre in 1572.

Skinner refrains from attributing any true originality even to these theorists: they may have helped to make the modern concept current, but they did not conceive it. Just as they had earlier borrowed the notion of a duty to resist from the Lutherans, so the Calvinists borrowed the notion of a *right* to resist from Catholic theorists, from "the Scholastic and Roman Law tradition of radical constitutionalism." From these sources the Calvinists drew the ideas of the "natural liberty" of the people and of government originating "in an act of true consent on the part of the whole populace" and thus left behind the "characteristically Protestant" view of government as a remedy for sin. Skinner concludes that "the main foundations of the Calvinist theory of revolution were in fact constructed entirely by their Catholic adversaries" (II.319–21).

Thus, although Skinner describes the theories of the Huguenots as "epoch-making," final credit for the epoch belongs to earlier, scholastic writers such as Mario Salamonio (I.148–152), whose arguments formed the true foundation of "a genuinely political theory of revolution, based on the idea of a contract which gives rise to a moral right (and not merely a religious duty) to resist." But behind such writers as Salamonio, Skinner discerns the far-reaching influence of Marsiglio of Padua, who along with his contemporary, the jurist Bartolus, developed a "theory of popular sovereignty . . . destined to play a major role in shaping the most radical version of early modern constitutionalism" (I.65). Saying that the political theory of the late Middle Ages became more and more modern is equivalent, it seems, to saying that it dared more and more to repeat the heresies of Marsiglio of Padua (II.132, I.42).[6] What is distinctively modern in Marsiglio's democratic argument is at bottom the same as the essentially modern element that Skinner later discerns in the concept *state:* both are thoroughly secularized (II.338, 352), free of any religious elements. According to Skinner, Marsiglio launched "the earliest full-scale attack on the Church's status as a *Regnum*," an attack that, when complemented by the later challenge to seignorial rights, led to the concept of a state that has "no rivals within its own territories as a lawmaking power and an object of allegiance" (II.351).

For Skinner, then, *modern* means essentially "naturalistic and secular" (I.50), words that he seems to understand simply as negations of "religious." Like Allen, Skinner seems to think that to know what the modern age is, it is sufficient to know that it is not medieval. Thus Skinner interprets modern politics—politics freed of religion—simply as "pure" politics: once the religious encumbrance is removed, the political is revealed to be a straightforward and unproblematic category. The essential unity of the various postmedieval political teachings seems to be assured by the mere fact that they are all political (that is, secular or naturalistic). The modern state exists "solely for political purposes" (II.352). Modern politics is political politics.

Political argument therefore becomes more modern as it becomes more "political" or secular. It follows that neither Calvin's theology nor any other specifically religious body of ideas can have contributed to the foundations of modern political thought; Calvinist political theory became modern only as it detached itself from Calvinism and became truly political. This was the achievement

of the Huguenots, who made the epoch-making move to "a genuinely political theory of revolution" (II.335), that is, one "founded
on a recognizably modern, secularized thesis about the natural
rights and original sovereignty of the people" (II.338).

Michael Walzer

Quentin Skinner considers Michael Walzer's *Revolution of the
Saints* to be "one of the most remarkable examples" of the interpretation of Calvinist politics he intends to refute. Walzer argues,
according to Skinner, that "the theories lying behind the rise of
modern radical politics were distinctively Calvinist in character"
(II.332–33). It is not clear, however, that Skinner's argument addresses the same questions as Walzer's. For, whereas Skinner (at
least insofar as he is true to his method) is concerned not with
choices to act but only with arguments used to mask actions
(I.xiii), Walzer is explicitly concerned with choices themselves.
He wants to grasp the possibility of choosing to be a Puritan (vii),
to understand "the concrete needs that sainthood served" and the
bases in routine reflection and day-to-day activity "of the strength
of character needed to experiment boldly in politics" and to shed
"age-old assumptions" and "traditional loyalties" (18).

Skinner's criticism of Walzer thus seems beside the point.[7]
Walzer argues not so much that Calvinism articulated a new
political theory as that it created a new political man, a disciplined
radical activist who may be seen as the prototype of the Jacobin
and the Bolshevik (312, 315–17). Thus Walzer in fact agrees with
Skinner's low estimate of the *theoretical* contribution of Calvinism to modern liberalism; he only adds that Puritanism was
important in terms of "historical preparation" (315).

In order to spotlight the historical importance of Calvinist radicalism without making claims for Calvinist theology, Walzer severs character and history from theory. His method consists in
subordinating theory to psychology. He attempts this by interpreting Calvinism as "a way out of anxiety" (308), as "a practical effort
to cope with personal and social problems" (316). That is, Walzer's
Calvinists were not anxious to discipline themselves because they

believed in a certain kind of God; rather, they believed in a certain kind of God in order to ease an anxiety at bottom nontheological and nontheoretical in nature.[8] By interpreting Calvinist anxiety as essentially nontheoretical, it is possible to detach the theoretical therapy from the psychological state of relief: if people believe only in order to find relief, then they are free to forget to believe as soon as they feel relieved—they can become liberals once Calvinism has cured them of their anxiety. Walzer seems to think that Calvinists, once cured of their anxiety, could become Lockeans by learning that what they really wanted was not to glorify God but to "cope," that what was important was not belief but relief.

Still, on closer inspection, it is not so easy to reconcile Skinner with Walzer. For Walzer elsewhere proceeds on the assumption that Calvinists' understanding of human nature was profounder than that of later liberals (320). *The Revolution of the Saints* often very skillfully exhibits a connection between character, or the order of the soul, and a general understanding of order; between psychology and cosmology. Walzer devotes most of a chapter ("The Attack upon the Traditional Political World") to themes quite far removed from modern psychology as well as from politics in the narrow sense—angels, for example—in order to show that Calvinism was "among the most important" sources of the politically divisive shift from an understanding of order as a "chain of being" to the view that order is "a matter of power and power a matter of will, force, and calculation." Indeed, Walzer's entire argument illustrates the interdependence of theory, character, and history. If Puritan character and Puritan organization are essentially similar to those of Jacobins and Bolsheviks, this is because these three groups have similar understandings of the world and their place in it: in sum, individuals in all three groups view their choice to enter a political struggle as a sign of their equal election to ultimate victory in a world-redeeming combat (317–18). This self-interpretation makes possible a new kind of action, "a novel view of politics as a kind of conscientious and continuous labor" (20). Walzer thus credits Calvinism not only with setting a practical precedent but with constructing "a theoretical justification for independent political action" (2). He affirms that this kind of action is distinctively modern.[9]

Walzer's unquestioned sympathy for modern radicals, however, frees him from fully scrutinizing the theoretical matrix of this radicalism and thus invites him to detach the question of the practical impact of Calvinism from that of its theoretical or theological content. Walzer interprets Calvin's writings not as theology or—as Calvin himself sometimes described them—as "Christian philosophy," but as ideology (22–30). He is concerned not with any claim to "offer believers a knowledge of God" or to "explain the world and human society as they are and must be" but rather with Calvinism's "capacity to activate adherents and change the world" (27). To be sure, Walzer seems to concede that the "content" of an ideology is always in part theoretical, "a description of contemporary experience as unacceptable and unnecessary" (27). But how far would Calvin's preaching have reached if he had dwelt on "contemporary experience" instead of on the eternal glory of God? His age was not ready for so much humility.

To understand the ideological capacity of Calvinism we may have to abandon the assumption that Calvinism is just an ideology. It is true that Walzer finds in Calvin's own writings a kind of precedent for the ideological approach. The Reformer's teaching is vigorously antispeculative; Walzer aptly describes Calvin's thought as "theology anti-theological" (24). But an antitheology is still something more than the absence of a theology. Walzer underestimates the value of examining the foundations of Calvin's teaching and their relation to the foundations of modern political thought. His comment that Calvin is "only barely interested in the internal ordering of the mind or in the construction of a philosophical position" (26) overlooks the possibility, which we will explore, of a theoretical position in which the problem of the "internal ordering of the mind" tends to disappear, not due to some accidental lack of interest but because of a definite orientation toward God and His order. Once one sees the distinction between a lack of theology and an antitheology, between an ideology and the founding of an ideology, it is necessary to raise afresh the question whether the founder of Puritan activism might contribute theoretically to the self-understanding of the modern age.[10]

This of course amounts to asking whether liberal theory by itself adequately represents the self-understanding of the civilization we call liberal. Before assuming that an age was at bottom invisible to itself, that it could give no account of itself, of the deepest roots of its habits and opinions, it makes sense to look beyond its political and economic theory narrowly understood. Walzer suggests but does not adequately explore the possibility that the theoretical contribution of a certain interpretation of Christianity to Western politics did not end with the beginning of liberalism.[11] He thus raises the question, which this book will pursue, of the ground of possible alliance between the holy zeal of the Calvinist saints and the unabashed acquisitiveness of the liberal-capitalist, a question the category of "historical conditioning" does nothing to answer but only obfuscates. To reflect on this question promises to yield a better understanding of the early modern or liberal period by suggesting how liberalism could have been built, as Walzer believes, on a Calvinist foundation (though not of course only on a Calvinist foundation). Granted that Calvinist theology and liberal theory are quite different, even directly opposed on many points, there is still a theoretical explanation to be sought for the possibility of a Protestant-liberal civilization: What, precisely, do liberal and postliberal theories share with Calvinism? Walzer chooses to set this question aside; this book addresses it, not only by examining how far Calvinism might fit into a liberal mold, but, more fundamentally, by asking whether certain basic but now inconspicuous aspects of liberalism might conform to a Calvinist mold.

Pure Politics and Religious Radicalism

What was the distinctively modern content of Calvinist "ideology"? Walzer does not explore this problem theoretically, but he does make this helpful suggestion: "The old order was imagined to be natural and eternal, but it is the nature of the new that it be regularly renewed. It is the product of art, of will, of human doing. If traditionalism was stable, modernity is founded upon change" (311). Change or revolution thus appears to be the representative phenomenon of modern politics.[12] But Walzer generally refrains from crediting Calvin or the Calvinists with creating the modern idea of revolution. He rather treats Calvinist "permanent warfare" as intermediate between the traditional right of resistance and the modern ideology of revolution (112). Elsewhere, however, he calls this idea of "eternal warfare" "revolution in its origins" (110) and ventures the assertion that "in a sense, modern politics begins in England with the return of the Genevan exiles" (113).

The basis of Skinner's difference with Walzer should now be clear. Whereas Skinner understands the beginning of modernity as the emergence of politics, pure and simple, from the encumbrance of religion,[13] Walzer, despite his hesitations, sees religion as contributing positively to a distinctively modern view of political activity.[14] Walzer has no intention of disputing Skinner's and Allen's basic assumption, namely, that modern political thought is most clearly distinguished from medieval by its fundamental secularism. On this view, the break between medieval and modern is that between the otherworldly and the worldly. But Walzer's main argument points to another basic difference between modern and premodern politics—and this way of explaining the difference seems to put Calvinism on the side of the moderns. Walzer proposes to understand modernity in terms of a break between an "old order imagined to be natural and eternal" and a new order "founded upon change."

Whether or not Calvinism or any theological view can finally be described as modern according to this scheme, the dichotomy between nature and motion points to an important defect in Allen's and Skinner's interpretation of modernity as essentially secular as opposed to religious. For clearly not all nonreligious thought is secular in their sense; a view of politics may be oriented toward the "natural and eternal" without making any commitment to revelation. Indeed, the revelation of God the Creator of nature obviously poses a considerable obstacle, to say the least, to the association of what is natural with what is eternal. In a word, nonreligious political thought need not be modern.

It follows that Skinner, like Allen, has failed to tell us anything positive about modernity; he has only told us that it is not medieval. Given that Skinner intends to discover the "foundations of

modern political thought," this represents a rather startling over-
sight. As we have seen, the argument of Skinner's second volume,
The Age of Reformation, is largely negative in character: the foundations of modern political thought are to be sought mainly in his
discussions of Marsiglio in volume 1, *The Renaissance*. Of what is
modern political thought the rebirth? In discussing Marsiglio,
Skinner argues that "the development of a modern, naturalistic
and secular view of political life" depended upon the "rediscovery
of Aristotle's moral and political writings" (I.50). Marsiglio's contribution consisted essentially in his importing Aristotelianism
into fourteenth-century Italy (I.52–53). It follows, of course, that
there is nothing fundamentally new about modern political philosophy, and Skinner does not shrink from explicitly asserting that
the core of the modern conception of politics only *appeared* new
because Christianity had caused it to be "lost to view" (II.349).
Aristotle, it seems, is the true founder of modern political
thought—which is to say that there is no such thing as "modern"
political thought, there is only medieval and nonmedieval
thought.

To respond to this remarkable interpretation, so blandly proposed, we need only notice that, whereas according to Skinner
"Aristotle's *Politics* treats the polis as a purely human creation,
designed to fulfill purely mundane ends" (I.50), Aristotle himself
writes that the polis exists by nature (*Politics* I.2) and that its end is
the highest good (I.1); the polis aims, therefore, at the good of the
soul, and not merely at external goods or goods of the body (VII.1).
Skinner asserts furthermore that Aristotle describes the polis as "a
self-sufficient ideal, never hinting at any further purposes lying
beyond it" (I.50). But Aristotle does more than hint; he argues in
the *Nichomachean Ethics* that political activity is instrumental to
contemplative activity, which alone is self-sufficient (X.7).[15]
Whereas for Aristotle the assertion that the polis is natural is only
the starting point of a lengthy reflection on the nature of politics,
Skinner proceeds as if the natural, which he equates with the
"purely mundane," were brought to light by the simple elimina-
tion of the supernatural (I.50).[16] A sign of the difference between
the natural view of politics and Skinner's "purely political" view is
that, as Skinner mentions, this "pure" view tends to proceed by

"depicting men in a pre-political condition" (I.322). This view therefore clearly implies that human nature is not political but pre- or subpolitical.[17] If Skinner can regard this naturalistic view of politics as "purely political," it can only be because the Aristotelian notions of nature and politics have been radically transformed. But what is the character of this transformation? Modernity is not simply Christian, certainly, but neither is it Aristotelian. So what is it?

This is a question which neither Walzer not Skinner undertakes to answer; yet they both begin to answer it. In our attempt to reconcile their implicit answers we will prepare ourselves to see how Calvin himself can illuminate the problem of the meaning of modernity.

The terms of Skinner's interpretation point to the minimalism of modern politics, to the modern attempt to restrict the political to the "mundane." Once the object of human choice is understood to be not some natural perfection but "a purely human creation," then that object appears as *merely* human. An obvious interpretation of the object that remains once the good of the soul is rejected as an end is the liberal one: politics is about self-preservation and "commodious living" (Hobbes). Pure politics, purely human politics, thus means the politics of the body.

As Skinner's book does not argue but shows, the modesty of this view claims to be compensated by a gain of clarity and precision. Pure politics may not be much, but at least there's no need to quarrel over what it is. To deny that human choice seeks a natural good is in one sense a bit humbling, but this denial claims finally to make choice or will perfectly transparent to itself and unproblematic. The politics of this world does not want much, but it knows what it wants.[18]

Walzer's perspective points to a different, apparently contradictory aspect of modernity. His main interest is not the minimalism of the "routine" periods of modernity but the radicalism of the periods of renewal. Thus the activists (such as Vladimir Lenin and John Knox) whom Walzer describes seem filled with a spirit entirely different from the sober secularism of Skinner's moderns or promoderns (such as John Locke or Jean Bodin). And yet Walzer believes that there is finally no contradiction between radicalism and secularism—for it is precisely radical secularism that Walzer attempts to understand. Revolution does not deny the *basic* principle underlying the modern routine, but reveals it by renewing it. It thus appears that the spirit of radicalism does not oppose this substance of secularism—rather, it makes this substance its own.

Just what Walzer would accept of Skinner's version of modernity and how he would amend it is apparent in the definition of modernity that I have quoted from Walzer's conclusion (311; see the beginning of this section). Walzer agrees with Skinner that modern order is secular, that is, "the product of art and will, of human doing." But he immediately goes beyond Skinner: "Modernity is founded upon change" (311). Whereas Skinner assumes that the politics of the human will are "mundane," Walzer will not allow such a static definition—worldly politics is the politics of motion. This is why Walzer can locate the origins of modern politics in *religious* radicalism: the *end* of modern political movements is secondary to the point of *moving.* "Revolution in its origins" can be understood as "the continuation of religious activity by military means" because this activity, with its means, seems detachable from any definite end. The Puritan activists, like later radicals, Walzer writes, are "presumably" committed to a "community of the future . . . But for the present it was warfare and not fellowship, military order and ideological discipline, and not Christian love that occupied his mind" (110). The point is not to understand the world (or the other world) but to change it.

If motion is the essence of modernity, then we must revise our previous formula describing the relationship between radicalism and modern politics. I suggested that Walzer's view implied that modern radicalism is needed to renew mundane modernism; that radicalism is the spirit which embraces secularism as its substance. But now it appears that it is the role of radicalism to reveal to a mundane age that secularism *is* renewal, that it is the essence of modernity to modernize. Whereas Skinner seems to assume that a state which is a "purely human creation" will be directed towards a static set of "purely mundane ends," Walzer suggests a direct connection between the radical freedom of the human will and the politics of change, of the new regularly renewed. For the will to be perfectly free, it must not be bound to any static view of this world or to the impersonality and omnipotence of the state that follows from such a view; radical freedom is free not only from the idea of the soul as ruler of the body but from the nature of the body as well. The will is purely free only when it is purged of any substance but its own; it is finally transparent to itself only when it is essentially nothing—but change.[19]

To give Skinner his due, however, it is clear that this process not only changes but "advances" in a certain direction. The end of the process of modernization may not be definite, but it is definitely this-worldly. Modern freedom may have no essence, but it is essentially opposed to the political claims of another world. Skinner's error thus appears to be one of tone or spirit: modern politics may not always be mundane, as Skinner thinks; but it is always *worldly*.

Thus, although Walzer's comparison of religious to modern revolutionaries calls our attention to the radical spirit of modernity, Walzer does not dispute Skinner's point that the ends of modern politics are altogether of this world. On this view, it appears impossible that Calvin or any primarily religious thinker contributed to the theoretical foundations of modern politics. We seem left with Allen's simple but sensible argument: modern politics denies the medieval view that politics must serve religious ends; and since Calvin made politics serve religious ends, Calvinist political theory is fully medieval, that is, not at all modern.

However, our discussions of the differences between Skinner's and Walzer's understanding of worldliness, and of the distance between Skinner's naturalism and Aristotle's teaching on nature, suggest the inadequacy of the simple dichotomy "religious" versus "nonreligious" for understanding the history of political philosophy. Walzer's argument, in particular, brings to our attention the problematic character of this distinction. For Calvin insists on the radical corruption of human nature and on the absolute subordination of human to divine ends. In Calvin's words: "There is no middle ground between these two: either the world must become worthless to us or hold us bound by intemperate love of it" (III.xi.2; 713). But Walzer, following Weber, points to a certain worldliness in the practical meaning of Calvinism. He writes of Beza, Calvin's loyal disciple and successor, that "his extreme preoccupation with worldly means gives a curious non-religious tone to his political writing, until it is understood that this very preoccupation had its theological reasons" (80). Walzer writes elsewhere, "The overcoming of anxiety became for Calvinists a specifically worldly, rather than an otherworldly, activity" (25).

Walzer thus indicates but does not attempt to elaborate or explain theologically the paradoxical worldliness of Calvin's otherworldliness. To illuminate this paradox and to situate Calvinism in relation to modern "secularism," we will examine not only the status of the worldly but the very meaning of *this world* in Calvin's theology.

My chief source in examining both Calvin's practical and his more strictly theological teachings is his monumental *Institutes of the Christian Religion*. This work in four volumes, intended as a complete account of the basis of Reformed Christianity, represents the labor of a quarter century; certainly it surpasses any other general theological statement by a sixteenth-century reformer in intellectual power and comprehensiveness as well as in historical influence. Calvin himself presents the *Institutes* as embracing "the sum of religion in all its parts."[20]

I begin my reading of the *Institutes* with the most straightforwardly political part of that work, the last chapter on "Civil Government" (IV.xx). In the first section of this chapter Calvin brings to our attention the problem of the union of two radically distinct realms, the spiritual and the political. This theme, the paradoxical union of opposites, emerges time and again throughout my reading of Calvin's political and moral teaching; to illuminate the nature and significance of this union is a central purpose of this book. I show in part 1 that Calvin's extreme rejection of the natural world, the world accessible to natural reason, implies not extreme otherworldliness but on the contrary, the rejection of otherworldliness in favor of a spiritual commitment to this world. Furthermore, Calvin's understanding of this world reveals his profound affinities with the rationalistic materialism commonly associated with such authors as Hobbes and Locke.

In part 2, I probe more deeply into the theological basis of Calvin's practical teaching. (More properly I should say the anti-theological basis; there is for Calvin no logos of God.) I argue that Calvin's pervasive tendency to distinguish radically and to unify emphatically the human and the divine realms is rooted in his view of the unity of self-knowledge (or consciousness of nothing-ness) with knowledge of God (or consciousness of absolute power). Thus Max Weber was more correct than he knew in suggesting an affinity between the Protestant ethic and the spirit of capitalism; he saw that Calvinism was associated with resolute activity in the secular realm but failed to discover the deep theological springs from which this particular affinity flows.

Thus I not only rehabilitate the modernist interpretation of Calvinism by addressing Calvin's teaching at a fundamental level, but I also demonstrate for the first time the intricate unity of Calvin's practical teaching with his theology and indeed, the rigor-ous internal unity of that theology itself.

This examination of Calvin's *Institutes* lays the foundation for a more comprehensive if necessarily tentative and incomplete re-flection on the nature and origins of modernity. The conclusion develops my views on this question by contriving a many-sided debate among authors who understand that the meaning of the secular is not so unproblematic as contemporary scholars such as Skinner and Walzer tend to assume. These authors recognize, that is, that modern secularism (or rationalism or materialism) is not a self-evident given but a problem as much practical as intellec-tual—as the raging of the idealistic spirit of materialism in the twentieth century makes all too clear.

Participants in this concluding discussion are Leo Strauss, Karl Löwith, Eric Voegelin, and Hans Blumenberg. The debate begins and ends with a consideration of Strauss's apparent view that, contrary to Weber, no religious body of thought can be accounted a direct source of modern rationalism. A comparison of Strauss's own interpretation of modern political thought with those of Eric Voegelin and Hans Blumenberg, however, suggests that *rational-ism* is by no means an adequate synonym for *modernity*. The rational materialism of the modern age is ever haunted by a nonra-tional idealism, the nature of which is exhibited more clearly in

Calvin than in Strauss's alleged founders. In my conclusion the question of the modernity of Calvinism is thus transcended by the problem of modernity itself; if Calvin cannot give a fully "modern" account of himself (which of course he cannot), then neither, it seems, can the canonical founders of modernity.

Thus I intend to put in question the very notion of modernity as susceptible of clear and complete exposition on its own terms. Although I appreciate what I take to be the profoundly practical motives behind Strauss's disagreement with Löwith and Voegelin on this point, it seems to me that Strauss himself gives us good grounds for appreciating Löwith's remark (1949) that modern vision is necessarily dim because "the modern mind sees with one eye of faith and one of reason" (207). As to where this reflection leaves us with regard to the practical problem of articulating a sound foundation for modern politics, I am able only to endorse— if it is not too late—Tocqueville's praise of the American marriage of a decent materialism with a prudent piety. Tocqueville shows us how to praise both progressive religion and the religion of progress without praising either too much.

The desirability of such an accommodation is intelligible only by reference to a good that transcends each accommodated element. In the last analysis, the critique of various understandings of modernity and the exposition of Calvin's antitheology are two dimensions of a single attempt to understand and to explicate (if not, obviously, to solve) a problem that is no more specifically modern than it is Calvinist, namely, that of the relation of human action and human interaction to what is above or beyond human power. One does not have to accept Calvin's purported solution to this problem (as I certainly do not), nor does one have to be a Christian or even a theist to learn something from Calvin about the nature of the problem itself.

PART ONE

Calvin's Practical Teaching:
Divine Glory in Human Action

The Sabbath was made for man, not man for the Sabbath.

The Gospel of Mark

The Right of Nature, whereby God reigneth over men, is to be derived . . . from his *Irresistible Power.*

Thomas Hobbes

Chapter 1

The Separation and Union
of Religion and Politics

We are now prepared to consult Calvin himself on the status of practical or worldly activity. Part 1 of this book takes its bearings from Calvin's thematic treatment of politics in the final chapter, entitled "Civil Government," of the final book of his monumental *Institutes of the Christian Religion* (IV.xx). I will digress from a direct study of this chapter, according to Calvin's own cues, or as the argument requires, to examine his teachings on providence, Christian freedom and church government (chapter 2), law and ethics (chapter 4), and human reason (chapter 5). In tracing the structure of Calvin's teaching in each of these areas, it is possible to discern the recurrence of the central theme to which I have already adverted: the radical distinction between and the union of the secular and spiritual. In every fundamental question that he addresses, Calvin rigorously distinguishes between the secular and the spiritual in order to join them fast together. In this, I suggest in the concluding chapter of part 1, Calvin's thought reveals surprising parallels to modern rationalism, whose materialistic assumptions are surrounded and supported by an often unrecognized idealism.

To introduce Calvin's practical teaching, it will be best to attend carefully to his own introduction to politics, contained in the first three sections of "Civil Government." It is well to note first that Calvin has described the *Institutes* as "a sum of Christian doctrine" or a "key to open the way for all the children of God into a good and right understanding of holy Scripture."[1] It is not immediately clear what place a political teaching has in a work with such a purpose. Calvin grants, in fact, that "this topic seems by nature alien to the spiritual doctrine of faith" (IV.xx.1; 1485). The doctrine of faith is concerned primarily with the spiritual govern-ment of man, which "resides in the soul or inner man and pertains to eternal life." (Calvin has discussed church government in the preceding nineteen chapters of this fourth book of the *Institutes*.) Spiritual government is to be rigorously distinguished from civil government, "which pertains only to the establishment of civil justice and outward morality." But Calvin promises to show, without sacrificing this rigorous distinction, that he is right in "joining" the spiritual and the political teachings.

Calvin argues, in fact, not only that he is "right" in joining a political teaching to his summary of Christian faith ("c'est à droit que je l'y conjoin"), but that "necessity compels [him] to do so." But the addition of an argument from necessity poses a problem for determining the sense of the argument from right. Does Cal-vin's right to join politics to religion derive from religion as he understands it—that is, does he mean by *right* something like "theologically consistent" or perhaps "pious"? Or does he mean that political necessity gives him this right or makes it right for him to join civil with spiritual government?

The next sentences suggest that Calvin bases his right to discuss politics on both piety and political necessity. Calvin first describes the political necessity of this joining: right order is threatened on the one hand by "insane and barbarous men" who would overturn it and on the other by "flatterers of Princes" whose praise of worldly powers goes so far as to offend against the rule of God himself. These opposing groups of extremists clearly threaten the temporal security of Christian peoples. But more than this; "un-less both these evils are checked, purity of faith will perish."

Thus the argument from political necessity appears itself to be rooted, or partly rooted, in Calvin's concern for true piety. Purity of faith—the success of the Reformation—depends on the uphold-ing of God's order in the realm of civil government. This order is threatened both by those who esteem political authority too little, because they do not recognize its divine foundation, and by those who claim too much for political authority—because they, too, fail to recognize that it depends upon God.

Calvin next spells out his more direct argument from piety for the right to join a discussion of politics to his "sum of Christian doctrine." "To know how lovingly God has provided in this respect for mankind" adds to our zeal and gratitude (1; 1486). Since Calvin understands piety as "that reverence joined with the love of God which the knowledge of his benefits induces" (I.ii.1; 41), he believes that to add to this knowledge of providence by describing the divine benefits of civil government will contribute to piety.

Calvin's intention in his chapter on "Civil Government" thus appears to be twofold: first, to complete his general account of God's providential care for mankind by setting forth the divine basis of political order, and thus to further encourage piety; second, to counter threats to this order from two opposing groups— on the one hand, those who would overturn it in the name of religion and on the other, those who refuse to subordinate this order to its author. Calvin's spiritual teaching is joined to a political teaching because the political order is part of the divine providential order, and because it is important, even urgent, both for piety and for politics, that this be recognized by men. It is as if, at least in the world of politics, the benefit of God's order depended on men's prudent care or defense of God's order.

The task of joining the spiritual and the political is made especially precarious by the danger of joining them too closely, of destroying the distinction between them. Thus, although as we have seen Calvin in a sense joins religion and civil government, he warns us of the error of those who "unwisely mingle" these elements, which "have a completely different nature" from one another (IV.xx.1; 1486). To mingle such elements is to fall into the error of those who "strive to overturn this divinely established [political] order." When people forget to distinguish "between body and soul, between this present fleeting life and that future eternal life," then they think "that nothing will be safe unless the whole world is shaped to a new form where there are neither courts, nor laws, nor magistrates, nor anything which in their opinion restricts their freedom." Such people commit the "Jewish vanity" of seeking "to enclose Christ's Kingdom within the elements of this world." It is true that the political order is part of the divine order; nevertheless, the two orders must not be conflated.

But neither must the two orders be regarded as antithetical; the distinction between spiritual and political "does not lead us to consider the whole nature of government a thing polluted, which has nothing to do with Christian men" (2; 1487). Body and soul, the temporal and the eternal, are distinct—"completely distinct," in fact—yet "we must know that they are not at variance." The Christian, whose overwhelming concern is of course for the life of the spirit, is not for that reason entitled to think himself above the requirements of politics. Calvin mocks those who think "it is a thing unworthy of us and set far beneath our excellence to be occupied with those vile and worldly cares which have to do with business foreign to a Christian man."

The error of this way of thinking seems to consist essentially in overestimating the perfection of believers in this life, and, consequently, in underestimating the necessity of laws and civil government. "Our adversaries claim that there ought to be such great perfection in the church of God that its government should suffice for law. But they stupidly imagine such a perfection as can never be found in a community of men" (2; 1487). Calvin grants that if it were true that "the Kingdom of God, as it now exists in us, extinguishes the present life"—that is, if the victory of the spiritual over the temporal were already complete—then civil government would indeed be "superfluous."

On closer inspection, however, it appears that Calvin's disagreement with the disparagers of civil government extends beyond the question of its necessity. It is possible, after all, to admit that government is necessary and yet to consider it low, of little dignity, and unworthy of what is best in men or in Christians. Thus Augustine argues that true peace and true justice are present only in the City of God, not in earthly cities (*City of God* XIX.13, 25, 27). And because earthly cities lack true justice, they would appear to be no better than criminal gangs (IV.4). On this interpretation, the so-called justice or the "peace of Babylon" obtaining within these gang cities is no more than "a kind of compromise between human wills about the things relevant to mortal life." Therefore, according to Augustine, the household that has faith in the accomplishment of true justice "looks forward to the blessings which are promised as eternal in the future, making use of earthly and temporal things like a pilgrim in a foreign land."

Augustine clearly does not dispute the necessity or usefulness of government as regards "things which are designed for the support of this mortal life." But he does imply that government is a necessity for fallen human nature, not a good for human nature simply: "God," he writes, "did not wish the rational being, made in his own image, to have dominion over any but irrational creatures, not man over man, but man over beasts" (XIX.15). Politics, on this view, appears to serve wholly as a very imperfect remedy for sin.[2]

Although Calvin agrees with Augustine that the political order is a remedy for sin, he also insists that government is not only necessary but noble; he gives politics a much higher status than did Augustine.

> It has not come about by human perversity that the authority over all things on earth is in the hands of Kings and other rulers, but by divine providence and holy ordinance. (IV.xx.4; 1489)

> [Magistrates] are occupied not with profane affairs or those alien to a servant of God, but with a most holy office, since they are serving as God's deputies. (6; 1492)

To deprive man of government, according to Calvin, is to "deprive him of his very humanity." The purpose of government extends far beyond man's physical interest in "peace and tranquility" to the protection of "the outward worship of God," the defense of "sound doctrine" and the promotion of "civil righteousness" (2; 1487).

> Its function among men is no less than that of bread, water, sun, and air; indeed, its place of honor is far more excellent. For it does not merely see to it, as all these serve to do, that men breathe, eat, drink, and are kept warm, even though it surely embraces all these activities when it provides for their living together. It does not, I repeat, look to this only, but also prevents idolatry, sacrilege against God's name, blasphemies against his truth, and other public offenses against religion from arising and spreading among the people; it prevents the public peace from being disturbed; it provides that each man may keep his property safe and sound; that men may carry on blameless intercourse among themselves; that honesty and modesty may be preserved among men. In short, it provides that a public manifesta-

tion of religion may exist among Christians, and that humanity be maintained among men. (3; 1488)

Government, it appears, is not only necessary but honorable and even excellent. It enables man not only to live but to live well. And living well here seems to have two parts: living according to "humanity" and living according to true religion. On this interpretation, the political order thus contributes to life, to the good life, and to the future life—to man's natural necessities, his natural purposes, and his supernatural purposes. Thus it is perhaps not surprising that Calvin should praise the calling of the civil magistrate as "not only holy and lawful before God; but also the most sacred and by far the most honorable of all callings in the whole life of mortal men" (4; 1490).

This reading of Calvin's view of the status of politics is not, however, without serious difficulties. In the first place, the magistrate's duty seems to be to protect only public manifestations of religion; and since Calvin distinguishes so sharply between body and soul, between outward and inward, it is not clear how this outward control can contribute to man's inward righteousness or salvation. Indeed, it is not obvious what significance "outward worship" has for God or man.

In section 9 of this chapter on civil government, Calvin seems to imply that the purpose of this outward worship is not religious but secular; he there agrees with certain philosophers that even on secular grounds it can be shown that piety is necessary to good government.[3] It is necessary not to "neglect God's right" even if one's purpose is to "provide only for men" (9; 1495); public welfare cannot exist without public worship. However, Calvin's purposes, although appearing to coincide partially with those of certain "secular writers," extend further. For Calvin does not assign to magistrates the task of establishing religion according to their judgment of its usefulness; he does not "allow men to make laws according their own decision concerning religion and the worship of God." Rather, Calvin enjoins magistrates to defend "the true religion," which is "outside of human decision" (3; 1488). It is still unclear, however, just what purpose, natural or supernatural, is served by this defense of the outward manifestations of piety.

Calvin may have good reason to refrain from illuminating his teaching on outward worship by referring it to the purposes it serves. For to illuminate an activity in this way would exempt it from the realm "outside of human decision." If human beings could grasp the purpose of outward worship, then it would be possible and right, at least within limits, for them to deliberate in order to "make laws according to their own decision concerning religion and the worship of God." And if such decisions affected man's highest ends, his supernatural ends, then men competent to make such decisions would be in a position to claim spiritual as well as temporal authority over other men; it would no longer be the case that "spiritual freedom can perfectly well exist with civil bondage" (1; 1486). We can be spiritually free while politically bound only if we do not understand politics as serving any spiritual purpose—only if human choice cannot affect the salvation of the soul.

Thus it is far from obvious that Calvin understands the political order as advancing spiritual or supernatural ends. Furthermore, the idea that Calvin understands government as facilitating the attainment of some natural end of mankind also becomes doubtful upon examination of the texts at hand. Calvin teaches that government is necessary to man's very humanity, but this humanity seems to consist in little more than the restraint of violence. Government makes it possible—barely, perhaps—for men to live among other men; it protects property and provides the conditions for "blameless intercourse." It seems to aim at no natural end or virtue beyond "honesty and modesty." The natural end of politics, according to the passages cited above, seems to be not the perfection of the human soul but simply the maintenance of peace.

Here Calvin may appear to be in agreement with Augustine, who writes that "all man's use of temporal things is related to the enjoyment of earthly peace in the earthly city" (City of God XIX.14). But Augustine understands peace as the right order which is the natural aim of all creatures; earthly peace for him is a great good because it imitates, albeit very imperfectly, the peace which is everlasting, wherein all things are rightly subordinated to the love of God (XIX.11–14). Thus, although politics rests for Augustine on a kind of "compromise between human wills about the things relevant to mortal life" (XIX.17; 877), this compromise would not be possible without some reference, however imperfect, to the divine or truly natural (created) order of things: "The peace of the rational soul is the duly ordered agreement of cognition and action . . . peace between men is an ordered agreement of mind with mind . . . the peace of the whole universe is the tranquility of order—and order is the arrangement of things equal and unequal in a pattern which assigns to each its proper position" (XIX.13).

In Calvin's teaching we find no attempt to link the political order with a comprehensive hierarchy unifying the natural and the divine. A radical depreciation of politics would seem to follow, but this is not at all the case. On the contrary, for Calvin politics is ordered by God—indeed, much more directly ordered, it appears, than for Augustine (at least in *The City of God*). Government does not arise from a mere compromise of human wills: magistrates have "a mandate from God, have been invested with divine authority, and are wholly God's representatives" (IV.xx.4; 1489). The political order is thus for Calvin very much God's own order. And yet there is no suggestion of anything intrinsically divine or partaking of the divine in this order itself. There is only a peace without transcendent purpose and a provision for "outward worship." Calvin's peace seems to have less in common with Augustine's than with the naturalistic peace of Hobbes, a peace without any purpose beyond the containment of war by the terror of the sovereign (*Leviathan*, chaps. xiii, xiv, xvii).

Calvin's puzzling combination of an elevation of the status of politics with a lowering of its substance or end has given rise to considerable confusion among scholars attempting to locate the essential character of the reformer's political teaching. Thus J. W. Allen, as we have seen, classifies Calvin among the otherworldly theorists of the Middle Ages but also observes that Calvin departs decisively from Aquinas in his view of human nature and therefore of the end of political order. Similarly, Quentin Skinner carelessly identifies Aristotle's "nature" with modern naturalism and thus cannot ask whether a rejection of the former might be compatible with an affinity with the latter. Michael Walzer more perspicaciously observes that Calvin at once viewed the state as

an "order of repression" and acknowledged its "independent value" (42), but he cannot explain how it was possible to value
repression so highly—that is, to regard it not only as a necessary
consequence of sin but as a positive manifestation of divine order.[4]

The author who goes furthest in arguing the elevation of politics
in Calvin's thought is Sheldon Wolin. A brief discussion of Wolin's striking claim (in "Calvin: The Political Education of Protestantism") that the Genevan reformer was the Protestant Aquinas
(190) and an heir of the political idealism of Plato and Aristotle
(192) will serve to clarify the problem of the status of the political
in Calvin's thought.

According to Wolin, Calvin "worked to restore the reputation of
the political order" (167) and stood at the end of a long tradition in
Christian thought in which "the idea of the community as the
custodian of virtue has been translated from a political to a religious setting" (175).

In order to recapture this older conception of the community, it
was necessary to "reconcile the several opposites created by the
split vision of the early reformers." Wolin writes, "He had to
resolve the conflict between the Christian cosmology and its so-
ciology; he had to reestablish the moral status of the political
order, but without making it appear as a substitute for religious
society; he had to soften the black-and-white contrasts between
the two forms of society" (180).

This conflict or contrast is none other than that created by the
fall of man and the consequent fall of the creation as a whole.
Wolin notices that "Calvin stood second to none of the Reformers
in his low estimate of man's nature" (181). But it would seem to
follow from this low estimate of human nature that Calvin did not
disagree fundamentally with Luther's view that the state is a
"mighty engine of repression" (cf. Wolin, 167). Here Walzer seems
more correct than Wolin. In any case, given such a low estimate of
human nature, that is, given the radical view of the fall that is
rightly associated with Calvin, it is not clear how the conflict
between the integrity and order of the creation and the corruption
and disorder of sin can in any way be "reconciled" within the
political realm. As Wolin himself points out, "the business of the
political order was to shape man to habits of civility and order; it

could not cure souls" (185). But to say that politics can contribute nothing to the cure of souls is, it seems, to say that Calvin's thought failed to heal the split between the divine order and the human order. Even if it is true that according to Calvin, man "must contain something beyond an irrepressible inclination towards disorder" (181), it still must be shown whether there is any kinship between the order of which human nature is capable and the order that God's sovereignty demands—that is, whether the political order, from the divine point of view, constitutes anything but sheer disorder.

Thus it is not clear what Wolin accomplishes by speaking of political virtue as "virtue of a second order," since the second (fallen) order seems radically alien to the virtues of the first; and it will not do to explain Calvin's apparent rehabilitation of the status of politics in Protestantism by saying that he "had to soften the black-and-white contrasts" between religious and political order.[5]

Wolin's interpretation of Calvin as the political educator, the institutionalizer—in a sense, the founder—of Protestantism, is very apt. It is true that Calvin is very much concerned to ground human institutions by establishing the political order as part of the divine order. It is far from clear, however, that he accomplishes this by any softening of contrasts. Indeed, a careful study of Calvin's political teaching will reveal that this grounding is accomplished precisely through a radicalization of the contrast between the human and the divine; Calvin joins religion and politics by intensifying their separation. The thoroughgoing absorption of the political by the religious requires a radical reduction of the political to the material. To see this we must now return to the text of Calvin's *Institutes*. But before pursuing further Calvin's thematic treatment of civil government, it will be useful to examine three subjects to which Calvin refers us in introducing his chapter on politics: providence, Christian freedom, and church government.

Chapter 2

Providence, Christian Freedom, and Spiritual Government

Providence

We have seen that Calvin justifies joining a discussion of politics to his "sum of Christian Religion" in part by arguing that government is a benefit of God's providence and that to signal this benefit is an incentive to piety. But what God has provided, Calvin seems to have suggested, it is necessary for men to recognize and defend. It thus appears that, at least in the world of politics, God's order depends on man's prudence and courage.

Can a benefit provided by God depend upon human virtue? To address this question, I turn briefly to Calvin's chapters on providence, entitled "God by His Power Nourishes and Maintains the World Created by Him, and Rules Its Several Parts by His Providence" (I.xvi) and "How We May Apply This Doctrine to Our Greatest Benefit" (I.xvii).

Calvin's main intention in chapter 16 seems to be to refute pagan beliefs in fortune or chance as well as false Christian interpretations that tend to reduce divine governance to a distant and impersonal force. Whereas "impious" or "profane men" are "compelled" from an observation of the natural world to infer the existence of an original creative power, the man of faith "ought to penetrate more deeply"; for "faith has its own peculiar way of assigning the whole credit for Creation to God." The man of faith refuses to dissociate the "Creator" from the "everlasting Governor and Preserver"; he insists that God not only "drives the celestial frame" (*la machine du monde*) but also that he "sustains, nourishes, and cares for, everything he has made, even to the least sparrow." In sum, Calvin presents in radical form the Christian subordination of nature to God by subordinating God's creation itself to providence. Far from limiting God's providence to the original act of Creation, Calvin understands the creation itself as a manifestation of providence; he sees "the presence of divine power shining as much in the continuing state of the universe as in its inception" (I.xvi.1; 197–98).[1]

In order rightly to acknowledge God's omnipotence, we must therefore understand that his power is "not the empty, idle, and almost unconscious sort that the Sophists [scholastics] imagine, but a watchful, effective, active sort, engaged in ceaseless activity" (3; 200). God not only foresees but actively governs the events of this world; providence "pertains no less to his hands than to his eyes."

Calvin is willing, it is true, to grant the conditional efficacy of natural causes. He grants that "the several kinds of things [*toutes espèces*] are moved by a secret impulse of nature, as if they obeyed God's eternal command, and what God has once determined flows on by itself." Calvin thus concedes that providence often operates through nature, but he will not grant that reason can grasp this operation or the end that links each natural kind of thing with divine purposes. The impulse of nature is secret; to claim to discern it is to deny that God "directs everything by his incomprehensible wisdom and disposes it to his own end" (4; 202–3). God's providence "not only flourishes among creatures so as to continue the order of nature, but is by his wonderful plan adapted to a definite and proper end" (7; 206–7). God gives nature order and purpose, but the fact that we can know or perceive this order does not mean we can know the purpose. The end of nature is not a natural end.

To claim to know the end that governs a natural species or the order of nature as a whole is in effect to subject God to his creation, "to enclose [God's governance] within the stream of nature" (3; 200), to reduce God to an impersonal "general principle of confused motion," a mere "first agent . . . and cause of all motion"; it is to imagine the ideal and unconscious being of the scholastics or

"Sophists." If God's purposes inhere in the order of nature, then, in effect, nature has no purpose. Either "all events are governed by God's secret plan," or the sun must "rise and set by a blind instinct of nature" (2; 199).

The purpose of the universe is a secret. And yet there is something we can know of it: "Because we know that the universe was established especially for the sake of mankind, we ought to look for this purpose in his governance also" (6; 2054). Calvin thus refers to his treatment of the purpose of the creation in chapter 14. There he has taught that "God's fatherly love toward mankind is shown in that he did not create Adam until he had lavished upon the universe all manner of good things" (xiv.2; 161–62).

These "good things" must, however, always remind us of their author: "God has destined all things for our good and salvation but at the same time to feel his power and grace in ourselves and in the great benefits he has conferred upon us, and so bestir ourselves to trust, invoke, praise, and love him" (22; 181). The universe is good because it is for the sake of man. And yet it could not be good for man unless it were full of "all manner of good things." Without this goodness, we have seen, the order of nature would in itself be alien to man—empty, unconscious, and moved by blind instinct. This implies that we cannot recognize God's providence without recognizing the goodness of nature. This goodness, however, is not natural but hidden in God's secret plan. How then can it serve "our good and salvation?"—unless our good and salvation consist in feeling "his power and grace in ourselves"—unless, in a sense, to know God's benefits means to feel his power in ourselves.

This problem points to a fundamental theological question that will require further reflection in part 2. In any case, it is clear that for Calvin, God's governing power is exercised especially for the sake of humankind. And this power of providence also applies emphatically to human action. Calvin quotes the prophet Jeremiah: "I know, O Lord, that the way of man is not his own, nor is it given to man to direct his own steps" (xvi.6; 204). Some would interpret this to mean that men "are governed by God's might but not by his determination"; that is, that God has given man a nature and left it to man "to act in accordance with the nature implanted in him." Some say "that man is moved by God accord-

ing to the inclination of his nature, but that he himself turns that
motion whither he pleases" (6; 204). In this way certain writers
attempt to give place both to God's omnipotence and to human
action, to "free choice." They "apportion things between God and
man" (4; 202).[2]

But this apportioning to make room for free choice does not
satisfy Calvin. In order to form the believer to "gratitude of mind
for the favorable outcome of things, patience in adversity, and also
incredible freedom from worry about the future" (xvii.7; 219), it is
necessary to affirm that "nothing takes place by chance." Only
then will the human heart "not doubt that God's singular providence keeps watch to preserve it, and will not suffer anything to
happen but what may turn out to its good and salvation" (6; 218).
According to Calvin, then, God governs everything, including
human action, not only indirectly by his power but actively and
continuously by his will.

It would seem to follow that divine providence leaves little
room for human action. But Calvin emphatically denies this in-
ference. He insists that "we are not at all hindered by God's eternal
decrees either from looking ahead for ourselves or from putting all
our affairs in order, but always in submission to his will" (4; 215–
16). Calvin seems here to be following the method of those who
"apportion things between God and man": part of God's providence consists in making room for human providence. Furthermore, the phrase "but always in submission to his will" is fundamentally ambiguous. Calvin has taught that man is in a sense
always in submission to God's will, whether he chooses to be or
not. So this phrase would seem to be a statement of fact. But it also
seems to be intended as a guide to choice, commending men to
provide for themselves in ways consistent with God's commandments. In any case, that man should rightly order his own affairs
for his own good obviously requires that he know what his good
consists in. But we have seen that Calvin teaches that God "directs everything by his incomprehensible wisdom and disposes it
to his own end" (xvi.4; 202). Calvin makes no exception for man,
although he teaches that the universe was created for the sake of
man. Man is the purpose of nature, but man has no natural or
knowable purpose. Man is commended to exercise prudence, but
wisdom is withheld from him.

How then will human beings care for themselves? How will they order their lives? Calvin here mentions only man's ability to preserve his physical existence and to guard against dangers to it: "The Lord has inspired in men the arts of taking counsel and caution, by which to comply with his providence in the preservation of life." Calvin denies man the power of free choice because he denies that man is competent to choose the good which only God knows or wills; but he teaches that man is not incapable of recognizing what is necessary to his self-preservation. The care of the body is an example of God's use of the natural order to accomplish his purposes: "God's providence does not always meet us in its naked form, but God in a sense clothes it with the means employed." In the activity of self-preservation, the mystery of providence is clothed in a form naturally accessible to man.[3] Self-preservation is the point where divine and human power coincide.

Christian Freedom

In the second section of his chapter on civil government, Calvin describes the relationship between the governments of the spiritual and civil orders. But in order to understand the relationship between these two governments, it is necessary to understand the relationship between the orders themselves. The relationship between politics and religion seems to correspond to the relationship between body and soul or between the temporal and the eternal. Thus Calvin reminds the reader, in introducing his discussion of civil government, that it is necessary to "keep in mind that distinction which we previously laid down" (IV.xv.1). The reader is referred to Calvin's chapter on "Christian Freedom," which in the original edition of the Institutes (1536) was combined with Calvin's discussion of ecclesiastical and civil government. Before continuing to examine "Civil Government," I will first heed Calvin's reminder and examine his chapter on "Christian Freedom" (III.xix) and then consider his teaching on spiritual government.

Calvin treats the subject of Christian freedom with caution, obviously well aware of intense controversies that surround it and of its vulnerability to misinterpretation. "As soon as Christian freedom is mentioned, either passions boil or wild tumults rise unless these wanton spirits are opposed in time, who otherwise most wickedly corrupt the best things. Some, on the pretext of this freedom, shake off all obedience toward God and break out into unbridled license. Others disdain it, thinking that it takes away all moderation, order, and choice of things." (III.xix.1; 834).

Nevertheless, the subject cannot be neglected; to explain Christian freedom is "a thing of prime necessity." Freedom is, after all, "an appendage of justification" (1; 833), and justification by faith, Calvin has written earlier, is "the main hinge on which religion turns" (xi.1, 7; 726). Thus, "unless this freedom be comprehended, neither Christ nor gospel truth, nor inner peace of the soul, can be rightly known" (xix.1; 834).

The doctrine of Christian freedom, Calvin explains, follows immediately from justification by faith. Since it is impossible for a human being to fulfill the requirement of the law that we "love our God with all our heart, with all our soul, and with all our strength" (4; 836), then "believers, in seeking assurance of their justification before God, should rise above and advance beyond the law, forgetting all law righteousness." We should "turn our attention from ourselves"—that is, from our own "works"—"and look only to Christ" (2; 834).

Christian freedom thus means freedom from the law. One can see why this characteristic Protestant teaching might have been the source of "wild tumults" and "disdain." Therefore Calvin hastens to add that it is wrong "to infer from this that the law is superfluous to believers." It is true that believers' *consciences* are free from the law, Calvin explains—it is true that the law is irrelevant to the believer's certainty of salvation. Still, the law "does not stop teaching and exhorting and urging them to do good." On the contrary, "the whole life of the Christian ought to be a sort of practice of godliness" (2; 834–35). The burden or threat of the law is eliminated for believers, but this only increases their ability to conform to the law, to the degree that fallen human nature allows: "consciences observe the law, not as if constrained by the necessity of the law, but that freed from the law's yoke they willingly obey God's will" (4; 836). Unbelievers are like servants "who think they have accomplished nothing and dare not appear before their masters unless they have fulfilled the exact measure of their tasks"; believers are like sons who, trusting in the generosity of their father, "do not hesitate to offer them incomplete and half-done and even defective works" (5; 837).

The analogy is attractive, but it points to a difficulty in Calvin's doctrine: if sons do not hesitate to present defective works to their fathers, this is not only because their fathers treat them generously but also because defective works, although imperfect, are not intrinsically worthless. And if one son is capable of a work "half-done," another son, or the same son making a better effort, might be capable of a work three-quarters perfect. Thus sons, in trying to please their fathers, do not turn their attention wholly from themselves, that is, from their work; they do not look exclusively to the grace of their fathers.

Calvin would of course object to this interpretation of his analogy. He wrote earlier that "so long as any particle of works righteousness remains some occasion for boasting remains with us." True faith "excludes all boasting" (xi.13; 743). However, a son who offers works that have some worth, although they are imperfect, would seem to be boasting. Thus Calvin must say or imply that imperfect works are—from God's point of view, at least— "entirely evil" (xix.4; 837). But then it is not clear why or in what spirit believers offer their works to God.

It would seem that works—the fruits of human efforts, what human beings can do—must either have some worth or be entirely worthless. But Calvin's argument is not constrained by this logic. On the one hand, according to Calvin, it is necessary to the purity of faith that works be worthless; if we allow them any intrinsic worth, however small, then we invite men to look partly to themselves for their salvation, an invitation which can only lead to tortured consciences, to the impossibility of being assured of one's salvation. And when man turns to himself, he in effect turns himself over to the power of other men; to depend on human works is to depend on human interpretation of works and thus to fall prey to "superstitions" in which "consciences ensnare themselves" (7; 838–39). Falling prey to these superstitions, men fall prey to the "savage tyranny and butchery" (IV.x; 1179; see also III.iv.17; 641) of popes and priests, whose claim to know what works are necessary to salvation exhibits a desire "to rule lustfully, licentiously, without God and his word" (III.iv.21; 648). The "Kingdom of Christ" is "invaded" by priests armed with so-called "spiritual" laws claimed to be "necessary for eternal life." This, "the freedom given by him to the consciences of believers is utterly oppressed and cast down" (IV.x.1; 1180).

Only by recognizing the worthlessness of works for salvation, by turning men's attention away from themselves and their own works and toward the grace of God, are they "released from the power of all men" (III.xix.14; 846).

On the other hand, as we have seen, Calvin denies that Christian freedom is freedom to disregard the law of God. The purpose of the law is to encourage us to do good, and so there must be some goodness in our obeying the law, however imperfectly we obey it. Furthermore, even in matters not specifically regulated by God's law, Calvin insists that Christian liberty is not license: "it is perversely interpreted . . . by those who allege it as an excuse for their desires that they may abuse God's good gifts to their own lust" (9; 840). God's gifts are good, and they are only rightly used when they are used according to their goodness. Christian freedom is not freedom to abuse the goodness of God's gifts.

But what precisely is the nature of the goodness of God's gifts? To know how to use a gift well, one must know what makes the gift good; and to act on this knowledge would be to accomplish some good by one's own efforts. But then human works would not be entirely evil; they would seem in fact to participate in the goodness of God by actualizing or perfecting the goodness of God's gifts. This would imply that men can by their own efforts contribute something to righteousness and that men are competent to determine what good works consist in.

Calvin does not draw these conclusions from his teaching on the goodness of God's gifts. He writes, "we should use God's gifts for the purpose for which he gave them to us, with no scruple of conscience, no trouble of mind" (8; 840); but he gives little consideration to the question of the nature of this purpose. In particular, he offers no suggestion as to how the goodness of God's gifts is related to God's goodness.

Calvin's main intention in explaining Christian freedom seems to be to discourage both superstitious asceticism and immoderate indulgence of the appetites. He provides little guidance for determining the proper or moderate use of God's gifts. He does, however, drop some hints:

> But where there is plenty, to wallow in delights, to gorge oneself, to intoxicate mind and heart with present pleasures and be always panting after new ones—such are very far removed from a lawful use of God's gifts.
>
> Thus let every man live in his station, whether slenderly, or moderately, or plentifully, so that all may remember God nourishes them to live, not to luxuriate" (9; 841).

One can gather from the first passage that a gift is not well used when it is used in a way that hinders the operations of "the mind and heart." This implies that the goodness of the pleasures referred to is inferior and subordinate to the good of the activities of the mind and heart. In this case, the knowledge of this superior gift would regulate the use of other gifts.

But the second passage does not corroborate this interpretation. For if the right use of God's gifts is simply the use of them according to one's station—if what is right is not determined by a good or a purpose—then all stations are equally right. It follows that a station is not a better station because it favors the proper activity of the mind and heart. "God nourishes them to live" thus means "to live in their stations," to live without concern for any purpose superior to their stations, without concern, notably, for any intrinsic purpose of the mind and heart. We are to use God's gifts for God's purposes, but we are not to inquire into God's purposes, ranking his gifts according to the respective purposes they serve. All we need to know about the goodness of God's gifts is that which is evident to anyone: food is for eating, for example, and wine is for drinking.

In order to free believers from the spiritual tyranny of human beings, Calvin thus seems to deny any knowable spiritual purpose to human action. But in order to check the apparent anarchic potential of this doctrine, in order to show that "spiritual freedom can perfectly well exist along with civil bondage" (IV.xx.1; 1486), Calvin, in concluding this discussion of "Christian Freedom," must rigorously distinguish between two kingdoms. "There is," he writes, "a twofold government in man. . . . There are in man, so to speak, two worlds, over which different kings and different laws have authority" (III.xix.15; 847). These worlds or kingdoms are the "spiritual" and "temporal realms," a dichotomy that Calvin here equates with that between the soul and the body (or "the present of life"), between "inner mind" and "outward behavior," and between the "forum of conscience" and the "outer forum" (15; 847–48). The believer finds all his spiritual needs in Christ alone; therefore he is spiritually subject to no man. But this spiritual freedom does not abrogate the necessity of a political kingdom or jurisdiction "whereby man is educated for the duties of humanity and citizenship that must be maintained among men"—an education that apparently pertains only to the body or outward behavior. Calvin specifies that the jurisdiction of "the present life" goes beyond, if not above, "food and clothing"; this jurisdiction also concerns "laying down laws whereby a man may live his life among other men holily, honorably, and temperately."

How it is possible for the realm of the body to extend not only to the temperate and honorable but even to the holy we will examine below, by looking first at Calvin's description of the spiritual kingdom and then again at his account of civil government.

The Spiritual Kingdom and Its External Means

The meaning of the spiritual kingdom seems clear in light of the doctrine of justification by faith and the "appendage" of this doctrine, Christian freedom. Believers, esteeming their own righteousness as nothing, turn their whole attention to the saving righteousness of Christ. Since they are wholly dependent on Christ, in whom their salvation is absolutely assured (for they are the elect of God, chosen by his free mercy before the creation of the world) (II.xi.1, 2), believers are wholly freed from dependence on all men and from themselves—that is, from concern for their own works. The spiritual kingdom thus seems to consist in the invisible community of all the elect, past, present, and future, in the "communion of saints." Christ is the king of this kingdom. He reigns over the elect and the damned alike (xv.3–5); but the elect are no mere subjects but partakers of the priesthood of Christ himself, "companions in this great office. For we who are defiled in ourselves, yet are priests in him, offer ourselves and our all to God, and freely enter the heavenly sanctuary" (6; 502).

Since believers are one with Christ, they depend on no one and on nothing else for assurance and support. Calvin's affirmation of the priority of individual belief over institutional authority could hardly be stronger: "the basis on which we believe the church is that we are fully convinced we are members of it" (IV.i.3; 1015).

Calvin is obviously describing here a spiritual communion, in which each individual fully and securely possesses the benefits of the whole, and not a human institution, in which the individuals are more or less incomplete and therefore dependent upon the whole. It seems to follow that, in this life, such a spiritual kingdom would exist only for individuals, since individuals may know that they are members of it (III.xxiv.6–7), whereas they cannot know whether anyone else belongs among the elect. The church or spiritual kingdom must necessarily be invisible.

This is not, however, what Calvin teaches. For when, near the end of his chapter on "Christian Freedom" (xix.15), Calvin begins an extensive treatment of "spiritual government," he is not mainly referring to the perfect communion of saints, to this invisible church. Instead, he is referring to a very visible institution existing here and now, to the ecclesiastical structure of true faith, to "the true church with which as mother of all the godly we must keep unity" (IV.i). The title of the fourth book of the *Institutes*, which treats "the church, its government, orders, and power; then the sacraments; and lastly the civil order" (i.1; 1012), is "The External Means or Aids by Which God Invites Us into the Society of Christ and Holds Us Therein" (1011). Why do believers need these external means? "In our ignorance and sloth . . . we need outward helps to beget and increase faith within us, and advance it to its goal," Calvin answers (1; 1011).

By spiritual kingdom, Calvin therefore means much more than the free and invisible community of the elect. In fact, he announces plainly that his subject is the visible church (4; 1016), pausing just long enough on the subject of the invisible church to make clear the distinction between the two (3, 7). It is necessary, therefore, to reconsider the meaning of the spiritual kingdom and its relation to Christian freedom. To what end does the internal kingdom employ external means? How is it that the believer, whose spiritual freedom appears to be perfect, is nonetheless subject to a religious institution? If the believer's assurance of his own salvation is the basis of his belief in the church, then how is it that the visible church is the "mother of all believers?" Calvin writes, "For there is no other way to enter into life unless this mother conceive us in her womb, give us birth, nourish us at her breast, and lastly unless she keep us under her care and guidance until, putting off mortal flesh, we become like the angels. Our weakness does not allow us to be dismissed from her school until we have been pupils all our lives. Furthermore, away from her bosom one cannot hope for any forgiveness of sins or any salvation" (4; 1016). Here Calvin appears to adopt the very terms of the popes and priests he attacks. What can he mean?

There appears to be a simple answer to the question how Calvin's doctrine of faith can coexist with his doctrine of the church as mother of believers: the church is the means by which God has chosen to make us believers; it is thus the instrument of authority by which we become free. The church employs pastors whose "preaching of the heavenly doctrine" enables us "to grow up in manhood," to achieve, perhaps, the absolute spiritual self-reliance described above (5; 1017). God has willed to employ the means of preaching in order to save those whom he has willed to save: "God breathes faith into us only by the instrument of his gospel, as Paul points out that 'faith comes by hearing.'" He has chosen to use "human means" to accomplish the salvation of the elect. As he once chose priests to interpret the law to his people, he now "prefers to address us in human fashion through interpreters in order to draw us to himself, rather than to thunder at us and drive us away" (5; 1017–18).

It seems, then, that the role of the pastor is equivalent to that of the priest under the Old Covenant—to mediate between God and man by interpreting God's word to his people. But Calvin later points out a fundamental difference between priest and pastor. Priests appearing in the Tabernacle "properly represented Christ" as mediators between God and man. However, "because the pastors of the church do not play this part today, it is pointless to compare them with the priests" (xii.25; 1251). Since Christ has completely fulfilled the mediating office of priest, there is no longer need for any further mediation between God and man; the Word (Christ as represented in scripture) suffices to reconcile man to God (see II.xv.6). Similarly, since the word of God has been revealed in the flesh, there is no longer need for prophets to serve as the channel of God's revelation to mankind. The "teaching of His Son" must be regarded as "the final and eternal testimony." Thus, "after himself he left nothing for others to say" (IV.viii.7; 1154–55; cf. iii.5; 1058).

If God has left nothing for man to say, however, it is not clear what the function of the ministry is. In what sense are human beings to serve as "interpreters"? Calvin's answer is that ministers speak nothing but what Christ himself spoke. God uses human means but without subjecting his Word to human weaknesses. God does not depend on human reasoning but simply "deigns to consecrate to himself the mouths and tongues of men in order that his voice may resound in them" (i.5; 1018). God "leaves nothing to ministers by themselves." The human means can claim no credit for the spiritual effect of preaching. "God, ascribing to himself illumination of mind and renewal of heart, warns that it is sacrilege for man to claim any part of either for himself" (6; 1021).

The relationship between ministers and Christians is therefore very different from that which obtained between priests and the people of Israel. When "crafty men," trying to overwhelm us "with great heaps of ceremonies," compare modern believers to the children of Israel, we should remember that the Jews were under the custody of the law. "But we are like adults, who, freed of tutelage and custody, have no need of childish rudiments" (x.14; 1192). The church is our mother, but we are adults. Calvin does not deny that ceremonies are useful to the "ignorant to help them in their inexperience." But he insists that "the means used ought to show Christ, not to hide him." And since we are adults, capable of worshipping "in spirit and in truth," the central function of the church is that of preaching. The "keys" or authority of the church thus consist in no human ruling but in the preaching of the divine word: "the power of the keys is simply the preaching of the gospel. . . . For Christ has not given this power actually to men, but to his Word, of which he has made men ministers" (xi.2; 1213; see also ii.10; 1051).

Since the authority of the church is the authority of the Word, there is no place for any rulership based on the virtue or wisdom of human beings. Thus Calvin rejects the word *hierarchy* as a description of church organization, "for the Holy Spirit willed men to beware of dreaming of a principality or lordship as far as the government of the church is concerned" (iv.4; 1072). Or, if one wants to call church organization a hierarchy, Calvin wants it clear that no analogy can be claimed between this order and some speculative notion of the universal order or cosmos: "Nor is there reason for our opponents to philosophize subtly over a comparison of heavenly and earthly hierarchies" (vi.9; 1110). Calvin denies in particular that the order of the church requires "the unity of the hierarchy under an earthly head" (v.17; 1118). To "Christ alone" belongs "the honor and name of the Head"; to each member this Head assigns "a definite and limited function, in order that perfection of grace as well as the supreme power of governing may remain with Christ alone" (vi.9; 1110). The order of the church is not a human order, for no human being is competent to order the whole of Christ's kingdom, to represent the unity of the church; rather, scripture "assigns particular functions to each member according to the measure of grace bestowed upon each" (cf. Wolin, 176).

The church thus has its unity and completeness only in Christ; as an earthly institution it can claim no perfection. It is no more perfect or holy than its members. "The church is holy, then, in the sense that it is daily advancing and is not yet perfect." The church's holiness indeed consists in nothing but the progressive sanctification of its members: "Christ daily sanctifies all his people, cleanses and polishes them, and wipes away their stains," but "it is obvious that they are still sprinkled with some defect and spots, and that something is lacking to their sanctification." The church's holiness is assured because Christ has sanctified it. But this sanctification is now invisible; it will appear only in the future and can now be glimpsed only in the daily process of the purification of its members. It is striking that Calvin affirms at once that "the church's spots and wrinkles have been wiped away" and at the same time that this is a daily process until Christ by his coming completely removes whatever remains (IV.viii.12; 1160–61). The church's holiness consists in its becoming holy.

However, if the church is at present no more perfect than its members, then why should members be subject to the authority of the church and dependent on it as on a mother—away from whose bosom "one cannot hope for any forgiveness of sins or any salvation?" (i.4; 1016). Calvin's answer is that the essence of the church is purity of doctrine, that is, the preaching of the gospel. The visible church, if it is the true church, possesses with certainty the pure doctrine of faith, even though the members of the church are imperfect and continue to require daily purification. Therefore, although it is ridiculous to claim that the church as a visible institution is infallible (viii.10–16), it remains true that "believers . . . cannot err or disagree with God's judgment, for they judge solely according to God's law, which is no uncertain or earthly opinion but God's holy will and heavenly oracle" (xi.1; 1214). Since God makes the "mouths and tongues of men" the mere instruments of his own voice, the imperfection of the church in no way hinders the perfection of preaching. And what does preaching consist in? "The sum total of the gospel is that we all, being slaves of sin and death, are released and freed through the redemption which is in Christ Jesus and that they who do not receive or acknowledge Christ as this liberator and redeemer are condemned and sentenced to eternal chains" (1; 1212–13).

A preliminary examination of Calvin's idea of the church thus refers us back to his teaching on the freedom of believers. It would appear that ecclesiastical authority does not limit Christian freedom but only proclaims it. It would follow that the spiritual kingdom is simply the invisible kingdom governed by Christ himself, a kingdom not administered but only announced by the visible church, by the external means of this inward communion of the free. In this way it seems possible to reconcile the earthly authority of the church with Calvin's defense of the inner freedom that results from turning our attention from ourselves and seeking our righteousness in Christ alone.

However, this argument falls far short of accounting for Calvin's complete doctrine of church government. For the function of the church, according to Calvin, does not consist only in the preaching of the gospel of salvation by faith and in the administration of sacraments which are "outward sign[s] by which the Lord seals on our conscience the promises of his good will toward us in order to sustain the weakness of our faith" (iv.1; 1277). The church is also an agent of discipline. "The whole jurisdiction of the church," Calvin writes, "pertains to the discipline of morals." And this jurisdiction is the most important ecclesiastical power "in a well-ordered state." No more than a political body can the church exist without discipline and ordered authority. "For as no city or township can function without magistrate and polity, so the church of God . . . needs a spiritual polity" (xi.1; 1211).

The internal, invisible order of the free communion of saints under the immediate kingship of Christ alone is not self-sufficient. It must be supported and preserved by a visible, external order of moral discipline, a "spiritual polity." The spiritual kingdom demands its own political order, without which everyone would go his own way. "Accordingly, as the saving doctrine of Christ is the soul of the church, so does discipline serve as its sinews, through which the members of the body hold together, each in its own place." To the "preaching of doctrine" must therefore be added "private admonitions, corrections, and other aids of the sort that sustain doctrine and do not let it remain idle." Calvin employs three metaphors to depict the function of church discipline: "a bridle to restrain and tame those who rage against the doctrine of Christ; a spur to arouse those of little inclination; and a father's rod to chastise mildly and with the gentleness of Christ's Spirit those who have more seriously lapsed" (xii.1; 1229–30). The saving doctrine of Christ is not alone sufficient to create the visible order its preservation demands; the bridles, spurs, and rods of discipline must sustain this doctrine and make it visibly effective—that is, not "idle." The soul, without sinews, cannot hold the body together in proper order.

What do these "sinews" of discipline consist in? Calvin recommends admonition—private admonition for private sins and public and "solemn rebuke by the church" for public sins (2–3). To correct grave sins, that is, "crimes or shameful acts," a more severe remedy is necessary, namely, excommunication (4), by which the church "condemns [the offender's] life and morals, and already warns him of his condemnation unless he should repent" (2; 1214).

But how is it that the Christian whose salvation is secure in Christ, and who is therefore free from concern for the worth of his own works, can be subject to the threat of condemnation by a church which is itself far from perfectly holy—"For faith consists in the knowledge of God and Christ, not in reverence for the church"? (III.ii.3; 545). To address this question adequately will require an examination of Calvin's doctrine of justification by faith and its relation to sanctification or regeneration (see chap. 6). At present let us notice that, although faith is sufficient to give believers perfect assurance of their salvation in the perfect righteousness of Christ and therefore to give them perfect freedom from "works righteousness" (III.ii.15, 16, 38–40; xi.11; xiii.3; xv.title, 7, 8; xix.2; xxiv.7), our justification by faith is nonetheless in need of perpetual renewal (ii.4, 23) and therefore of external means or "outward helps to beget and increase faith within us, and advance it to its goals" (IV.i.1; 1011). "Faith must be perpetually begotten and increased, because even right faith is always surrounded by error and unbelief" (III.ii; 4). And faith needs help to "advance it to its goal," because its goal is "newness of life" or "actual holiness of life," and this is distinct from the "proper object of faith, namely, the free imputation of righteousness" (iii.1,19; 592–93, 614) "The Lord freely justifies his own in order that he may at the same time restore them to true righteousness by sanctification of his Spirit" (19; 613).

According to Calvin, the "signs of repentance" are evident in the "whole of life" of the believer. Still, "when we have to deal with God nothing is achieved unless we begin from the inner disposition of the heart" (16; 609–10). But the heart of man considered in itself always falls infinitely short of God's standard of righteousness: "All human works, if judged according to their own worth, are nothing but filth and defilement" (xii.5; 759). It follows that "whatever is praiseworthy in works is God's grace; there is not a drop we ought by right to ascribe to ourselves" (xxv.3; 990). Because it is inconsistent with the "flesh," that is, with human nature itself, to conform to God's holiness, our regeneration or vivification presupposes the mortification or destruction of our present natures, which cannot be complete in this life (III.iii.8–9). "So long as we dwell in the prison house of our body we must continually contend with the defects of our corrupt nature, indeed with our own natural soul" (20; 614). For this reason sanctification is for us more a process than an end; we possess it mainly in the sense of desiring it and striving for it. The evidence of repentance is not a state of holiness but an earnest measuring of one's life "by the standard of God's law" (16; 609).

"Vivification" is not "the happiness that the mind receives after its perturbation and fear have been quieted" but "the desire to live in a holy and devoted manner" (ii.3; 595). "The life of a Christian man is a continual effort and exercise in the mortification of the flesh," and it is a mark of progress to be "very much displeased" with oneself (x.20; 615). Citing Augustine, Calvin argues that central to the saints' "perfection" is the recognition of imperfection, both in truth and in humility" (xvii.15; 820).

Inward conformity to the absolute demands of God's law is impossible for man—the natural soul cannot please God. Thus we can only show our subjection to these demands by claiming no credit for ourselves and by demonstrating an intention more inward than the natural soul to overcome the limitations of our whole nature. This intention bears visible fruit in our outward subjection to God's law, in "works" that are not in themselves meritorious but are indications of Christ's progressive work of regeneration in the heart of the believer.

Although the Christian should rely, not on works, but "wholly on the free promise of righteousness," Calvin does not "forbid him from undergirding and strengthening this faith by signs of the divine benevolence toward him" (xiv.18; 785). The fruit of continuous justification by faith is the continuous process of sanctification exhibited in the believer's inmost heart by his disgust with his soul, his attendant striving for God's impossible holiness, and in his outward behavior by conformity to the outward demands of God's law.

Clearly the freedom of the Christian from the burden of the law is anything but freedom from concern for the law. The believer's salvation is secure, but this security manifests itself in a relentless struggle by which God inwardly reveals his own holiness and the soul's depravity and outwardly subjects the believer to obedience. The believer is free from concern for the goodness of his works; but he is not free from his holy duty to perform them, even though they are devoid of intrinsic merit. This is why the spiritual kingdom is also a kingdom of outward order.

To understand the connection between the inward freedom of the spiritual kingdom and the discipline of "external means," we must return briefly to Calvin's discussion of Christian freedom in the third book of the *Institutes*, and in particular to his treatment of "conscience." (Much of this treatment is repeated in IV.x.3–5.) Calvin insists, as we have seen, that "the consciences of believers, in seeking assurance of their justification before God, should rise above and advance beyond the law, forgetting all law righteousness" (III.xx.2; 854). "Freed from the law's yoke [believers] will obey God's will" (4; 836). But later it appears that this freedom or willingness can also be described as a kind of bondage and subjection. The freedom of conscience which seemed to be inward freedom from all law, and from the demands of God's law in particular, now appears as "freedom of conscience from all *human* law" (xix.14; 846, my emphasis). "Christ's death is nullified if we put our souls under men's subjection" (846), but subjection to God and to his laws (administered, of course, by men) is consistent with— indeed, bound up with—the freedom of the believer. And since God wills the subjection of believers to human laws—"as concerns outward government" only, of course—"bodily servitude" is perfectly consistent with freedom "according to the Spirit" (15; 847). The freedom of the Christian means not that he is free to disobey human laws or divine laws (except those "snares of Observances" by which papists trap souls by promising to improve them), but only that in obeying these he regards God alone and not other men. "Hence it comes about that a law is said to bind the conscience when it simply binds a man without regard to other men, or without taking them into account." Freedom of conscience is thus consistent with being "bound by guilt before God" (16; 849).

This link between conscience and active guilt is an essential part of Calvin's understanding of the nature of conscience. He defines conscience as "a certain mean between God and man" (15;

849). In book 4 (x.5; 1103) Calvin calls this mean "the tiny little spark of light" that remained after the fall, "while the whole world was shrouded in this densest darkness of ignorance." This might suggest that part of human nature, even after the fall, partakes of God's goodness and raises humanity just a little toward divinity. But this is not Calvin's meaning. The mean between God and man that exists in the mind of man is not sufficient to lead to God but only to convince man of his insufficiency, that is, of his need for mediation, for "Christ's grace." The "little spark of light" is not a divine apex to the natural soul, which might give a measure of divinity to nature, but rather a consciousness wholly different from "understanding" and "higher than all human judgments" (IV.x.5; 1183) of the depravity of all that is human.

Thus a "good conscience" is not a sinless conscience, and certainly not the consciousness of a sinless soul, but a conscience free of the "accusation of sin" precisely because of its awareness of the impossibility of being sinless. The "inward integrity of heart" is not a condition of the soul itself, a perfected inward order, but an ever-renewed inward awareness of sin, yielding continuous outward works of obedience. Thus "good conscience," which seems to describe a stable inner condition, in fact "signifies a lively *inclination* to serve God and a sincere *effort* to live piously and holily" (III.xix.16; 849; my emphasis). The end of holiness as a condition of soul is impossible; man's sanctification consists in a process of intention and action, with only a negative regard for condition.

It is clear, then, that "even believers have need of the law" (II.vii.12; 360). First, they need the law "to learn more thoroughly each day the nature of the Lord's will to which they aspire, and to confirm them in the understanding of it." Second, believers need the law for exhortation. "The law is to the flesh like a whip to an idle and balky ass, to arouse it to work . . . the law remains a constant sting that will not let him stand still" (12; 361). The sting or threat of the law troubles the soul with fear, which leads the believer to the delightful sweetness of the "accompanying promise of grace." However, grace does not exactly remove the sting; it sweetens it by making it a relentless motive for actions, never allowing the believer to stand still.

It is fitting, then, that the Christian freedom proclaimed by the preaching of the church be supplemented by subjection to God's law as enforced by the disciplinary sanction of the church. These sanctions (admonishment, rebuke, and excommunication), serve three purposes: first, to protect the name of the church from disgrace by excluding those of "filthy and infamous life"; second, to prevent the good (that is, those in whom the sting of conscience is effective) from being corrupted by association with the bad; and third, "that those overcome by shame for their baseness begin to repent" by being "awakened when they feel the rod" (IV.xii.5; 1232–33). The external rod employed by the visible church is therefore a useful supplement to the inward sting of the law. Because the believer grasps the soul of the church, the "saving doctrine of Christ" (1; 1230), only in response to the ever-renewed sting of the law, this soul can make use of the sinews of discipline.

Calvin rigorously distinguishes the disciplinary means employed by the church from those proper to civil government. Since "the church does not have the right of the sword to punish or compel," Calvin regards church discipline a voluntary chastisement. Thus, Calvin claims to respect the different natures of civil and spiritual order: "The church does not assume what is proper to the magistrate; nor can the magistrate execute what is carried out by the church" (xi.3; 1215).

This distinction between ecclesiastical and political jurisdiction represents an elaboration of the distinction Calvin insists on in his chapter on Christian freedom (III.xix)—the very distinction of which he reminds us in introducing his chapter on civil government. "There is a twofold government in man: one aspect is spiritual . . . the second is political . . . two worlds, over which different kings and different laws have authority" (III.xix,15; 847). This argument dividing authority into two distinct governments which (to recall our earlier discussion) Calvin bases upon an emphatic distinction between body and soul, or between the spiritual and the temporal, seems to be directed against two different kinds of errors. On the one hand, there are those (anabaptists) who, confounding the two worlds, "think that nothing will be safe unless the whole world is reshaped to a new form" wherein Christian freedom is made politically effective (IV.xx.1; 1486). These people "claim a perfection of which not even a hundredth part is seen in them" (5; 1490). Their error consists essentially in illegitimately transferring a doctrine concerning the spiritual realm into the temporal realm.

On the other hand, Calvin directs his rigorous distinction of the two governments against those who transfer a view of authority appropriate to the temporal realm into the spiritual realm. This group includes those who would give magistrates or emperors authority in spiritual matters (xi.3, 5), as well as those ecclesiastical authorities who claim for themselves the power of the sword and, therefore, the proper functions of the prince or civil magistrate (7–9). Emil Doumergue calls the first group *cesaropapists* and the second *theocrats* (V.405; cf. Chenevière, 247–48). In either case the effect is the same: the spiritual jurisdiction is ruled as if it were a political order; that is, force is applied where only "voluntary chastisement" is appropriate. But in the last chapter of the *Institutes*, Calvin does not hesitate to lend the arm of the state to spiritual government. One of the "chief tasks and burdens of civil government" is to provide that "a public manifestation of religion may exist among Christians" (IV.xx.3; 1488). In this discussion of the government of the soul, immediately after marking the distinction between the voluntary order of the church and the coercive political order, Calvin writes that "the magistrate ought by punishment and physical restraint to cleanse the church of offenses." The political and spiritual "functions ought to be so joined that each serves to help, not hinder, the other" (xi.3; 1216). Further on Calvin expands on this point, explaining that there is nothing wrong with the prince's intervening in church affairs "provided it was done to preserve the order of the church, not to disrupt it; and to establish discipline, not to dissolve it." The reasoning is simple: though "the church does not have the power to coerce, and ought not to seek it (I am speaking of civil coercion)," it still finds coercion useful. Thus "it is the duty of godly kings and princes to sustain religion by laws, edicts, and judgments" (16; 1228–29).

This apparent ambivalence concerning the spiritual use of coercion has been the source of much confusion among interpreters of Calvin's political and ecclesiastical teaching. For Sabine (*A History of Political Theory*), much as for Allen, Calvin's employment of political means to religious ends is enough to make Calvinism a clear case of "hierarchy," of "extreme medieval ecclesiasticism" (363). William Dunning (*A History of Political Theories from Luther to Montesquieu*) believes that Calvin's theory, along with those of the other great sixteenth-century reformers, was "in the strictest sense medieval and scholastic." Calvin for him is an advocate of hierarchy, a new Innocent III (32–34). Mercier also finds that the term *theocracy* applies to Calvin: "If he is careful, along with the scholastic theologians, to maintain the distinction between these two regimes, this is certainly not to the advantage of the temporal power" (37).

Chenevière likewise describes Calvin's political teaching as "profoundly theocratic" (178, 244); however, he distinguishes his own etymologically precise use of the word ("a regime in which all authority . . . is supposed to come from God"; 244) from the common usage ("a political regime that implies direct domination of the state by the clergy"), which does not apply to Calvin. Doumergue, on the other hand, insists that the received meaning of the term theocracy is indeed the only legitimate one (V.410 n. 2) and that Calvin was by no means a theocrat. On the contrary, the "Christian state" is an alternative both to theocracy and to cesaropapacy (v.411). This doctrine of the Christian state is for Doumergue "the foundation of the modern world" because it establishes "the autonomy of the state"—that is, the view that "church and state [are] two powers equal by their origin" (v.403 n. 6).

Wolin's treatment of this problem is perhaps the most penetrating in the literature, though it is not without its own difficulties: "the order that emerged was not a 'theocracy,'" he argues, "but a corporate community that was neither purely religious nor purely secular, but a compound of both." "In adopting the Lutheran idea of a community-in-fellowship," Wolin explains, "Calvin departed from the dominant medieval tradition; in enveloping that community within a structure of power he departed from Luther" (175–76).

No more than the other authors, however, does Wolin succeed in determining why Calvin insists, against medieval views, on the spiritual and "voluntary" nature of religious order, only to add almost immediately that the coercive power of secular government is to be used to establish and enforce this order. One is indeed entitled to wonder how this view differs practically from the views of cesaropapists and theocrats. And yet one must attend to the fact that Calvin understood his teaching to be very different from these. He writes, "For, when I approve of a civil administration that aims to prevent the true religion which is contained in God's law from being openly and with public sacrilege violated and defiled with impunity, I do not here, any more than before, allow men to make laws according to their own decision concerning religion and the worship of God" (IV.xx.3; 1488). The core of Calvin's disagreement with cesaropapists and with theocrats consists in his insistence that religious laws, laws touching the soul, be in no way dependent on any human choice. It is choice, not force, that Calvin considers inimical to spiritual freedom. Calvin attempts to establish the authority of God in religion *and* in politics without granting authority to priests or princes as God's intermediaries. Thus, some commentators have rejected theocracy as a description of Calvinist politics in favor of "bibliocracy" or "Christocracy" (Doumergue, V.410 n. 2). And yet Calvin does grant certain authority to men considered as God's intermediaries, his external means. The key is that he grants them authority precisely *as* his *external* means, and no more. Or one might say that whereas God finally keeps all authority for himself, he grants to certain men his power.

The central fact for understanding Calvin's ecclesiastical teaching is that he considered it beyond human capacity to improve the human soul; this incapacity is the basis of the freedom of believers from the tyranny and butchery of priests. It is because the human soul cannot approach perfection by human choice that Christian souls are not subject to human decisions. If "the office of pastor is distinct from that of a prince," this is because the realm of the spirit and the realm of human control must not touch. To be sure, religion and politics serve a single end, since God rules over both orders, but this is an end that no human being can know; thus it is impossible for a human being to unify the two callings in a single order. Furthermore, the impossibility of a human order or hierarchy unified by its end comports well with Calvin's insistence that the spiritual jurisdiction itself must not have a human head, that it must be administered "not by the decision of one man but by a lawful assembly" (IV.xi.5; 1217; see Wolin, 178, 191).

Since men are not competent to know the divine end of human action, they must decide according to the beginnings they can know. Thus Calvin, in condemning "human traditions" that have claimed authority in God's church, makes it clear that he is condemning only those human elements that claim authority over souls. "Our contention is against these, not against holy and useful church institutions, which provide for the preservation of discipline or honesty or peace" (IV.x.1; 1180).

It is in the beginnings of human action, not in the ends of the soul, that the spiritual and temporal jurisdiction have a common ground: fear. The temporal realm must use fear because "the insolence of evil men is so great, their wickedness so stubborn, that it can scarcely be restrained by extremely severe laws" (xx.2; 1487). Walzer is not wrong to call the Calvinist state "an order of repression" (30). Similarly, as we have seen, the sanctification of the believer proceeds by a continual reawakening of the fear of God: "For nothing so moves us to repose our assurance and certainty of mind in the Lord as distrust of ourselves, and the anxiety occasioned by the awareness of our ruins" (III.ii.23; 569). The sting of the law is the constant motor of faith. And this motor can be engaged by the external means of which the church disposes; the rod can "awaken" men to their dependency on God (IV.xii.5; 1244). Thus it appears that fear of God and fear of men have enough in common that the external human means may be used to awaken fear of God. Recall that in a passage in which Calvin denies the church the power of coercion, he adds, "I am speaking of civil coercion" (xi.16; 1229).

Of course human beings possess other arms of restraint, other rods than shame. This is why Calvin's account of the coercive power of government appears as a part of book 4 on the external means of the spiritual kingdom. If public rebuke can awaken fear of God, then so can the more immediate threat of physical harm. A "constrained and forced righteousness," or the moral law of God as enforced by human means, is at once necessary in order "that everything be not tumultuously confounded" and useful as a "tutelage" (pédagogie) of sanctification (II.vii.10; 359). Thus it is possible to join what has been rigorously distinguished—the spiritual kingdom and temporal force. This is why Walzer finds it difficult to separate "the state as Christian discipline" from "the state as order of repression." It is this common ground of fear that explains that "the defense of secular repression and the assertion of 'the claims of God' are so closely woven together that it is extremely difficult to disentangle them" (46). It is the essential place of fear in the order of the state as well as in the economy of sanctification that makes it possible for Calvin to bring conscience and coercion together (47). This fusion is grounded in Calvin's understanding of free conscience as an ever-renewed inner compulsion.

Thus I must agree with Wolin that, in a sense, the difference between "the two powers was not one of substance but of application." However, Wolin fails to see that Calvin does not arrive at a joining of spiritual and temporal coercion by softening the contrast between the two forms of society. If the contrast is in a way overcome in practice, it is not because it is softened but because it is hardened to the limit. Calvin does not make human means effective in securing spiritual ends by bringing spiritual ends closer to humanity, but by pushing them infinitely far away. It is because human action can contribute nothing of positive worth to the soul that its negative force can be so effective in turning man to the perpetual quest for God's grace.

Wolin is therefore altogether wrong to say that Calvin's political teaching represents an "effort to recapture an older conception of the community as a school of virtue and the total agency for the realization of individual perfection" (175; see also Mercier, 35–36). The Calvinist church and state were effective agencies of Calvinist sanctification precisely because they did not aim at human virtue or perfection. Calvin expressly repudiates forms of discipline that aim at perfecting the believer (IV.xiii.11, 16; 1265; 1271). For him discipline does not aim at perfection or merit but at an awakening to God's impossible holiness. The whole of life must be a sort of fast without merit (xii.18; 1244). Calvin did not break with Luther by denying that government was "a mighty engine of repression" (Wolin, 176), but by seeing more clearly than Luther the "spiritual" uses of repression. He did not ensure the collaboration of church and state by teaching that "a graduated social hierarchy ... was but the civil counterpart to the divine principle that sustained the universe" (183); rather, he denied that reason was competent to know any divine hierarchy (IV.xi.9, 1111) and drew the conclusion that the only commensurability between the human and divine orders is visible in the continued need to restrain chaos—or, as Wolin himself notices, "to prevent men from wallowing in 'universal confusion'" (183).

According to Wolin, "the tight corporate quality of [Calvin's Church] recalled the ancient polis, yet the underlying element of mystery was a reminder of that transcendent strain utterly alien to the classical community" (176). But little continuity exists between Calvinist politics and the classical idea of the polis. The order of Calvin's Christian state is much "tighter" or more repressive than in the classical idea of the polis precisely because, in Calvin's thought, transcendence has become so utterly mysterious or remote from human powers as to nullify its political relevance as transcendent; that is, it is no longer relevant to human choice. The good ceases to order politics as the object of choice; an infinitely transcendent God can only use political fear as a preparation for the fear of holiness.

Recall that the doctrine of Christ is the soul of the church and that the sinews of the church are discipline (IV.xii.1; 1230). But for Calvin, to say that Christ is the soul of the church is in effect to say that the church has no soul but Christ, whom it does not possess but is ever reaching toward. The sinews of the church cannot make souls like Christ's, they can only remind believers how unlike him they are—and thus commend them ceaselessly to works that are holy only because God receives them as holy. The soul lives; the sinews work. But the life of the soul is not in the sinews or in its works.

Chapter 3

Government and the People

Forms of Government

Having discussed the immediate theological and ecclesiastical background to which Calvin refers us in introducing his specifically political teaching, I return to the text of Calvin's chapter on civil government. The first three sections, discussed in chapter 3, constitute an introduction in which Calvin first distinguishes and then joins spiritual and civil government and sets his discussion of civil government in the context of his teaching on providence, Christian freedom, and the church (IV.xx.1–2) and then briefly describes "the chief tasks and burdens of civil government" (3).

At the end of these introductory paragraphs, Calvin outlines the body of his chapter on politics, proposing to divide the subject of civil government into three parts: "the magistrate, who is the protector and guardian of the laws; the laws, according to which he governs; the people, who are governed by the laws and obey the magistrate" (3; 1488).

This twentieth chapter of part 4 of the *Institutes* contains thirty-two sections. Calvin's treatment of magistrates extends from section 4 through section 13. I have already had occasion to notice some of the main themes of this discussion: the magistrate is "ordained of God"; he is "invested with divine authority"; his office is not an effect of "human perversity" but is indeed "the most sacred and by far the most honorable of all callings in the whole life of mortal men" (4; 1489–90). The coercive character of the magistracy is no argument against the holiness and dignity of this office (7; 1492–93). Princes are entitled to tribute and taxes, which they may use for "the magnificence of their household, which is joined, so to speak, with the dignity of the authority they exercise" (13; 1501). Those who deny the authority of princes and magistrates on "Christian" grounds "betray not only their ignorance but devilish arrogance, when they claim a perfection of which not even a hundredth part can be seen in them" (5; 1490).

Calvin does not detail the duties of magistrates, for, as he explains, "it is not so much my purpose to instruct the magistrates themselves as to teach others what magistrates are and to what end God has appointed them." And yet, in defending the dignity of magistrates by explaining their function to their subjects, Calvin cannot completely avoid giving instruction to magistrates themselves. He tells them that "they are ordained protectors and vindicators of public innocence, modesty, decency, and tranquility, and that their sole endeavor should be to provide for the common safety and peace of all" (1496). The magistrates' recognition of the divine ordination of their calling "can greatly spur them to exercise their office and bring them remarkable comfort to mitigate the difficulties of their task." Calvin urges magistrates to "remember that they are vicars of God" and to strive "to represent in themselves to men some image of divine providence, protection, goodness, benevolence, and justice" (6; 1491).

We have seen that Calvin summarizes the functions of government as providing "that a public manifestation of religion may exist among Christians, and that humanity be maintained among men." This is to say that the duty of magistrates "extends to both tables of the law" (9; 1495), that is, to man's duty to God as well as to his duties to other men. Thus God "entrusts the condition of the church to their protection and care" (5; 1491). He appoints magistrates not only to "decide earthly controversies" but to see "that he himself should be fully worshipped according to the prescription of his law" (9; 1495). Magistrates are forbidden, however, "to make laws according to their own decision concerning religion and the worship of God" (3; 1488).

I have examined Calvin's teaching on secular government as it pertains to the first table of the law, that is, as one of the "external means" of spiritual government. Calvin's teaching on the office of magistrates in regulating affairs among men will best be considered in connection with the second division of his chapter on civil government, the part on law (14–21). But before turning to Calvin's thematic treatment of law, I will consider section 8 on "the diversity of forms of government," which will lead me to matters treated under "the people" (22–32).

Calvin's discussion of the forms of government in the *Institutes* takes up a single section. This brevity as well as the way in which Calvin treats the subject have led many students of Calvin's thought to dismiss this chapter as of little importance.[1] I will not argue that Calvin's treatment is original or profound; but profound questions surround the interpretation of this section. The problem of determining the historical significance of Calvin's political teaching is often so closely connected with that of interpreting his position on forms of government that it is useful to examine and interpret that position. The very paucity of Calvin's reflections on this subject is worthy of reflection in the broader context of his teaching.

The section that Calvin devotes to the topic of "the diversity of forms of government" (IV.xx.8) is framed by introductory and concluding remarks, both present in the original version of the *Institutes* (1536), which in effect argue that there is no point in discussing this topic. Such a discussion would be "an idle pastime" for men holding no political authority, whose duty it is simply to be "compliant and obedient to whomever he [i.e., God] sets over the places where we live" (8; 1493, 1495). This argument for brevity already proves too much—that is, that the whole section is "needlessly spoken," at least to private men. The forms of government that actually exist are the forms God has provided, and it is impious to question God's providence. What God has done there is no need for man to deliberate.

Nevertheless, Calvin does not altogether refrain from discussing the relative merits of the various forms of government. In a passage dating back to the 1536 edition of the *Institutes*, he argues that there is "no simple solution" to the question of the best form of government, because each has its characteristic faults and because particular circumstances largely determine which form is most suitable. Thus the question "requires deliberation" (8; 1493). Those capable of such deliberation are capable of some understanding of the wisdom of providence, which, in view of the "particular inequality" according to which "countries are best held together . . . has wisely arranged that various countries should be ruled by various kinds of government" (8; 1494). It would seem that men capable of seeing the wisdom of providence would be capable of some measure of providence themselves. But Calvin, as we have seen, immediately forestalls this line of thought, directing the readers' attention from God's wisdom to his will.

In later editions of the *Institutes* Calvin stretches just a little further the tether that binds his political teaching to the will of God. In 1543, on the basis of both human experience and scriptural authority, he ventures the opinion that "aristocracy, or a system compounded or aristocracy and democracy, far excels all others." "No kind of government" he continues, "is more happy than one where freedom is regulated with becoming moderation and is properly established on a durable basis" (8; 1493, 1494). Although Calvin commends aristocracy or a mixed regime as far superior to other forms of government, he cautions that this superiority is no grounds for changing the form of government that God has appointed. "Even to think of such a move will not only be foolish and superfluous, but altogether harmful." The only practical conclusion that Calvin allows to follow from his praise of a certain form of government is that this form ought to be vigorously maintained by those who already enjoy it and, in particular, that it ought to be diligently defended by magistrates appointed as its guardians (8; 1494).

Clearly a tension exists within Calvin's treatment of the forms of government: on the one hand, the will of God as manifest in the actual existence of regimes is sufficient; on the other hand, deliberation, informed by experience and confirmed by the authority of scripture, is competent to judge certain existing regimes as superior to others. This tension has given rise to contradictory interpretations of Calvin's thought on this point. Marc-Edouard Chenevière insists that Calvin's political teaching can be to enjoining submission to the will of God as represented in whatever regimes actually rule; he thus goes to great lengths to minimize the importance of any political preferences expressed by Calvin himself.[2] "This discussion of the different political regimes," he writes, "appears to us of little importance." The essence of Calvin's thought is simply that "every state, whatever its form of government, comes from God" (228–29).

The fact remains, however, that Calvin made many statements relevant to the question of the best form of government; nor did he always frame these merely as personal preferences. Emil Doumergue has amply documented these statements.[3] Furthermore, without denying that for Calvin God is equally the author of every form of government, he builds an impressive case that Calvin's interpretation of scripture constitutes an endorsement of representative democracy. To be sure, in the text now under consideration (*Institutes* IV.xx.8) Calvin refers favorably only to an "aristocracy, or a system compounded of aristocracy and democracy . . . where freedom is regulated with becoming moderation" (8; 1493–94). He offers no explanation in the *Institutes* of what this "compound" of aristocracy and democracy might consist in. But Doumergue demonstrates from numerous other texts that what Calvin has in mind as an ideal regime is one in which magistrates are elected by the people. This is shown clearly in the *Sermons on Deuteronomy* (1553–56), where Calvin explains the superiority of the Israelite regime, which in the *Institutes* is described simply as "an aristocracy bordering on democracy" (8; 1494). "It is an inestimable gift, when God gives to people the freedom to elect judges and magistrates. And, in fact, when God gave such a privilege to the Jews, he thereby ratified his adoption and the fact that he had chosen them as heirs; and that he wanted their condition to be better and more excellent than that of all their neighbors, where there were kings, princes, and no freedom" (Doumergue, V.445).

Doumergue concludes on the basis of such evidence that Calvin was far from indifferent to the question of forms of government. "Calvin was as much favorable to democracy as he was opposed to monarchy" (V.44). Doumergue means *modern* democracy or more precisely, what is good and sound in modern democracy; Calvin is the founder of stable and powerful (*fermes et puissantes*) democracies (V.388), a defender not of "egalitarianism" but of "equality before the law" (V.452).

Various strong and interrelated objections to Doumergue's thesis have been advanced. Consider first the fact that the regime Calvin calls "aristocracy, or a system compounded of aristocracy and democracy" (IV.xx.8; 1493) becomes, for Doumergue, simply "democracy." Charles Mercier, who believes "it would be a grave error to claim to find in Calvin a precursor of modern democracy," discerns rather an "aristocratic tendency" in Calvin's thought, a preference not for simple equality but for "proportional equality." For Calvin, as for Aristotle and Cicero, the interest well understood of the faithful themselves requires that they be governed by the best men (31). This proportion, in Calvin's case, varies with the unequal distribution of God's gifts to mankind. All cannot be equal in the church or in civil authority, because God has not endowed all men equally. And God's gift of a superior aptitude is an indication of God's calling (26–27). The people's election of a minister or a magistrate is not, therefore, an exercise of the people's authority but a ratification of God's choice. Ministers and magistrates are, properly speaking, chosen by God, and not by the people: "Those elected are in no way the people's representatives; they may be elected by the people, but they are God's representatives" (28). "In the final analysis, it is in the diversity of gifts that Calvin, like Aristotle, places the foundations of authority" (26).

Wolin is in essential agreement with Mercier on this point. He argues that the Calvinist "system of vocations" constituted a "graduated social hierarchy, clearly defined in terms of offices and obligations," which "was but the civil counterpart to the divine principle that sustained the universe" (1830).

These are strong and rather obvious objections to Doumergue's democratic interpretation of Calvinism. And yet the assimilation of Calvinist to Aristotelian conceptions of order itself raises serious questions. For clearly political inequality has a much different significance for Aristotle than for Calvin. For Aristotle, competence in a political office is inseparable from the capacity to know and choose the good and to order inferior capacities so as best to attain this good. Since "the end of politics is the good for man," politics is "the most sovereign and comprehensive master science" (*Nichomachean Ethics* I.2; see also *Politics* I.ii.8). The political capacity is not just one gift among many; the man of practical wisdom or prudence, the man possessing "a truthful rational characteristic of acting in matters involving what is good for man" (VI.5; 154) is entitled to rule other men precisely because he knows how to rule himself—thus he knows and acts according to what is good for man. Aristocracy is the rule of the best, both in the sense that the best are rulers and in the sense that the end of the regime is what is best (*Politics* III.vi.3). The goodness of this form of government is inseparable from the goodness of its ruling part; the rulers truly represent or, one might say, embody the goodness of the regime. Thus, political excellence or, more precisely, the excellence of ruling and human excellence converge: "in the case of the ruler, the excellence of the good citizen is identical with that of the good man" (9).

This linking of political virtue with what is truly best in man is wholly foreign to Calvin's thought. A complete severance of political virtue from the highest excellence of which man is capable follows from Calvin's refusal to understand political order as determined by an end accessible to man. Thus the authority of political rulers, according to Calvin, is not grounded in the good they are supposed to know and to represent but is a sheer right to command, having no final reason beyond the command of God. Calvin emphatically distinguishes office from man: all authority resides finally not in any human being but in a divine calling. Although "the first duty of subjects toward their magistrates is to think most honorably of their office," the magistrates themselves may deserve no honor at all: "I am not discussing the men themselves as if a mask of dignity covered foolishness, or sloth, or cruelty . . . but I say that the order itself is worthy of such honor and reverence that those who are rulers are esteemed among us, and receive reverence out of respect for their lordship" (IV.xx.22; 1510).

It is misleading to liken the virtue of the Aristotelian aristocrat to the political calling or "gift" of the Calvinist official. The man of virtue embodies the good which he represents; the official is a conduit of the will of God, which he cannot possibly embody. The critical difference is this: the aristocrat is supposed to know the comprehensive end, "what is good for man," the intelligible principle of the whole political order. The official does not rule in the name of any end but by the will of God; in this case the political order is not intelligible in the light of a purpose. Thus it is incorrect to refer to Calvinist order as "a graduated social hierarchy," for the various orders of a hierarchy are ranked by reference to the relative comprehensiveness of the ends they govern. No true hierarchy, no authoritative ranking of orders according to their ends is possible if no knowledge of the comprehensive end is possible. Thus, for Calvin, as Wolin notes, "Hierarchy . . . was equivalent to arbitrariness" (176). Where there is no knowledge, order is sheer assertion.

Wolin is therefore wrong, however, to argue that Calvin "was not so much anti-hierarchical as anti-monarchical" (176). A community without a visible ruling part, or without an end accessible to human nature, cannot be ordered hierarchically; it cannot be ruled but only led. As Wolin himself writes, "The pastor was a leader, not a ruler" (178).

Wolin thinks Calvin was opposed to hierarchy only because he was opposed to monarchy. I suggest that he was opposed to monarchy because the rule of one is closely associated with the hierocratic idea: the idea that human affairs can be ruled according to a single, comprehensive idea of what is good for man.

When there is no end by which to rank the various activities within the life of a community, then although differences among these activities remain notable—some have the power to command and others do not—still they appear as essentially equal. Thus despite the diversity of God's gifts to man, Doumergue is right to say that Calvin's teaching is fundamentally democratic. Although he quotes Calvin's view that equality is inconsistent with unity, that the unity of the body requires the diversity of its members, Doumergue still maintains that Calvin taught "not the identity of individuals [but] the equality of classes, of estates" (V.442n. 1). This equality obtains in the ecclesiastical as much as in the political community: "Laymen are equal among themselves, pastors are equal among themselves; laymen and pastors are equal among themselves" (V.442). All are equally subject to the word of God, and the custodians of the Word are not rulers but leaders, because they claim nothing for their own virtue or wisdom but are wholly the instruments of God.

It is true, then, that in a sense Calvin's teaching is more "democratic" than Aristotle's. But this still falls far short of establishing Doumergue's claim that Calvin is the founder of *modern* democracy. To see Doumergue's difficulty it suffices to note that, in adducing passages to show that Calvin was a proponent of "liberty, equality, and fraternity," he quotes this Calvinist defense of liberty: "The pastors of the Word of the Lord can force every glory and every rank to obey its majesty; and by this Word they can govern everyone, from the highest to the lowest" (V.441). This liberty of the Word is obviously different from the personal freedom we associate with modern liberal democracies. And this difference, as Mercier points out, clearly arises directly from a radically different view of the ultimate source of authority. "The principle of popular sovereignty . . . which is the basis of modern democratic theories," he writes, "is wholly foreign to [Calvin's] thought" (38–40; see also Chenevière, 190). However democratic certain aspects of Calvin's thought may appear, a vast chasm, it seems, separates Calvinist politics from modern politics: the chasm between the defense of the sovereignty of God and the assertion of the sovereignty of man.

Whatever form of government may be most desirable when the preference of men is considered, it seems that the argument must finally return to the will of God, that is, to the pole of Calvin's discussion of forms of government that Chenevière insists is essential. If the sovereignty of God is the fundamental source of all authority—if the "will of the Lord is enough"—then indeed "all these things are needlessly spoken." It may be that all callings are fundamentally equal, but this is precisely because they are all equally commanded by God and subject to him. Thus it seems that this equality does not have egalitarian practical implications: equality under God's will binds men to their respective callings; it does not liberate them as political actors.

However, an examination of the exceptions Calvin is willing to make to his identification of present political powers with the will of God will reopen the question of the relationship between divine and human sovereignty as well as the question of the relation of Calvinism to the foundations of modern politics.

Authority and Resistance

The concrete political implications of Calvin's thought appear profoundly undemocratic. This is apparent in the very manner in which Calvin organizes his chapter on politics: first he treats the magistrate, then the laws according to which he governs, then "the people, who are governed by the laws and obey the magistrate." Magistrates govern, people obey: this fundamental separation between public and private callings pervades Calvin's political teaching. It is the basis of Calvin's very severe doctrine of nonresistance to established authorities: "The magistrate cannot be resisted without God being resisted at the same time. . . . Moreover, under this obedience I include the restraint which private citizens ought to bid themselves keep in public, that they may not deliberately intrude in public affairs, or pointlessly invoke the magistrate's office, or undertake anything at all politically" (IV.xx.23; 1511). This duty of obedience applies not only to faithful and upright princes "but also to the authority of all who, by whatever means, have got control of affairs, even though they perform not a whit of the prince's office" (25; 1512). The ruler's unfaithfulness is not the business of the ruled, who "ought . . . not to inquire about another's duties, but every man should keep in mind that one duty which is his own" (29; 1516). From the divine point of view, it may be that all earthly callings are equal; but from a political point of view, some are clearly more equal than others.

The people have no right to resist their political superiors. All rulers represent God; just and unjust "equally have been endowed with [his] holy majesty," though, to be sure, in different ways: "Those who rule for the public benefit are true patterns and evidences of this beneficence of his . . . they who rule unjustly and incompetently have been raised up by him to punish the wickedness of the people" (25; 1512). This seems sufficient to show that Calvin's idea of the absolute sovereignty of God is incompatible with the modern idea of the sovereignty of the people, practically as well as theoretically. Whatever form of government may be preferable, according to Calvin, the primary political fact is that we have no right to choose what we prefer; we can only submit to what God has willed.

Nevertheless, however severe Calvin's teaching on the duty of obedience may be, it is not without qualifications. First there is the famous exception made for inferior magistrates, an exception that figured significantly in the development of "Calvinist" political argument after Calvin. In section 31 of his chapter on civil government, Calvin explains that unlike "private individuals," certain "magistrates of the people, appointed to restrain the will-fulness of kings" are not only permitted but in fact solemnly obligated to "withstand . . . the fierce licentiousness of kings" and thus to protect "the freedom of the people" (31; 1519). Calvin compares such magistrates to Spartan ephors, Roman tribunes, and Athenian demarchs. In making this exception, McNeill (1949) argues, "Calvin sets ajar the iron gate of the defenses of existing absolute governments." "This single intentionally emphatic and dynamic paragraph, found in all editions of the *Institutes*," Mc-Neill writes, "links Calvin with the more radical Calvinist politi-cal writers of the sixteenth and seventeenth centuries" (162, 163; see also Skinner, II.230–34, 315–16, 324–26).

It is undeniable that Calvin's appeal to inferior magistrates is echoed in many of the arguments of later and politically less cautious Calvinists. But it seems that Calvin's teaching must be fundamentally altered—indeed abandoned—in order to make pos-sible a truly modern defense of the right of resistance. For one cannot forget that the principle of the sovereignty of God, not that of the sovereignty of the people, stands behind Calvin's limited defense of the right of resistance. If certain magistrates are given prerogatives which are denied to "private individuals," they are given them from God. Thus Chenevière insists that "the magis-trates treated here may be established for the defense of the people, but they are not representatives of the people" (353).

An examination of this paragraph, however, particularly the examples cited, shows that Chenevière's argument is too simple: Calvin clearly has in mind magistrates who are elected by the people as well as ordained by God (McNeill, 163–64; Skinner, II.232). This suggests that in Calvin's mind, the sovereignty of God may not exclude the sovereignty of the people, as Chenevière assumes. This also points to a possible inconsistency in Calvin's teaching on public and private callings. For if the people, the wholly "private" class, are entitled to elect magistrates; if there are "magistrates of the people" such as ephors, tribunes, de-marchs, and the French Estates General; then the people them-selves must make politics their business, at least in periodic elec-tions. And if God has made politics the people's business in this way—if God has given the people the authority to defend themselves by electing magistrates to represent them—then who can say that he has not given them whatever authority is necessary for their own defense? Here, to be sure, I am suggesting implications that Calvin himself was too prudent to reveal; my point is simply that Calvin's appeal to "popular magistrates" tends to undermine his otherwise rigid distinction between public and private callings (cf. Doumergue V.502–03).

Another qualification attached to Calvin's teaching on the duty of obedience directly modifies the public/private distinction. For after insisting that rulers, good and evil, are the direct representatives of God, in the final section of the *Institutes* Calvin asks his readers, whatever their political status, to look beyond these representatives to the superior authority of God himself. "We must obey God rather than man" (IV.xx.32; 1521). Whereas once Calvin enjoined believers to revere and esteem even a wicked ruler, since "in his hands . . . noble and divine power resides" (x.25; 1513), he now denies that "God has made over his right to mortal men, giving them the rule over mankind" (xx.32; 1520). Each man, whatever his station, is individually responsible to God. Our subjection to rulers "is never to lead us away from obedience to [God], to whose will the desires of all kings ought to be subject" (1520). God has given certain men power over other men, but even private men must withdraw obedience from God's supposed representatives when this would require disobedience to God himself. Thus God's ordination does not finally remove the political responsibility of each individual.

It would be a mistake, however, to associate Calvin's teaching on this point too hastily with modern individualism. For Calvin does not authorize men to rise up against rulers who threaten their interests but only to disobey those who would prevent them from accomplishing their sacred duties. Calvin does not invite readers to throw off any authority that displeases them; he enjoins them rather to "suffer anything rather than turn aside from piety" (1521). Or, to use Skinner's terms, what Calvin argues here clearly falls within the category of a *religious duty* to resist and not of a *modern* or *secular right* to resist. Furthermore, Chenevière argues that for Calvin, the impious commands of a prince give his subjects the right, or rather the duty, to disobey only those particular commands: the prince himself retains his authority in all other cases.[4]

But as Skinner points out, the argument of this 1559 addition to *Institutes* (partially quoted above), is "highly equivocal" on this point (I.219). To quote further: "For the king had exceeded his limits, and had not only been a wrongdoer against men, but, in lifting up his horns against God, had himself abrogated his power" (IV.xx.32; 1520). Skinner notes that "this passage does contain the clear suggestion that a ruler who goes beyond the bounds of his office automatically ceases to count as a genuine magistrate." He goes on to cite passages from later writings to show that Calvin advanced what Skinner calls a "private-law argument," that is, an argument that permits private persons to resist an unjust prince. The strongest of these passages is from the *Sermons on the Last Eight Chapters of the Book of Daniel*, published posthumously in 1565. There, Skinner shows, Calvin clearly teaches not only that Daniel "committed no sin when he disobeyed the King" but that impious rulers "are no longer to be counted as princes" and even that "it is necessary that they should . . . be laid low" (II.220). Doumergue seems to agree with Skinner on this point: "When the honor of God is concerned, one must disobey publicly, actively" (V.498). The duty of *passive* resistance applies only in cases that are "religiously and morally indifferent" (V.499). I know no way of making Calvin's various statements on the subject of resistance to authority cohere perfectly with one another; Calvin is often equivocal, and when he is not he sometimes simply contradicts himself. Despite the strong language of the *Sermons on Daniel* (quoted above), as Skinner remarks, Calvin "never deleted from the *Institutes* any of the contradictory passages in which he continued to uphold the duty of nonresistance" (II.221).[5] But if perfect theoretical consistency is not to be found in Calvin's teaching on the right to resist authority, considerable practical sense can be made of his various statements by keeping in mind that the *Institutes* was Calvin's most public and therefore most cautious writing, the text in which he was most at pains to distance himself from the Anabaptists, who were widely considered fanatical and politically dangerous (see Chenevière, 300–301, and McNeill, 155–56). Calvin was apparently convinced that the interests of the Reformation were best served in the *Institutes* by an emphasis on the duty of obedience, and he exercised restraint in outlining the limits of this duty.[6] Behind the diverse aspects of Calvin's teaching lay a constant practical motive: the survival and dissemination of a "purity of religion" that might well require the arms of the secular magistracy (Höpfl, 212) but might also require resistance to him.

As Pierre Mesnard remarks in *L'essor de la philosophie politique au XVIᵉ siècle*, two basic postulates underlay Calvin's political teaching, postulates that do not obviously or necessarily converge: "all power comes from God" and "power exists only to lead men according to God." Calvin attempts to hold these principles together, but "according to circumstances and especially the necessities of practical action, Protestants (*réformés*) will have a tendency, sometimes to be aware of one postulate, sometimes of the other" (281; cf. Allen, 52). These two principles correspond to the poles of God's will and human action referred to above. I would only insist more strongly than Mesnard on the significance of the fact that Calvin attempts to hold these two principles together or rather that he sees them as belonging together, as convergent. Both power and resistance to power may exhibit the glory of God; this thought, although it takes account of or employs circumstances, is not merely an effect of circumstances.

The unity behind the tension in Calvin's teaching on political authority resides in the fact that for him the reason behind all authority remains hidden in God; there is no reason but God for authority. We cannot know God's reasons but can only obey his will; this will Calvin believes is indicated by the sheer existence of power. God's authority is revealed to us as power, and we must grant authority to the powers that be "by whatever means [they] have got control of affairs" (IV.xx.25; 1512). To trust in God is to trust in the divine authority behind the greatest power. Doumergue thus argues (V.420), correctly, I think, that Calvinist "divine right" is directly opposed to the traditional (*historique*) theory of divine right, the theory that established authority on the basis of heredity: a crown prince holds a rightful claim to the throne because he possesses the right from birth; the prince does not merely seize power but claims authority on the basis of a standard above his power. For Calvin, however, there is no standard above power. Calvin denies the legitimacy of birth (V.420), because there is no legitimacy but power. In Doumergue's words, "c'est l'authorité de fait" (V.421).

But the authority of the factual, as Walzer has noticed, (58–59), is ambiguous. Facts change. To obey the powers that be may mean to obey the powers that come to be. The greatest power may not be the power that now appears greatest. Power is only known by the test of power, by becoming actual. To leave politics to God in this radical sense is to leave it to history. The tension that we have noticed within Calvin's thought, between the authority of existing powers and the divine mission of politics, is fundamentally a dynamic tension within a single idea: the divine authority of the factual. For the factual is not an eternal and stable reality but a field of change. The authority of power is the authority of what exists, but more fundamentally it is an authority of the potentially existent. What *is* has authority because in it is hidden what is *coming to be.* The authority of the present is the authority of the future emerging from the present.

The authority of the present and of the future can be contained in a single idea, can emanate from a single spirit, only because the authority of the future itself is not established by reference to some stable reality, accessible to human reason, but only by the effective will of God by the absolute power. If it were possible to know the goodness of the future, then it would be possible also to judge the present against the standard of this goodness and to choose to model the present, as far as possible, according to that standard. But various human choices would then raise themselves up to contest the authority that must be granted to God in history. On the other hand, if for lack of a standard above power and history human beings are incompetent to order their present lives according to a deliberate choice, then no one has reason to obstruct the effectiveness of God's power in pushing the future out of the present. Calvin attaches divine authority to presently visible powers not because of what they are but because of what God can do with them. And if God should will to exhibit his power by other means, then Calvin is in principle ready to welcome the change.

Thus Calvin is willing to welcome the power of inferior magistrates who "have been appointed protectors by God's ordinance" (IV.xx.31; 1519), that is, who have been empowered by History. These powers indeed appeared to Calvin to be God's most likely instrument in working his will in France and the world. But he also left open the possibility that God might empower other agencies to serve him. This leads us to a third qualification that Calvin attaches to his teaching on the people's duty to obey—a qualification that reveals the full potential of Calvin's defense of the authority of the actual.

> For sometimes he raises up open avengers from among his servants, and arms them with his command to punish the wicked government and deliver his people, oppressed in unjust ways, from miserable calamity. Sometimes he directs to this end the rage of men with other intentions and other endeavors. . . . For the first kind of men, when they had been sent by God's lawful calling to carry out such acts, in taking up arms against kings, did not at all violate that majesty which is implanted in kings by God's ordination; but, armed from heaven, they subdued the lesser power with the greater, just as it is lawful for kings to punish their subordinates. (30; 1517)

God may effect his will either through specially called servants or by unwilling agents. The former act "by God's lawful calling"; when they take up arms against kings they are "armed from heaven" to subdue a lesser power with a greater. It may appear that by "God's lawful calling" Calvin is referring exclusively to a category of public persons such as the inferior magistrates of section 31. But the example of Moses, which Calvin uses here (30), hardly seems to correspond to the ephors, tribunes, and demarchs of the next section. The providential avengers discussed in section 30 thus include powers armed by God from outside the category of regularly constituted authorities.[7] To be sure, Calvin also insists, in a text quoted by Chenevière (331), that "when God works outside the common rule, founded in his Word, it is a privilege which must not be usurped." But of course there can be no rule according to which to test God's action outside the rule. Here as in every case, finally we have no rule but the will of God, and our recognition that his power will prevail in history. If Calvin judges that God has not called a providential avenger to deliver his contemporaries, this is because he does not yet see any friendly force great enough to displace powers hostile to the Reformation. It is obvious that an omnipotent God cannot will an endeavor that cannot succeed. For Calvin, questions of expediency and of authority are joined, not simply because it is expedient to join them but because this union follows from Calvin's understanding of authority. Thus, in response to the question whether the Israelites were right or wrong to save Jonathan's life by swearing an oath to oppose King Saul's oath that he should die, Calvin declares, "these questions are vain, useless, and even impious. . . . Let it suffice that God willed that by this means Jonathan be snatched from death . . . and thus to punish the tyranny of Saul" (Doumergue, V.499).

The authority of the factual thus underlies both Calvin's defense of the power of kings and his more guarded suggestions (very guarded in the *Institutes*) that God might use the people to defy kings; the right of powers that be extends to powers that are coming to be. The opposition between the authority of worldly powers and the mission of these same powers to defend pure religion is not a theoretical contradiction but an indication of a dynamic tension within historical reality. Or one might say that what appears as a practical contradiction between what must be and what ought to be is overcome theoretically by Calvin's confidence that what must be, ought to be, or that what ought to be, will be—not by any human choice, but by God's power. The contradiction is overcome practically when men are called, that is, empowered to be God's agents. For such men action becomes its own argument.

Still, however one assesses the revolutionary potential of the Calvinist duty to resist, one cannot assume that it is equivalent to a secular right to resist. Calvin sometimes seems to encourage men to rise up in defense of the glory of God. But this is not to say that he grants men—and surely not "private" men—a right to take such action in defense of their material interests or their lives (Doumergue, V.499). Thus we are drawn back to the basic fact that the sovereignty of God is the source of all authority, according to Calvin. From this it seems to follow that resistance to authority is legitimate not to achieve mere human purposes but only to recall the political order to its divine mission. Even if Calvin's bolder statements sometimes tend to threaten existing authorities and even to undermine the distinction between public and private upon which he insists elsewhere, this is far from saying that he articulates a modern idea of political authority: God's glory and not man's needs or purposes remains the fundamental motive of the argument, whether the argument favors submission or resistance. To repeat Mercier's point: "The mission of the civil power [is] primarily a religious mission" (38). The state, as we have seen, is one of the external means of the spiritual kingdom.

Our discussion of the right of resistance therefore appears inconclusive regarding the status of Calvin's teaching on forms of government. The authority of the factual may encompass both the power of the state and its religious mission, but it is not clear that it can reconcile the tension we first noticed in examining section 8, the tension between God's will and human choice in the various forms of government. Perhaps Chenevière is right that whatever form of government Calvin happened to prefer, the essence of his teaching is simply that all forms of government equally come from God.

We have already seen, however, that Calvin does not praise elective aristocracies merely on the basis of his or any other human preference. In the *Institutes* and much more boldly elsewhere, as Doumergue demonstrates, Calvin tends to associate his praise of such aristocracies and his antipathy for monarchies with his specifically religious teaching. The freedom to choose judges and magistrates is the gift by which God ratified his election of the Jewish nation. Doumergue argues elsewhere that Calvin's democratic teaching is firmly grounded in his religious teaching. The doctrine of the sovereignty of God, "the supreme dogma of Calvinist theology," and the associated doctrines of election and of universal sin have the effect of abasing princes and thereby elevating subjects. Furthermore, the egalitarian idea of the church, in which, according to Doumergue, "the idea of the clergy is abolished," serves as a model for political liberty and educates believers in the habits of republicanism (V.387–89).

Chenevière would argue that it is illegitimate to read Calvin's ideal of religious order into his political teaching. And Calvin himself writes that while considering either the spiritual or the political kingdom, "we must call away and turn aside the mind from thinking about the other" (*Institutes* III.xix.15; 847). But as David Little has noted, neither Calvin himself nor his followers could resist seeing both kingdoms in one field of view (54; see also Höpfl, 154). In that case, Calvin and his followers, as God's empowered agents, would not act according to any human view of what a good order is but would act as God's instruments in bringing forth his irresistible order. To those who are called, the prohibition against viewing the historical whole does not apply, for then it is not their view but God's. In any case, God's agents do not claim to comprehend the whole; they claim only that they advance the order that God wills; they are representatives not of God's goodness but of his power.

The direction if not the end of this power is more or less visible in Calvin's work, although this is less true of the more public *Institutes* than of other writings. In the *Institutes* Calvin is more cautious and tends to emphasize the authority of present powers and to give his remarks about alternative orders the appearance of secondary, human, preferences. Yet it is clear that he tends to apply a single, fundamental understanding of order to both the political and the religious spheres. "For as no city or township can function without magistrate and polity, so the church of God needs a spiritual polity" (IV.xi.1; 1211). We have seen that Calvin opposes hierarchy and favors a kind of equality in both realms, and yet the realization of this equality requires the application of force in both realms. Not only does the religious notion of a voluntary community serve as the motive or spirit for political action, but the coercive power characteristic of politics is the practical reality of the voluntary community. Conscience and coercion, will and power are opposites, but they are joined. And power is more than the means to the end of the will; it is also its reverse face (see chapters 8–9, below). This is the key to Calvin's ability, according to Troeltsch's classic account (in *The Social Teachings of the Christian Churches*), to join the organizational principles of *church* and *sect* (II.602).

As Höpfl says (126, 171), there is a clear parallelism or "homology" between Calvin's teaching on politics and on church organization. McNeill (1949) notes that Calvin, "with a complete absence of embarrassment . . . associates theocratic with democratic concepts and blends the patterns of government for church and state" (165). Calvin's teaching therefore finally favors a form of government in which the sovereignty of the people and the sovereignty of God are joined. This joining manifests itself in the realm of human action. Calvin's teaching is not hostile, in the last analysis, to human action, but it is hostile to human choice—for human choice implies human authority.

Doumergue therefore mistakes the significance of the passage he quotes in support of his democratic interpretation of Calvin (V.432) that refers to the antimonarchic preference of "men of excellent and noble spirit" (IV.xx.7; 1492; see n. 3, below). Calvin's theocratic democracy is not based on the human virtue of excellence or nobility but, as Doumergue himself shows, on the equal and active subjection of all human authority. God's glory exhibits itself in history without any respect to human authority. The meaning of history is the laying low of human authority; this is accomplished by humans empowered by God.

Chapter 4

Law and Ethics

Law

What is the meaning of human power that asserts itself, not on the authority of any purpose known to human beings, but as the manifestation of the will of God? To address this question I turn to the second of the three parts of Calvin's discussion of civil government: "the laws, according to which [the magistrate] governs" (IV.xx.3; 1488).

Recall that in describing the spiritual polity Calvin employed the metaphor of the individual human being. He compared the saving doctrine of Christ to the soul of the church and represented discipline, or the application of laws, as its sinews (xii.1; 1229–30). To introduce his discussion of civil laws, Calvin recurs to the same metaphor: "Next to the magistracy in the civil state come laws, strictest sinews of the commonwealth, or, as Cicero, after Plato, calls them, the souls, without which the magistracy cannot stand, even as they themselves have no force apart from the magistracy" (xx.14; 1502). Laws may be represented either as the sinews or as the soul of the commonwealth: the soul of the commonwealth is its sinews. The laws as soul therefore have no force apart from the laws as sinews—apart from the magistrate's *enforcement*. But neither can the magistrate activate the sinews unless the sinews of the commonwealth are understood as its soul.

"Accordingly," Calvin concludes this introductory paragraph,

82

"nothing truer could be said than that the law is a silent magistrate; the magistrate, a living law." This formula, as McNeill, the editor, suggests (1502n. 35), recalls an argument articulated by Cicero in his own name (Marcus) in the *Laws:* "For as the laws govern the magistrate, so the magistrate governs the people, and it can be truly said that the magistrate is a speaking law, and the law a silent magistrate" (III.i; 461). The magistrate is a mediator between the laws and the people. Elsewhere Marcus argues that only the divine mind as known by the perfected or wise man truly deserves the name of law (II.iv; 383–87). The divine mind becomes true law for human beings through "the reason and mind of a wise lawgiver applied to command and prohibition" (II.iv; 381). The divine mind is the "reason inherent in nature" (vii; 389). The wise man, the man who has perfected his rational nature, can use his knowledge of nature to make other men better, that is, more perfectly what they are, more natural. "For virtue is reason completely developed; and this is certainly natural" (I.xvi; 347). "Knowledge of the principles of right living is what makes men better" (xi; 333). The end of true (natural) law is the perfection of human nature. Nature itself is silent, but since it is rational, it can be made to speak naturally by a rational nature. Rational nature, according to Marcus, is the link between the silent law and the speaking magistrate.

"The laws govern the magistrate": The true law is the standard or governor of laws that are the life or soul of the commonwealth (II.vi; 379), the laws that "bear the title of laws rather by favour than because they are really such" (v; 383), just as reason is the best and ruling part of the human soul, the part in virtue of which it is truly called human (I.vii–ix; 323–27). The laws govern the magistrate because the magistrate is rational insofar as he is in accord with the rational principles of nature. "The magistrate governs the people" by speaking to them the rationality of laws in the form, natural "by favor," of "commands and prohibitions." The magistrate needs the laws, for without them his commands and prohibitions, the sinews of the commonwealth, cannot speak to the rational natures of the people. On this view, what Calvin says does not follow: the laws "have no force apart from the magistracy." Cicero praises the noble bravery of the "heroic Cocles" whose virtue, in the absence of a written law, obeyed the silent commands of rational nature. The authority of the law as spoken by the magistrate depends upon the higher authority of the law the magistrate speaks. Whereas Cicero's magistrate is "a speaking law," Calvin's is "a living law." For Cicero, the force of the magistrate is not the life of the law; the silent law is not dead but too alive, too perfect, until the magistrate speaks it, to be useful in the commonwealth. Sinews or forceful commands are not the soul of the commonwealth but only an adjunct to the rational commands of the magistrate; positive laws are the inferior part of the commonwealth's soul, not that part in virtue of which it is truly called a commonwealth.

Calvin's introduction to his discussion of law thus suggests an understanding of the civil order very different from that presented in Cicero's *Laws*. Calvin associates the sinews of the commonwealth with its soul, the force of the magistrate with the authority of the law, and the voice of the law with its very life. The hierarchy formed by (1) the silent authority of nature, which governs (2) the human authority, which in turn forms by speech (3) the obeying part of the humanity is replaced by a view in which the life of the law seems to be reduced to the forceful speech, the sinews, of the magistrate. But Calvin does not attempt to ground the authority of the law in a human magistrate: the fundamental assertion of Calvin's political teaching is that civil government is a "divinely established order" (IV.xx.1; 1485). The magistrate therefore does not assert his power in his own name but has a "mandate from God" (6; 1489). It would seem to follow that the laws of the magistrate are only true laws insofar as they conform to the standard of the divine order. But if a divine order exists as an independent standard of the civil order, then it must have some force or life apart from the sinews of the magistrate.

Calvin seems reluctant to describe any standard above the positive law. Indeed, he writes, "I would have preferred to pass over this matter in utter silence" (14; 1502). He would have preferred not to attempt to speak the silent law to the living magistrate. But Calvin is impelled to speak because "there are some who deny that a commonwealth is duly formed which neglects the political system of Moses and is ruled by the common law of nations."

Calvin, then, takes up the defense of God's ordinance in the common law of nations against the "seditious" notion that this law must be measured against God's law published by Moses. He thus must address the question "with what laws a Christian state ought to be governed," although he cautions that "this is no reason why anyone should expect a long discourse concerning the best kind of laws." Calvin gives two reasons for not attempting such a discourse: first, it would be "endless"; second, it would "not pertain to the present purpose and place." Since Calvin's purpose is to exhibit political order as an aspect of God's providence (1; 1485–86) which "has wisely arranged that various countries should be ruled by various kinds of government" (8; 1494), it would be presumptuous to penetrate the wisdom behind this variety ("the will of the Lord is enough") and impossible and useless for the "present . . . place" to describe the endless variety itself.

Calvin thus refrains from a discourse on "the best kind of laws." But since the seditious must be answered, he notes "in passing . . . what laws can piously be used before God, and be rightly administered among men" (14; 1502). Calvin turns from the question of the best law to that of laws are not forbidden by God. His main concern is to dissociate himself from the dangerous attempt to model contemporary governments on the judicial laws of the Old Testament. He does this not as Thomas Aquinas does, by distinguishing the natural law to which all men are bound from the divine law (Old and New) (*Summa Theologiae* I–II.96.2, 4–5; 98.5, xcviii.a.5), but by using Aquinas's distinction between the three parts of the law of Moses (moral, ceremonial, and judicial) to argue that only the moral part of this divine law is an essential expression of God's will. Only this divine moral law, which Calvin also identifies with "natural law" (IV.x.16; 1504), is "an unchangeable rule of right living" (16; 1503). The ceremonial and judicial parts of the law were merely servants of the moral laws, fitted to the peculiar circumstances of the Jews. In different circumstances they could be "abrogated while piety remained safe and unharmed," that is, while "the perpetual duties and precepts of love could still remain" (15; 1503).

It is therefore to the moral law that one must turn to know what right or pious laws must be. Here Calvin is careful to insist that "every nation is left free to make such laws as it foresees to be profitable for itself." The only limitation on this freedom is that all laws "must be in conformity to that perpetual rule of love." This divine moral rule "is contained under two heads" and governs man's relation to God as well as to men. "The first part of the law simply commands us to worship God with pure faith and piety; the other, to embrace men with sincere affection." Thus the moral law, or the "eternal and unchangeable will" of God, is "that he himself indeed be worshipped by us all, and that we love one another" (15; 1503). This rule of love is the standard by which all laws are to be judged. Its twofold command recalls Calvin's summary of the function of civil government: "It provides that a public manifestation of religion may exist among Christians, and that humanity be maintained among men" (3; 1488). I have examined this function from the standpoint of church government. Now I must consider the specifically civil function of law, although it should be clear that this is not separate from its religious function.

Calvin also calls this rule of love a "purpose," and in section 16 equates this rule with "natural law," with "that conscience which God has engraved upon the minds of men" and with "equity," which "must be the goal and rule and limit of all laws" (16; 1504). Thus divine law, moral law, the rule of love, natural law, conscience, and equity are all equivalent terms.

But it is not clear how the rule of love can serve as the goal and therefore the standard of political laws. Under what kind of law is the love of God and man most in evidence? Calvin offers little explanation on this point; his concern is always to emphasize that diversity of civil laws is compatible with conformity to the law of God. His examples suggest only a minimal standard and do not clarify how laws serve the end of love. Thus Calvin refuses to regard as true laws any "barbarous and savage laws such as gave honor to thieves [or] permitted promiscuous intercourse" (15; 1503). Similarly, he asserts that "all laws tend to the same end," but he mentions no end but the punishment of "murder, theft, adultery, and false witness" (18; 1504–05). Thus although the law of God interpreted as the rule of love would appear to set an extremely high standard for civil laws, this rule in application seems to amount to little more than the punishment of acts universally recognized as abhorrent and specifically forbidden in the second table of the Jewish Law.

A fuller discussion of the moral law is contained in book 2, chapter 8. Here the requirements of the law again appear to be very high. "Through the law," Calvin writes, "man's life is molded not only to outward honesty but to inward and spiritual righteousness." The law is "spiritual"; it "requires an angelic purity" (II.viii.6; 372, 373). These passages and others seem to suggest that the purpose of the law lies far above external actions, above practically useful activity. "The purpose of the whole law, according to Calvin, is the fulfillment of righteousness to form human life to the archetype of divine purity" (51; 415). Elsewhere he explains that "the worship of God [is] the beginning and foundation of righteousness." Without such righteousness, practical virtues such as "equity, continence, or temperance [are] in God's sight empty and worthless" (11; 377). Equity, or the love of humanity, is subordinate to the love of God. This suggests that, according to Calvin's standard, the best laws are those that most favor activities cultivating love of God in men's souls and that properly subordinated activities merely useful to human beings as human beings.

This, however, is not Calvin's meaning. "Our life shall but conform to God's will and the prescription of the law," he writes, "when it is in every respect most fruitful for our brethren" (54; 417). Since we cannot benefit the Lord, "he does not confine our duties to himself, but he exercises us 'in good works toward our neighbor'" (53; 417). The rigorous spirit of the law thus flows from the first table, from the requirement of pure love of God, but the practical effect of the law is visible primarily in the second table, in love of humanity. Since "the intention of the heart did not show itself" in the law of worship, it was vulnerable to exploitation by "hypocrites" who "continually busied themselves with ceremonies." It is thus only in "works of love" that "we witness real righteousness," only in the practical virtues that we show "through signs real evidence of . . . the fear of God" (52; 416). The spiritual requirement to love God in purity is fulfilled inwardly by a pure intention; this intention is visible only in right conduct toward humanity.

The rule of love is the final standard of Calvin's politics; and yet the harder one looks at Calvin's idea of love, the harder it is to see it. Love of man is founded on love of God; but love of God points back again to love of man. Without the love of God, the love of humanity is impossible and any appearance of right conduct toward men is "in God's sight empty and worthless" (11; 377). Human beings in themselves "more often engender hate than love"; therefore, humanity "should be contemplated in God, not in themselves." Only when men are so contemplated is it possible "to embrace the whole human race without exception in a single feeling of love" (55; 419). The contemplation of God thus appears to be the ground of our love of humanity. However, the contemplation of God appears to be exhausted in the practical embracing of humanity in God; the inward activity of obedience is not a self-sufficient end but an intention that itself points to an activity—the active love of humanity.

Thus in Calvin's argument as in his examples, it is impossible to locate the purpose of his politics. It is appropriate, then, that Calvin should frequently refer to his standard as the *rule* of love; love as a rule takes the place of love as an end or goal; there is no love superior to that which is actually practiced as a rule. The spirit of the law is not above the law; spirit is set in opposition to law, the eternal opposed to the temporal, the "spiritual kingdom" to the "civil jurisdiction" (IV.xx.1; 1486) only to allow the spirit completely to infuse the law; they are rigorously distinguished only to be more perfectly joined. "The purpose of the whole law," we have seen, is "the fulfillment of righteousness to form human life to the archetype of divine purity." And yet this purpose of the law is not the reason for the law but the very meaning of the law itself: "For God has so depicted his character in the law that if any man carries out in deed whatever is enjoined there, he will express the image of God, as it were, in his own life." The image of God is in the deeds themselves, not in any end above the deeds—notably, not in the end of the perfection of the soul, for the soul knows no perfection but that which God grants to its deeds. Thus, Calvin argues, it would be a mistake to long for some spiritual righteousness above the law, "since you cannot desire a greater perfection" than that expressed in the law" (II.viii.51; 415).[1]

It would be misleading, however, to characterize Calvin's teaching as legalistic. Certainly he attaches fundamental importance to law, but this law is understood not as a set of particular commands but as the motive that unites them, as "the perpetual rule of love." Calvin turns the attention of believers from passive contemplation to deeds, but he does not necessarily understand by *deeds* any very detailed pattern of life. For Calvin "every nation is left free to make such laws as it foresees to be profitable for itself." Calvin's understanding of the divine and natural law does not determine for individual cases what is profitable. Although Calvin assumes the universal necessity of certain kinds of law guaranteeing a minimal standard of order, he indeed leaves much scope to human reason to decide what is profitable and how to achieve it. He does, however, deny to human reason the power to determine purposes appropriate to human nature. Human virtues are "empty and worthless" (11; 377) unless contemplated in God. Recognition of this emptiness is necessary in order for the soul to be "entirely filled with the love of God." But since the soul that is filled remains in itself an entirely human—that is, worthless—being, this fulfillment is not effective in the intrinsic perfection of the individual soul but in the intention of the soul to practical activity: "From this will flow directly the love of neighbor" (51; 415).

This point will become clearer through a closer examination of Calvin's section on "love of neighbor" (54). Love of neighbor and God are here radically opposed to love of self. There is nothing good in self-love and there is certainly no need to command it, for men are universally "all too much inclined to self-love." Love of self is precisely that inborn human characteristic against which the law is directed: Only the evil man "strives for his own advantage" whereas "he lives the best and holiest life who lives and strives for himself as little as he can" (54; 417). The purpose that guides right action therefore cannot be "one's own advantage."

Calvin here explicitly opposes his teaching to what "certain Sophists [scholastics] stupidly imagine." One of the sophists who argues the position derided by Calvin is Thomas Aquinas. Aquinas differentiates love of self as a rational nature desiring spiritual good for himself both from the mere universal desire for self-preservation and from the desire of the wicked to gratify what they mistakenly take to be their true selves—their corporeal and sensitive natures. It is only this last kind of self-love that is essentially sinful (Summa Theologiae II–II.25.7). Aquinas further argues that man, who loves God as the principle of all good, ought to love himself as possessing a share of God's goodness in love or charity more than he does loves neighbor, who is a partner in that share; it is natural and right for a man to love his own soul more than his neighbor's just as he ought to love God more than his neighbor by reason of the greater goodness by which God is the cause of happiness (26.4). If there is any sense in which we ought to love our neighbor more than ourselves, it is only that we ought to love our neighbor's soul more than our own body (a.5).

All of this is wholly alien to Calvin's viewpoint. Calvin gives no place to self-love because he does not believe it consistent with man's nature to desire to possess a share of God's goodness. He does not distinguish between true, rational or spiritual goods and false, sensitive or corporeal goods but condemns all alike as "the advantage of his own flesh": "The reasoning of these sophists is not worth a hair: that the thing ruled is always inferior to its rule" (II.viii.54; 418). The so-called ruling or rational part of the soul is spiritually no better than the irrational part. The problem for Calvin, then, is not to get man to seek his true advantage but to enjoin him to forget himself and his own good as far as is possible.

However, if a man does not act in view of a good that is a good for his own soul, on what principle should he act? In view of what good? In order to secure someone else's good, it would appear—"to benefit our neighbor," Calvin says (54; 418). But what is our neighbor's good? And if it is truly good, then is it not good for a man to seek it for himself? Calvin cannot say what our neighbor's good consists in, because to say this would be to say that human beings are capable of sharing in some good above the depravity of the "flesh." There is only one solution: the goods with which a man must seek to benefit his neighbor are the very goods that he considers devoid of any spiritual goodness. "The Lord . . . shows that the emotion of love, which out of natural depravity commonly resides within ourselves, must now be extended to another, that we may be ready to benefit our neighbor with no less eagerness, ardor, and care than ourselves" (54; 418). We can possess no goods above our depraved nature. We can only demonstrate our love of God by extending our desire for depraved goods to our neighbor. The natural and divine law therefore jointly command, under the perpetual rule of love, that each man benefit his neighbor's flesh as much as in his own, without asking what the good is. The spirit, to subdue the claims of the flesh as natural soul, infuses and universalizes the flesh as body.[2]

Calvin associates love of God with faith in him and with fear of him (11, 53). Fear, we have seen, is the perpetual sting necessary to keep faith active (III.ii.23). Aquinas taught that man's love of God is a friendship based upon a likeness between God and man, a likeness between human virtue and divine goodness (*Summa Theologiae* I–II.99.2). But for Calvin no likeness between human virtue as such and divine goodness is possible: there is no properly human goodness but only God's will to manifest his holiness in the deeds of human beings. Therefore divine love is not a good that human beings can grasp firmly; it is accessible to us only as the union of the opposite yet mutually intensifying feelings of fear and faith. The effect and sign of this dynamic union is the love of mankind. In this sense the love of God (faith activated by fear) produces the love of mankind. Thus Calvin seems to argue that faith is superior to love: "It is certain that the law and the prophets give first place to faith and whatever pertains to the lawful worship of God, relegating love to a subordinate position" (II.viii.53; 417). Divine love experienced as faith is the foundation of human love. However, since divine love is now experienced only as faith, it cannot serve as an intelligible guide or standard for human love. This explains why the love inspired by faith itself appears to be not at all inspiring but rather merely useful or practical. Thus Calvin immediately adds that "the law only enjoins us to observe right and equity toward men, that thereby we may become practiced in witnessing to a pious fear of him" (53; 417).

Therefore, although Calvin's identification of love with very practical notions of "right and equity" may seem uninspiring, it would be more faithful to Calvin to say that he intends to inspire practical activity without pointing to a good or purpose above the practical: the love of God is the foundation of the love of man but not the end of it. When the love of God is identified wholly with faith in God there is no place between God and man for friendship based on some degree of likeness. Since we cannot love God except in fearful faith, we cannot love human beings except by benefiting their flesh. The believer finds no repose in the goodness of love: he is perpetually driven by fear to a faith active as utility.

Ethics

The tendency of Calvin's thought to ally a rigorous unworldliness with a certain thoroughgoing commitment to practical concerns is clearly exhibited in his treatise on "The Life of the Christian Man." This treatise, which constitutes chapters 6–10 of book 3 of the *Institutes,* is proposed quite explicitly as an alternative to philosophical treatments of ethics. The basis of this alternative is, of course, "the law of God," which Calvin interprets essentially as "the perpetual rule of love." This ethical treatise represents a further explication of the rule of love: "Because our slowness needs many goods and helps," Calvin explains, "it will be profitable to assemble from various passages of scripture a pattern for the conduct of life" (III.vi.1; 684). The repentant believer needs more than zeal; he needs a pattern "to show . . . how he may be directed to a rightly ordered life, and . . . some universal rule with which to determine his duties" (1; 685).

Calvin is well aware that already "philosophers have fixed limits of the right and the honorable"; but he will show that "Scripture is not without its own order in this matter, but holds to a most beautiful dispensation, and one much more certain than all the philosophical ones." Philosophical ethics may on the surface be more impressive than the less methodical plan of scripture, but this is only because philosophers "were ambitious men, [who] diligently strove to attain exquisite clarity of order to show the nimbleness of their wit" (1; 685).

The stylistic virtuosity of the philosophers is in fact associated with a defect of substance. Because they are ambitious, concerned with their own honor, "in their commendation of virtue, [they] never rise above the natural dignity of man" (3; 687). Since they fail to rise above natural dignity, the philosophers fail to rise above reason; "they set up reason alone as the ruling principle in man, and think that it alone should be listened to; to it alone, in short, they entrust the conduct of life" (vii.1; 690). Philosophers attempt to make the life of reason self-sufficient by contending "that virtue should be pursued for its own sake" (2; 691). That is, they argue that a life ruled by reason is in itself a good life. "Thus, each individual, by flattering himself, bears a kind of kingdom in his breast" (4; 694).

This inward kingdom is the declared enemy of Calvin's ethics: "There is no other remedy than to tear out from our inward parts this most deadly pestilence of love of strife and love of self" (4; 694). Calvin proposes to aim much higher and thereby to offer a more certain and more effective rule of life, one that will at once "penetrate the inmost affections of the heart" and "affect the whole man a hundred times more deeply than the cold exhortations of the philosophers" (vi.4; 688). Calvin thus promises a teaching at once more inward and more outward than that offered by reason: "For it is a doctrine not of the tongue but of life. It is not apprehended by the understanding and memory alone, as other disciplines are, but it is received only when it possesses the whole soul. . . . It must enter our heart and pass into our daily living, and so transform us into itself that it may not be unfruitful for us" (4; 688). Calvin's doctrine is more inward than the accounts of philosophers because it demands a holiness absolutely detached from man's natural self-interest, a "life of righteousness to which we are not at all inclined by nature." And since this holiness is alien to our nature we can never achieve "our union with God . . . by virtue of our holiness. Rather, we ought first to cleave unto him so that, infused with his holiness, we may follow whither he calls" (2; 686). To become a vessel of this divine holiness, the believer must be emptied of all attachment to human goods; as far as possible he must forget himself and all natural virtue. According to Calvin, in order truly to put off selfishness we must erase from our minds not only "the yearning to possess, the desire for power, and the favor of men, but also ambition and all craving for human glory and other more secret plagues" (vii.2; 691). To repent you must "give up all thought of self and, so to speak, get out of yourselves" (5; 695). The law commands us "to put off our own nature and deny whatever our reason and will dictate" (3; 692).

We must "accustom ourselves to contempt for the present life and . . . be aroused thereby to meditate on the future life" (xi.1; 712). In looking for happiness on this earth we sink to the level of "brute beasts, whose condition would be no whit inferior to our own if there were not left to us hope of eternity after death." Without our regard for a righteousness that utterly surpasses our nature "the whole soul [is] enmeshed in the allurement of the flesh." "If you examine the plans, the efforts, the deeds, of anyone, there you will find nothing else but earth." Without the spirit of regeneration the soul's powers of transcendence are dead; there is nothing in the natural soul by which it can rise above this world. "Indeed, either the world must become worthless to us or hold us bound by intemperate love of it" (2; 713). This agrees with Calvin's remark in book 2, "The spirit is so contrasted with flesh that no intermediate thing is left" (II.iii.1; 289).

Since this world is in itself worthless, we must look wholly to God for the rule of our life. "We are consecrated and dedicated to God in order that we may thereafter think, speak, meditate, and do, nothing except to his glory" (III.vii.1; 690).[3]

God's glory is thus the only lawful goal of human life. It would seem to follow that the life of the Christian would consist in withdrawing as far as possible from practical affairs, from activities that aim at earthly goods. And Calvin indeed teaches that we ought "to travel as pilgrims in the world that our celestial heritage may not perish or pass away," that we should "meditate, amid earth's filth, upon the life of the angels" (3; 696). If this world is worthless filth, then "let us despise this life and long to renounce it . . . whenever it shall please the Lord." Until that moment, we should "burn with the zeal for death and be constant in meditation" (xi.4; 716).

On closer inspection, however, it is clear that by "meditation on the future life" Calvin means the very opposite of withdrawal from practical activities. First, an ethic that required such withdrawal would be incompatible with Calvin's injunction, "let *all* the parts of our life . . . strive toward him" (my emphasis) (1.690). As long as human beings live, they must give some attention to their practical needs; it is impossible wholly to withdraw from the concerns of this life. If it is possible to glorify God in "all the parts of our life," then practical activity must somehow be included among activities that glorify God. Furthermore, to attempt to withdraw from practical activity implies that human beings are capable of some activity that transcends the practical, that the human soul is capable of some meritorious activity superior to the desires of the flesh. But Calvin of course denies this. The contemplative life is not possible for man; when philosophers claim to transcend this world, they are only exposing their vanity and ambition. And when monks claim to be exercising the best parts of their soul, they are really doing nothing at all; Calvin debunks as mere "idleness" the claim to an excellent and near-angelic "sanctity" of those who practice the so-called contemplative life. No one is entitled to claim detachment from every "earthly care" in order to "philosophize in retirement, far from intercourse with men." Rather than "hatred of the human race," "Christian meekness" requires attention to "those duties which the Lord has especially commanded," that is, to "a definite calling" (IV.xii.10, 16; 1264, 1271). If all parts of life and all stations in life are to refer equally to God, it is necessary not only to include practical activity under "meditation on the future life" but in fact to exclude contemplative meditation. Human nature is incapable of the virtues necessary to contemplate God's goodness or holiness; therefore the believer must "contemplate the divine will." Since the righteousness of this will is wholly alien to human nature, this nature can in no way find completion and repose in God: "In this life we are to seek and hope for nothing but struggle" (III.xi.1; 713).

If this world is worthless and if there is no way for human nature to rise above it, then how is the Christian to live? How can the believer conform to the standard of God's holiness? Since it is contrary to human nature to be guided by a divine end, it is necessary that "a rule be set forth for us that does not let us wander about in our zeal for righteousness" (vi.2; 685). Calvin sometimes expresses this rule in a purely negative form: the "goal of our calling" is to "have no fellowship with wickedness and uncleanness" (2; 686). But what, in a positively sense, are believers to do? Since all concern for self is excluded, including concern for so-called "virtue" and for philosophical "contemplation," the believer can only turn his attention to preserving or increasing the worldly goods of other men. To consecrate ourselves wholly to

God means "to devote ourselves to God and our brethren" (vii.3; 693). "The benefits we obtain from the Lord"—what Calvin has just called "earth's filth"—must "be applied to the common good of the church. And therefore the lawful use of all benefits consists in a liberal and kindly sharing of them with others" (5; 695). What is filthy becomes clean, indeed "sanctified," when it is shared. And since it is of course impossible literally to practice generosity toward the Lord, "you must, as the prophet says, practice it toward the saints on earth" (5; 696). Still, the outward performance of generosity is not sufficient; it must be accompanied by "a sincere feeling of love" (7; 697) for men—or, more precisely, for "the image of God in all men," not for what "men merit of themselves," because "the great part of them are unworthy if they be judged by their merit" (6; 696).

When worldly goods are shared with sincere generosity, God puts no limit on the worldly resources Christians may acquire or possess (7; 698), as long as there is no dishonesty involved in their acquisition. We must not "greedily strive after riches and honors," but it is permissible "to look to the Lord so that by his guidance we may be led to whatever lot he has provided for us." God may, of course, lead us to our lot by our own enterprises. Profitable undertakings are not in themselves alien to Christian life, but we must "pursue only those enterprises which do not lead us away from innocence" (9; 699).

If this world must become "worthless" to believers, then what reason do they have to engage in worldly enterprises? Calvin argues that the world, which from one point of view is filthy and worthless, must be esteemed a great benefit when considered as God's creation and gift to man. "Let believers accustom themselves to a contempt of the present life that engenders no hatred of it or ingratitude against God" (xi.3; 714). "Something that is neither blessed nor desirable of itself can turn into something good for the devout" (4; 716). Worldly benefits are good for the devout because they allow us "to taste the sweetness of the divine generosity in order to whet our hope and desire to seek after the full revelation of this" (3; 715).

But if these benefits are not good in themselves, how can they represent God's goodness? If there is no commensurability between the desires of the flesh and the divine sweetness—if "no intermediate thing is left"—then how can the satisfaction of these desires whet our taste for that sweetness? Calvin is thus led to grant, in apparent contradiction with his other assessments of the present life, that this world does possess some intrinsic goodness, that it is full of daily benefits or "lesser proofs" of the Fatherhood of God that remind us of "the inheritance of eternal glory." "Since, therefore, this life serves us in understanding God's goodness, should we despise it as if it had no grain of good in itself?" (3; 715). But what precisely does this intrinsic goodness of the world consist in? And how can we best enjoy this goodness? Calvin addresses these questions in the last chapter (10) of his ethical treatise: "How We Must Use the Present Life and Its Helps."

As a principle for guiding our use of "God's gifts" in the present life, Calvin teaches that all benefits must be "referred to that end to which the Author himself created and destined them for us, since he created them for our good." But how are we to understand this good? We have already seen that it cannot be any good dictated by natural reason, that it cannot be "the natural dignity of man" or any human virtue considered as intrinsically good. Is nothing left to this world but sheer physical survival? Calvin sees more than this: "Now if we ponder to what end God created food, we shall find that he meant not only to provide for necessity but also for delight and good cheer. Thus the purpose of clothing, apart from necessity, was comeliness and decency. In grasses, trees, and fruits, apart from their various uses, there is beauty of appearance and pleasantness of odor. . . . Did he not, in short, render many things attractive to us, apart from their necessary use?" (x.2; 720–21). Calvin therefore explicitly opposes those who would limit the Christian use of this world to the minimum necessary for the preservation of the body. Since "we also cannot avoid those things which seem to serve delight more than necessity . . . we must hold to a measure so as to use them with a clear conscience, whether for necessity or delight" (1; 719).

It is not clear, however, what is to serve as the "measure" of our delights; it is not clear what moderation means when "no intermediate thing is left." Calvin says that the good for which God created things ought to govern their use, but he denies that human reason is capable of knowing a good that might order the other goods of human life. In fact, Calvin's whole teaching is directed against the characteristically human attempt to found a kingdom in the breast, to order life according to some idea of what is good for man: this "love of self" necessarily implies a "love of strife" that we cannot simply redirect or moderate; we must "tear [it] out from our inward parts." Since Calvin denies the possibility of a hierarchical ordering of the goods of the present life, he must believe that each earthly delight contains its own principle of moderation within itself, that each can rule itself without reference to any superior good. Or perhaps he means that any desire is moderate that does not claim to rule another—a sort of liberal democracy of delights. In the final analysis, Calvin has no objection to this world as a mass of benefits necessary and delightful, but only to the human attempt to interpret these benefits as a world, that is, as a whole, a "kingdom" ordered toward an intelligible end.

In order to oppose the presumptuous erection of human orders, the attempt of human ambition to subordinate various activities to a single end, Calvin must reduce the order of human life to the discrete practical activities to which God, through history, has called man. Without "the Lord's calling" as the "beginning and foundation of well-doing . . . there will be no harmony among the several parts of this life" and all will be "turned topsy-turvy." And since there is no final reason for human activities but God's will, all callings must be considered equal, since they are equally willed by God. No task is "so sordid and base" that considered as a calling "it will not shine and be reckoned very precious in God's sight" (xi.6; 724–25). There is thus no order to human life except the unintelligible order represented by the actual distribution of practical callings among men.

Calvin's teaching on callings may appear essentially conservative: men are bound to their stations in life. But simply to accept this impression would be to mistake profoundly the significance of Calvin's teaching. Far from a mere endorsement of the way things are, Calvin's ethics represents an attack on "the kingdom in the breast," the hierarchical view of the world and human action embedded in fallen human nature. We have seen that this attack tends to favor a liberation of practical and material activities from any allegedly higher ends. To be sure, the radical potential of Calvin's teaching is somewhat constrained by the emphasis on activity in a "definite calling," that is, the calling that one happens to have. But the limitations of this constraint become clear in recalling (from chapter 3) the most fundamental classification of callings, namely, that which distinguishes between private and public, or political, vocations. Calvin reminds us, in the last chapter of his ethical treatise, that although "to free one's country from tyranny" may be considered a supremely noble deed, "yet a private citizen who lays his hand upon a tyrant is openly condemned by the heavenly judge" (6; 724).

To grasp the importance of the distinction between private and political callings in Calvin's thought, one must consider that the political calling consists in the control and at times in the reordering of the overall distribution of callings. The public calling is that in which God's historical activity is most clearly manifest. And there is no natural measure of fitness for this calling, or natural limitation on membership in it. There is, in fact, no final public basis for defining or constituting a public calling. God calls whom he will to historical activity, and historical activity is itself the sign of this calling. Furthermore, it would appear that since the public or historical calling is limited by no authoritative end, whoever claims such a vocation may with good conscience order private callings so as best to provide the necessities and delights in which we see God's continuous providence. In the next chapter I will show that those powers who best serve the rational self-preservation and prosperity of the people in fact most fully exhibit the glory of God.

Chapter 5

Reason, Rationalism, and History

It is now possible to see how Calvin can understand the moral law, or the perpetual rule of (practical) love, as being at once a divine and a natural law. Calvin's quite frequent appeal to natural law, despite his consistent emphasis on the depravity of nature, has long presented an obstacle to efforts to provide a complete and coherent account of Calvin's political teaching. Given Calvin's overriding emphasis on the absolute sovereignty of God, one can understand that August Lang was led to conclude that "natural law plays no role in Calvin's judgment on legal and social conditions of life" and that the relations of Calvin's theory with natural law are "exterior and superficial."[1]

We have seen, however, that Calvin himself very clearly and with no embarrassment identifies natural and divine law. To ask how this identification is possible, we must first ask what it means. A divine law is a law revealed by God; a natural law is a law accessible to natural reason. To identify the two laws would seem to imply either that there is no law but revealed law or that all law is accessible to natural reason. Either the Bible is the sole and indispensable guide to right living, or anyone endowed with natural reason has no need of the Bible as a practical guide.

Calvin does not seem to hold to the first view, since he does not subject positive laws to any detailed biblical standard but leaves men free to make laws as they judge most "profitable" (IV.xx.15; 1503), subject only to the very broad "rule of love." This would seem to leave a wide area for the discretionary exercise of human reason. However, in the first section of his chapter on the Ten Commandments (I.viii), Calvin argues that although what the revealed law asserts is the same as what is available in the "inward law . . . written, even engraved upon the hearts of all," this inward or natural law, conscience, is ineffective by itself. It is ineffective because it has been "shrouded in the darkness of errors" and ignored out of the blindness of self-love. Thus, owing both to our "dullness" and to our "arrogance, . . . the Lord has a written law to give us a clearer witness of what was too obscure in the natural law, shake off our listlessness, and strike more vigorously our mind and memory" (II.viii.1; 367–68).

It would seem to follow that natural reason finally has no moral role. Chenevière draws this conclusion: "The Decalogue therefore in effect (*pratiquement*) replaces the conscience, at least for the Christian" (80). "The conscience no longer . . . serves as a moral rule" (83).[2] Calvin, however, interprets the scriptural standard very broadly as the rule of love and quite deliberately leaves room under this rule for human judgment in determining what is profitable. What is the basis of human judgment, if the natural or inward law has been rendered ineffective by our dullness and arrogance? To address this question I turn to Calvin's thematic treatment of the powers of human reason.

Fallen Reason as Conscience

In chapter 15 of book 1 of the *Institutes*, Calvin discusses "The Original Integrity of Man's Nature," that is, the state of human nature before the fall. He defends the perfect integrity of human nature as created and criticizes the philosophical view of the soul according to which one part is by nature inferior and in need of restraint by a more perfect part (see below, chap. 8). Turning to the condition of fallen man, Calvin does not dispute the philosophers' claim that human nature is in need of a ruler. Rather, he questions whether fallen reason is fit to be that ruler. Those who distinguish between "sensitive" and "rational" parts of the soul, pointing out the "great disagreement" between them, speak "as if reason itself did not also disagree with itself and were not at cross-purposes with itself, just like armies at war" (I.xv.6; 193). Reason cannot agree with itself because it has access to no authoritative purpose. This is what the philosophers overlook: not recognizing the conflict which besets reason itself, "they always imagine reason in man as that faculty whereby he may govern himself aright" (6; 194).

Calvin clearly has strong reservations, to say the least, concerning the power of reason to rule the soul in fallen human nature. Chenevière seems right, then, that human beings must turn wholly from natural law to revealed law for moral guidance. Calvin, however, admits that what philosophers teach may be "true, or at least probable," that "they seem to be asserting something probable," that their teachings may be "profitable to learn" (6; 193). He also points to the intellectual experience of fallen human beings as evidence of the substantiality of the soul, which clearly implies that even fallen reason is not without significant powers. A "vestige" of the soul is evident in man's sense of shame, which proceeds from a "regard for what is honorable," in turn proving that men "understand themselves to have been born to cultivate righteousness, in which the seed of religion is enclosed" (6; 192). Elsewhere Calvin cites other experiences or powers of fallen man as evidence of the transcendence of the soul: he mentions interest in astronomy, the "nimbleness of the soul" with respect to space and time, imagination, skill in inventing "marvelous devices," and dreams (v.5; 57). He even argues that "the conscience, which, discerning between good and evil, responds to God's judgment, is an undoubted sign of the immortal spirit" (xv.2; 184).

What, then, is the status of the soul of fallen man, according to Calvin? "In another place," Calvin promises, "we shall see how firmly the understanding now governs the will" (7; 195). Calvin here refers the reader to the discussion of the effects of the fall in the first three chapters of book 2. His final answer to the question of the status of fallen reason is not, however, easily derived from these chapters. Indeed, Calvin often seems flatly to contradict himself here.

Calvin begins by insisting on the absolute and thoroughgoing corruption of fallen human nature. He goes so far as to speak of the "death" of the soul and the obliteration of the "heavenly image" in man (II.i.5; 246). The effects of the fall extend to every part of human nature: "We are so vitiated and perverted in every part of our nature that by this great corruption we stand justly condemned and convicted before God. . . . whatever is in man, from the understanding to the will, from the soul even to the flesh, has been defiled and crammed with concupiscence" (8; 251–52). In chapter 2 Calvin states the practical conclusion of this radical doctrine of the fall. Against the scholastics, he argues that it is alien to human nature to seek after the good (ii.6; 263). Since "the whole man lies under the power of sin," it is impossible "that men should have, apart from grace, some impulses (however puny) toward good" (27; 288). Though one might argue, with the philosophers, that "all things seek good through a natural instinct," this has nothing to do with "the uprightness of the human will." For man's "natural sense of good" is identical in kind with the nonrational "inclination of . . . nature" which all animals possess. Indeed, this "desire of good . . . no more proves freedom of the will than the tendency of metals and stones toward perfection of their essence proves it in them" (26; 286–87). Human action is no more a proof of the ruling powers of human reason than the falling of a stone is a proof of its rationality.

In chapter 3, Calvin continues to emphasize his point: "The whole man is flesh." "Whatever he have from nature . . . is flesh." "The Spirit is so contrasted with flesh that *no intermediate thing is left*" (iii.1; 289; my emphasis). The "intermediate thing" excluded by the contrast between the regenerating power of the Holy Spirit and the corruption of the flesh is the human soul. The soul is not only "diseased"—this would imply that "some vigor of life yet remains." Rather, "the soul, plunged into this deadly abyss, is not only burdened with vices, but is utterly devoid of all good" (2; 291–92). It appears that, for Calvin, the impotence of the human soul is absolute and clearly established; it would seem to follow that the natural law can in no way be effective as a guide to human beings.

But this is not Calvin's position. We saw in book 1 that Calvin intends to grant some place in his teaching to the philosophical idea of the ruling power of reason and that he points to certain traces of the soul's power in the intellectual experiences of fallen

man. Calvin has not forgotten these arguments. In the very chapters in which he insists on the total depravity of man, Calvin
repeats and indeed amplifies these apparently contradictory arguments. He claims, for example, that even fallen human nature
"possesses some power of perception, since it is by nature captivated by love of truth" (ii.12; 271). And in summarizing this
discussion, Calvin returns to the essential distinction between
human and animal nature: "We see among all mankind that reason is proper to our nature; it distinguishes us from brute beasts"
(17; 276).

Furthermore, although it would seem clearly to follow from
Calvin's doctrine of total depravity that the human mind is entirely powerless to govern human nature, Calvin explicitly and
emphatically avoids this conclusion. He in fact recurs to the traditional Christian distinction between natural and supernatural
gifts: "The natural gifts were corrupted in man through sin, but
. . . his supernatural gifts were stripped from him." Thus it appears
that certain parts of human nature partially escaped the effects of
the fall; gifts that are "natural" or "inseparable from man's nature" were preserved. Calvin even writes that "reason . . . by
which man distinguishes between good and evil, and by which he
understands and judges, is a natural gift . . . and could not be
completely wiped out" (12; 270–71). Fallen reason is therefore not
entirely worthless, "especially when it turns its attention to
things below," that is, to "earthly things." Calvin writes, "I call
'earthly things' those which do not pertain to God or his Kingdom,
to true justice, or to the blessedness of the future life; but which
have their significance and relationship with regard to the present
life and are, in a sense, confined within its bounds" (13; 271–72).
In these passages Calvin thus seems clearly to grant a place to the
governing power of reason within fallen human nature. But how is
this to be reconciled with his doctrine of the depravity of every
part of human nature and of the virtual death of the soul?

Does Calvin affirm or deny that human beings are by nature
capable of seeking truth? Immediately after asserting that men are
"by nature captivated by love of truth," Calvin fundamentally
qualifies this assertion: "Yet this longing for truth, such as it is,
languishes before it enters upon its race because it soon falls away

into vanity" (12; 271). It is true that human beings desire truth and are therefore different from animals. However, since mankind is "incapable of seeking and finding truth," the bare longing for truth cannot provide a basis for true transcendence. The natural longing for truth leads nowhere; this natural desire in no way partakes of the true, spiritual good of man. One might say, then, that fallen human beings transcend beasts in only a purely formal sense: they desire truth, which beasts do not, yet they are no more capable than beasts of truly ascending to truth. Men desire *a* truth, but the truth they desire has nothing at all in common with *the* truth. It is only rationality as a *mode* and not the *end* of reason that links man with his original condition as the image of God. Thus even the so-called philosophers are finally incapable of true love of wisdom. In essence, "they were ambitious men, who diligently strove to attain an exquisite clarity of order to show their nimbleness of wit" (III.xi.1; 685). The philosopher is "like a traveler passing through a field at night who in a momentary lightening flash sees far and wide, but the sight vanishes so swiftly, that he is plunged again into the darkness of the night before he can take even a step, let alone be directed on his way by its help" (II.ii.18; 277).

Similarly, man's sense of shame, or "regard for what is honorable," indeed proves that humans are capable of being oriented toward the divine, that they are "made for meditation upon the heavenly life." But it does not prove that man has any access to God: even in his discussion of the original excellence of human nature (I.xv, from which these last passages are drawn) he clearly distinguishes between the presence of these seeds of religion and the possibility of their germination: "If human happiness, whose perfection is to be united with God, were hidden from man, he would in fact be bereft of the principle use of his understanding" (II.xv.6; 192). And since, as we learn in book 2, man's supernatural gifts have been extinguished, it follows that man is in fact "bereft of the principle use of his understanding." The transcendence implied in man's sense of shame must remain purely formal, an empty possibility. In book 2, Calvin therefore lists shame and a striving "towards virtue" among those qualities through which God restrains corrupt human nature without regenerating it, that is, by which "the Lord merely restrains [the nonelect] by throwing a bridle over them" (iii.3; 292–93). Calvin immediately makes it clear that this inward restraint in no way raises man above corruption: "Because, however excellent anyone has been, his own ambition always pushes him on . . . anything in profane men that appears praiseworthy, must be considered worthless." The virtues that "have their praise in the political assembly and in common renown among men" have nothing in common with the "zeal to glorify God" and "shall be of no value . . . before the heavenly judgment seat" (4; 292–94).

Calvin's treatment of man's regard for truth and honor clearly shows that the promise of transcendence implied in this regard must remain unfulfilled in unregenerated human beings, for this "truth" and "honor" are purely human and utterly removed from, even hostile to, the truth of God's honor. Fallen human nature fails to rise above animal nature, because human honor is merely an "inclination of nature" like the inclination of metals or stones to their proper "essence." Men are bound to "desire their own well-being" (ii.26; 286–87), and this well-being has nothing in common with God's glory.

It must be added, however, that the necessity which enslaves human beings is not identical to animal or material necessity, for humans may be restrained by shame or impelled by ambition. This characteristically human desire for honor and glory indeed differentiates men from beasts and stones. But it does not raise man above other creatures unless it is transformed by the Holy Spirit into a desire for God's honor and glory. Indeed, without this transformation man is not only infinitely inferior to God, along with the rest of creation; he is the only creature who actually opposes God by setting up his own honor and glory as rivals to God's. The characteristic purpose of human reason is radically alien to God; it is only human reason as the formal possibility of the glorification of God that distinguishes man from the irrational creation. No rational human purpose links man with God. One might say that man is linked to God not by reason but by sheer consciousness.

It follows that Calvin's natural law is a law of reason only in the special sense of a law of consciousness or conscience. We have seen that conscience, the "tiny spark of light" (IV.x.5; 1183) that remains in fallen man, the only natural "mean between God and man" (III.xix.15; 848), is not based on a likeness between God and man but consists precisely in man's consciousness of his absolute alienation from God (see above, chap. 3). This consciousness of guilt seals Calvin's argument that conscience is a proof of human transcendence. Humanity transcends itself only in the bare consciousness of its inability to transcend itself. "For how could a motion without essence penetrate to God's judgment seat, and inflict itself with dread at its own guilt?" (I.xv.2; 184). The soul is dead in all but its ability to recognize its own death. It knows good and evil because it knows that God is absolutely good, and that the human soul is absolutely evil—to the point of being incapable of desiring good. The natural soul cannot desire good; it can only know that what it desires is evil.

Calvin consistently identifies this conscience, or consciousness of depravity, with natural law. "It is a fact that the law of God which we call the moral law is nothing else than a testimony of natural law and of that conscience which God has engraved upon the minds of men" (IV.xx.16; 1504). It is because this conscience is ineffective by itself that God reveals his law in unmistakable terms in order to awaken man to full self-consciousness: "Knowledge of ourselves [requires] . . . that, empty of all opinion of our own virtue, and shorn of all assurance of our own righteousness— in fact, broken and crushed by the awareness of our own utter poverty—we may learn genuine humility and self-abasement. Both of these the Lord accomplishes in his law" (II.viii.1; 367). Man's natural consciousness of self is "so puffed up with haughtiness and ambition, and so blinded by self-love, that he is as yet unable to look upon himself and, as it were, to descend within himself." The revealed law is necessary, not to add anything to the natural law, certainly not to clarify any purpose inherent in human nature, but precisely to shatter man's confidence in his own purposes, to destroy man's efforts to raise himself above the rest of creation. "The Lord has provided us with a written law to give us a clearer witness of what was too obscure in the natural law, shake off our listlessness, and strike more vigorously our mind and memory" (1; 368).

Reason and the Instinct of Self-Preservation

If the natural law is equivalent to consciousness of nothingness, then its practical function must be purely negative—practically, it must tell human beings not what we ought to do but
what we cannot do. But this does not represent Calvin's whole
intention; natural law has for him a positive practical function as
well as the negative theoretical function I have just described.
Indeed, Calvin is acutely aware of the potential of the radical
doctrine of depravity for destroying the springs of human action,
and he very deliberately hedges his teaching against this potential. "When man is denied all uprightness, he immediately takes
occasion for complacency from that fact, and holds all pursuit [of
righteousness] to be of no consequence" (II.ii.1; 255). The obvious
alternative is to grant that man can accomplish some righteousness by his own powers; but it is of course a fundamental premise
of Calvin's teaching that this is false: "Nothing, however slight,
can be credited to man without depriving God of his honor, and
without man himself falling into ruin through brazen confidence."
    Calvin seems caught in a hopeless practical dilemma. But he
sees in this hopelessness the grounds for an unprecedented hope:
man must be "instructed to aspire to a good of which he is empty,
to a freedom of which he has been deprived." This expresses in
essence the whole practical program of the *Institutes*: man must
aspire to a good which by nature he is wholly incapable of desiring
as good—which it is wholly impossible for him to know as good.
The impossibility of such human knowledge and desire are converted by Calvin from a hindrance to human activity into an im-
measurable boon. To deprive man of a soul with a purpose not only
honors God but activates man, it is "both fundamental in religion
and most profitable for us"; to abjure "all credit for our wisdom
and virtue . . . is no less to our advantage than pertinent to God's
glory." To claim any such credit is to be "born aloft on a reed stick,
only to fall as soon as it breaks" (1; 256). To recognize the impossibility of human wisdom and virtue thus does not hinder but increases the activity of human beings; man "may thus be more
sharply aroused from inactivity than if it were supposed that he

was endowed with the highest virtues" (1; 255). "Man's power is rooted up from its very foundations that God's power may be built up in man" (1; 256). Human activity is wonderfully increased when it is freed from the encumbrance of human purposes. Precisely because man can *be* nothing, there is no limit to what he can *do*.

What, then, will he do? What can guide human action if not a human purpose, or some purpose in which human beings are capable of participating? Calvin's answer again involves his teaching on natural law, but an aspect of this teaching distinct from the negative, liberating function of conscience. Natural law as conscience frees man from human purposes; it remains to see how natural law can be a positive guide to action. This guide is reason, understood as concerned only with earthly things, as "confined" within the bounds of "the present life." When it is understood within these bounds, Calvin is willing to grant the competence of human reason and to consider the philosophic account of the soul as true, or at least probable, and as profitable.

Yet it is clear that the practical truths accessible to fallen reason are not what the philosophers claim them to be, truths regarding man's true nature. Calvin is careful to limit the scope of his defense of fallen reason by indicating not only that philosophical truth regards the present life but that this truth is "in a sense confined within its bounds."[3] The philosophers themselves understand their accounts of human nature to be in principle full accounts, or as full as possible; they understand themselves to be discussing, if not exactly the highest things, then certainly the highest human things, and they demonstrate that such discussions necessarily open into reflections on the whole or the divine. Plato's political teaching, for example, includes a consideration of the problem of the idea of the good itself (*Republic*, VI). And Aristotle, who is intent on confining the moral virtues to their own sphere as far as possible, in the final book of the *Nichomachean Ethics* nevertheless asserts that the contemplative life is the happiest and most divine. For both philosophers, the practical question of how one ought to live cannot be wholly separated from the theoretical question of the purpose of the whole of nature. Therefore, in saying that the philosophic account of human nature is probable and profitable only as confined to earthly things, Calvin understands this account very differently.

When Calvin attempts to confine worldly things rigorously to this world, he causes them to appear in a new light. When human activity is totally severed from divine goodness, it takes on a new meaning. The human quest for truth becomes just another form of human ambition, and human ambition becomes just another form—indeed, a particularly perverse form—of human self-interest. Since all self-interest is alien to God's law, the law cannot aim at honor or at truth. What, then, is the aim of the law?

This aim, we have seen, is defined by "the perpetual rule of love." The meaning of this rule becomes clearer upon examining more closely Calvin's description of the powers of fallen reason in book 2. On the one hand, Calvin argues that reason is incompetent to govern human conduct because it has no access to an authoritative purpose; reason is at cross-purposes with itself. On the other hand, Calvin grants that reason is competent to govern man in temporal things, including political matters (II.i.13; 272). But how can reason govern without a purpose? Calvin's answer is that man, as "a social animal, tends through natural instinct to foster and preserve society." This instinct is the source in "all men's minds" of "universal impressions of a certain civic fair dealing and order." Thus, all men understand the necessity of laws and "comprehend the principles of these laws" (13; 272). Reason does not need a purpose in order to govern man, because purposeless "natural instinct" takes the place of purpose.

The connection between natural instinct and the preservation of society by laws is so obvious that those who "think unjust what some have sanctioned as just . . . and contend that what some have forbidden is praiseworthy" have no claim to the authority of reason: "They fight against manifest reason." Men fight against the manifestly rational connection between natural instinct and the preservation of society "on account of their lust." But they oppose rational preservation not in the name of lust but in the name of honor, freedom, or justice—in the name of some good supposed to be superior to the preservation of society. Here the most virtuous natures (from a human point of view) are most at odds both with the rationality of natural instinct and with the will of God: "A man of the most excellent disposition finds it utterly senseless to bear an unjust and excessively imperious domination," Calvin writes, "but the Lord condemns this excessive haughtiness and enjoins upon his own people a patience disgraceful in men's eyes" (24; 184). The will of God and the rational recognition of the instinct of preservation make a common front against the man of "most excellent disposition," against "heroic and nobler natures" (IV.xx.7; 1492). "The light of nature" that God has given all mankind in the form of rational instinct opposes "the natural man," "the common judgment of human reason" based on a lustful and haughty appeal to justice, honor, or freedom.[4]

These passages provide a key for understanding the central paradoxes of Calvin's practical teaching. Nature here is opposed to nature, and reason to reason. Calvin defends nature as the social instinct of self-preservation against nature as lustful ambition; and he defends reason as the rational acknowledgement of this instinct against reason as the presumptuous creator of standards above this instinct. "The light of nature," which means the consciousness of the soul's worthlessness, also indicates the rationality of collective self-preservation. Calvin's doctrine is not opposed to reason as such but only to the idea of the intrinsic goodness of reason, to the rational soul that pretends to govern by virtue of its own goodness. It is opposed not to modern rationalism but to classical reason. Thus it is possible for Calvin's doctrine of natural law as consciousness of nothingness to be joined to a doctrine of natural law as a rational rule of action. The sheer form of consciousness is therefore not the only link between God and man to survive the fall—the only divine spark in depraved human nature—there is also the rational instinct of self-preservation.

Calvin argues that man's "supernatural gifts" have been stripped away (II.ii.12; 270) and that "the rule by which we conform our lives to . . . the knowledge of God" falls under "heavenly things" and not "earthly things." But he then makes an exception for this rule: there is one element of heavenly knowledge that is accessible to fallen reason: "The human mind sometimes seems more acute in this [the rule for the right conduct of life] than in higher things" (22; 281). Further on, Calvin explains that "men have somewhat more understanding of the precepts of the Second

Table because these are more closely concerned with the preservation of civil society among them" (24; 284). To be sure, the natural knowledge of the means of preserving society is not practically effective without the support of revelation. The revealed majesty of God's law is needed to defend rational collective self-preservation against the haughty self-assertion of fallen reason. If man is in one sense naturally social—because instinctively inclined to self-preservation, for which he depends on society—he is in another sense, by the fall, naturally opposed to society. If nature tells man that society will be overthrown if he does not submit to princes, it also tells him that he is the equal of any prince and therefore not bound to obey him. Calvin thus teaches that it is absolutely contrary to our nature to submit to princes (Doumergue, V.466, 467, 493, 494). Men may, by the power of natural reason, "agree on the general conception of equity." But without the authority of revelation they "dispute about individual sections of the law" (II.i.13; 273). "Herein is man's ignorance: when he comes to a particular case, he forgets the general principle that he has just laid down" (23; 282). Without the revealed law it is impossible fully to rationalize self-preservation; apart from the fear of God men do not preserve equity and love among themselves. Furthermore, whatever collective self-preservation is secured apart from the fear of God is infected with the motive of private self-preservation and is of no spiritual worth. When fear of God is removed, "whatever equity, continence, or temperance men practice among themselves is in God's sight empty and worthless" (viii.11; 377). The revealed law is necessary to secure the rational universalization of self-preservation and thereby to infuse the instinct of nature with supernatural worth.

Chenevière's insistence on the nonrational character of Calvin's practical teaching is therefore misleading. He believes that the identification of natural law with the law perceived by the conscience implies the total separation of this law from reason and from the order of nature (61–67). He describes conscience as the God-given faculty, obscured by the fall and thus effectively superseded by the Decalogue, by which man distinguishes good from evil, not according to any general principle, but case by case (69–70). But this view fails to explain Calvin's numerous appeals to reason and particularly to nature (see Doumergue, V.466–70). It overlooks the possibility that the law of God might oppose the assertion of human virtue implied in a teleological understanding of reason and nature precisely in order to secure the manifest rationality of the natural instincts created by God.

Chenevière fails to see that a standard of political order which is in one sense irrational is in another manifestly rational. God's law seems to require an obedience completely beyond human understanding and completely unrelated to human needs or purposes; the powers that be are ordained of God and therefore we must obey them. The political order, like the order of nature, consists in nothing but sheer obedience to unintelligible power. "The order of Nature," Calvin writes, "is nothing but the obedience rendered to him by all the parts of the world, that his sovereign power may everywhere shine" (Doumergue, V.471). Thus the authority of God is simply the authority of fact (V.421). No human being can presume by his own powers to question the divine authority of fact in the name of human justice, freedom, or honor.

On closer inspection, however, the authority of fact is more manifestly rational than any human reason because it is more closely bound to the instinct of human nature for self-preservation. Thus Chenevière himself notices that, besides the appeal to revelation, "Calvin also knows some good reasons which can facilitate the obedience of the most lukewarm." These reasons reduce to collective self-preservation. Chenevière quotes Calvin's explanation of the usefulness even of princes who "abuse their power in tormenting the good and innocent." Such tyrants thus "retain some semblance of just domination" because "there can be no tyranny which does not in part and in some way serve to maintain human society." Chenevière notes, furthermore, that Calvin frequently insists even the worst tyranny is better than the anarchy that would result from the absence of authority.[5] Even the worst rulers are God's servants despite themselves, for by preventing through their very cruelty the war of all against all, they protect the natural and God-given instinct of self-preservation against the natural equality of men.

It follows that any positive law, by virtue of its very existence, conforms to the minimal standard of the divine and natural law of collective self-preservation. The enforceable command of the sovereign is the effective manifestation of the perpetual rule of love. Calvin's position tends toward that of Hobbes: the law of nature and the civil law contain each other (*Leviathan*, 26).[6]

Rationalism and History

It is possible on the basis of this analysis to solve the contradiction that stands as a final obstacle to coherence in Ernst Troeltsch's brilliant discussion of Calvinism in *The Social Teachings of the Christian Churches*. "There is," Troeltsch argues, "an inner contradiction within [Calvin's] whole theology, which on the one hand recognizes to a great extent the rationalism of the *Lex Naturae*, and on the other hand asserts the irrational character of the Divine Will." From Calvin's irrationalism it follows that "all government seems to be simply appointed by God, and the whole duty of subjects seems to consist in the exercise of self-humiliation." Calvin's rationalism, on the other hand, leads to the idea that "authorities are bound by the Law of Nature and they are to be controlled by those who have called them to their office." Troeltsch can only conclude that "this discord goes right through Calvin's teaching." He believes, though, that "as time went on, the [Calvinist] conception of the State became more rational" (II.897n. 349). However, Troeltsch's "inner contradiction" dissolves when one realizes that in Calvin's thought rationalism and irrationalism are not enemies but allies in a joint attack on purposive reason. For Calvin as for Hobbes, the impotence of reason with regard to purposes must be established as a condition for the rationalization of human society (*Leviathan*, 6, 17, 18). It is true that the politics of the rationalization of the instinct of self-preservation may take various forms—the basic idea is as compatible with Hobbes's emphasis on the people's duty of obedience as it is with Locke's defense of the people's right of resistance. And Calvin indeed hesitates between these two positions. But this hesitation does not point to an inner contradiction in Calvin's theology; the difference between obedience and resistance is not a difference between irrationalism and rationalism—in both cases human power is interpreted as divine power in order to lay low human authority; in both cases supernatural spirit infuses naturalistic needs to defend them against natural purposes. The duty of obedience and the right of resistance represent different ways of implementing a single law of nature understood as grounded both in the will of God and in rational human instinct, just as Hobbesian absolutism and Lockean constitutionalism are both derived from an assertion of a natural right more powerful than any purpose.

It is misleading, furthermore, to suggest that the difference between the two poles of Calvin's politics (submission and resistance) is a difference between "self-humiliation" and self-assertion or between the acceptance of a duty and the assertion of a right. In both cases the haughty self-assertion of fallen human nature is humbled or laid low in favor of human nature considered as more truly natural, indeed divine—or rather, as willed by God. "For there is no danger of man's depriving himself of too much," Calvin explains, "so long as he learns that in God must be recouped what he himself lacks" (II.ii.10; 267). He who loses his will shall find it—he who loses his free will shall find a will empowered by God:

> Nothing now prevents us from saying that we ourselves are fitly doing what God's Spirit is doing in us, even if our will contributes nothing of itself distinct from his grace. . . . For any mixture of the power of free will that men strive to mingle with God's grace is nothing but a corruption of grace. It is just as if one were to dilute wine with muddy, bitter water. . . . Yet because we are by nature endowed with will, we are with good reason said to do those things the praise for which God rightly claims for himself: first because whatever God out of his loving kindness does in us is ours, provided we understand that it is not of our doing; secondly, because ours is the mind, ours the will, ours the striving, which he directs toward the good. (v.15; 335–36)

God activates the human will toward a good it cannot know by purifying it of all claims to act in view of a good it can know.

Although this view of human action underlies Calvinist submission as well as Calvinist resistance, it does not appear with equal clarity in both. Cruel tyrannies exhibit the glory of God despite themselves, for they serve the God-given instinct of self-preservation only through the impious self-glorification of the tyrant. How much more brightly, then, will the glory of God shine in the laying low of human authority and the liberation of human activity for the manifest needs of human nature. In submitting to powers that be, subjects obey indirectly the will of God to glorify himself in the preservation of humanity; but how much more glorious to submit to or to constitute the powers that are coming to be, powers that directly and consciously submit to and enact God's glory in his creation. If self-preservation is glorious, then how much more glorious is a full prosperity undiluted and unrestrained by assertions of mere human goodness. If God's majesty shines in the commands of every king or prince, then how much more will it shine in the laws of those who acknowledge that "the world was not created for kings; they were rather created for the multitude" (Doumergue, V.424).

Calvinist politics would therefore tend to develop not from an irrational to a rational conception of the state, as Troeltsch suggests, but from a less clear to a more clear expression of irrational rationalism. One cannot say that such a development occurred in Calvin's own politics; he seems to have judged to the end of his life that in France at least the moment had not come in which his idea of God's glory could begin to become directly effective in the authority of the actual. He continued to try to use existing powers, including inferior magistrates and princes of the blood, to protect the Huguenots from persecution. After the massacre of Vassny (1562), he went so far as to authorize the taking up of arms by Protestants and even the use of foreign soldiers, but only on the grounds that they were fighting not against the king but against usurpers (the Guises; see Chenevière, 337–49; Doumergue, V.503–6). To the end of his life, Calvin continued to insist upon the duty of submission: "We find Calvin completely dissociating himself from the various conspiracies being hatched by his more irresponsible followers in France" (Skinner, II.302).

It does not follow, however, as Chenevière argues, that the "monarchomachs betrayed the profound thought of their master, by giving his doctrine of inferior magistrates and his whole political thought in general a revolutionary character that it did not have" (349). Nor is it evident that in order to create a modern, secular understanding of political authority it was necessary, as Skinner argues, "to abandon the orthodox Pauline contention that all the powers that be must be seen as directly ordained by God." For it is possible to interpret the powers that be so as to include the powers that are coming to be and to understand the power of God in history—that is, in human action—as directed toward collective self-preservation and toward a prosperity that powerfully exhibits God's glory by confining itself strictly to this world. Furthermore, the spiritual or idealistic striving for worldly prosperity may be more comprehensively characteristic of modern politics than is the idea, to quote Skinner, "that any legitimate political society must originate in an act of free consent on the part of the whole populace" (see above, chap. 2). Humanitarian theorists from Hobbes to Marx have made it clear that modern democratic freedom refers more fundamentally to the secular objective than to the political means. Even for Locke, the effectual truth of "free consent on the part of the whole populace" is of course the actual power of the majority, of "the greater force" (*Second Treatise*, VII.96). Calvin, Hobbes, Locke, and Marx are in fundamental agreement that there is no higher authority than the greatest power manifest in human activity, in what Marx calls "History."

In any case, it would be hard to find a more far-reaching application of the contractual theory of authority than Calvin's remarkable gloss on these words of the prophet Hosea: "then shall the children of Judah and the children of Israel be gathered together and appoint themselves one head." Calvin writes "when we believe the gospel, we choose Christ for our king, as it were, by a voluntary consent" (*Comm. Hosea* I.11, quoted in Doumergue, V.483). Doumergue notes that the contractual theory of authority was put in practice by Calvin himself in founding his church in Geneva in 1537; this church was based on a written constitution to which every member consented. But Doumergue chooses not to dwell on the means Calvin was ready to employ to create his "voluntary" society. The contract bore the title, "Confession of Faith which all the citizens and inhabitants of Geneva and the subjects of the country must promise to keep and hold"; and those who did not choose to consent to this manifesto of Christian freedom were free only to leave the city.

The fact that in Calvin's thought politics is grounded in the will of God is therefore not conclusive evidence that his thought is fundamentally hostile to modern political activism. Indeed it is possible that only interpreting human activity as the will of God in history made it possible to free this activity from restraints based on finalistic interpretations of human nature. Skinner, like Chenevière, overlooks this possibility because he assumes that modern rationalism is continuous with classical reason and modern naturalism with Aristotle's idea of nature. Thus he believes that a providentialist argument must be foreign to a secularist argument, and he does not see that providence may serve as an argument for pursuing, unrestrained by human authority, objectives understood at once as manifesting God's glory and as radically confined to this world.

Perhaps only by joining the glory of God to the rational self-preservation of humanity could rationalism overpower the idea that the end of politics is the natural perfection of the human soul. This is essentially Doumergue's view, although he is so inspired by the Calvinist combination of religious fervor and worldly prosperity that he is not at all aware of the loss of the view of human action that is excluded by this combination. Doumergue argues that all natural law before Calvin remained ineffective because it was never fully put in practice in positive law: "In order for something great—from a modern point of view—to come out of natural law, a new spirit was necessary" (V.463–64). Calvinism, according to Doumergue, supplied this spirit necessary to make natural law effective in history. And Troeltsch remarks that in Calvinism "the historical and natural law point of view is [sic] united" (II.897n. 348). George DeLagarde and Hans Baron agree that although the political arguments of Calvinist republicans after Calvin were often copies of old scholastic theories, the spirit or, as Lagarde says (128–29), the "form and color" of these arguments were new and powerful.[7] The foregoing discussion suggests that this spirit is not some mysterious and irreducible historical energy; instead it flows from a certain view of God and man that can be articulated theoretically on the basis of Calvin's arguments. It is beyond the scope of this study to determine the degree of continuity between Calvin's fundamental political teaching and the views of later Calvinists thought to be much more radical and modern than

Calvin himself. I hope it is clear, however, that this question cannot be properly examined as long as it is simply assumed that arguments which appeal to the authority of revelation are necessarily opposed to rationalistic arguments, or that the authority of God's power necessarily excludes the right of the people as agents of history.

Calvin radically distinguishes the divine and the human, the spiritual and the temporal, precisely for the purpose of joining them together more powerfully than ever before.[8] He must teach that "there are in man, so to speak, two worlds, over which different kings and different laws have authority" (III.xix.15; 847) in order to establish that there is only one world and that it is all God's. In radically separating the political and spiritual worlds, Calvin denies that either forms an intelligible whole for human beings, denies that either order is ruled by a principle in which human nature partakes. Calvin opposes the spiritual kingdom and the political kingdom in order to wage a two-front war against the kingdom in the human breast—against the rational soul. When the soul is excluded, along with all "intermediate things," it is possible completely to unite divine activity and human activity. Since Hegel, at least, we have called this union History.

PART TWO

Calvin's Antitheology: Transcendence without Another World

They who attribute (as they think) ease to God, take from him the care of mankind; take from him his honour: for it takes away men's love, and fear of him; which is the root of honour.

—Thomas Hobbes

In democratic ages, therefore, it is particularly important not to confuse the honor due to secondary agents with the worship belonging to the creator alone.

—Alexis de Tocqueville

Chapter 6

Justification and Sanctification

I have shown that Calvin's politics and ethics are embedded in his religious teaching. On the basis of the fundamental Protestant belief in justification by faith alone, Calvin radically severs the human and divine realms in order to make possible their fusion in historical activity.

In part 2 I examine more fully the pivotal doctrine of justification by faith, tracing its roots in still deeper levels of Calvin's thought. An examination of the idea of justification by faith alone will lead to the question (chap. 6) of the meaning of holiness or santification and thus to the question (chap. 7) of the right constitition of the human soul in relation to God.

This right order is of course authoritatively and comprehensively represented for Calvin in the person of Christ himself. I will argue, however (chap. 8), that it is possible to look beyond the simple revelation of the person of Jesus in Calvin's theology to the "secret energy of the Spirit." Finally, I claim that the meaning of the Holy Spirit is in turn grounded in Calvin's understanding of right order as the pure consciousness of absolute power. Calvin's pervasive tendency to distinguish radically as well as to unify emphatically the human and divine realms is thus rooted in his understanding of the radical separation and intimate union of self-knowledge (or consciousness of nothingness) and the knowledge of God (or consciousness of absolute power).

To trace Calvin's joining of divine and human activity to the deepest foundations of his theology will first require a more careful examination of his doctrine of justification by faith alone, which he calls "the main hinge on which religion turns" (III.xi.1; 726), "the pivotal point of our disputation [with the papists]" (xix.11; 778), and "the sum of all piety" (xv.7; 794). Justification is the key, because it is through this teaching that "you . . . grasp what your relationship to God is"; it is the "foundation on which to establish your salvation" (xi.1; 726).

According to the doctrine of justification by faith alone, which Calvin of course learned directly or indirectly from Luther, the relationship between God and man is wholly the work of God; man contributes absolutely nothing to it. This doctrine teaches man "to seek righteousness outside himself" (23; 753), that is, to look for no righteousness in himself but to depend solely on God's acceptance of him, in Christ, without any regard for his merit. "We explain justification," Calvin writes, "simply as the acceptance with which God receives us into his favor as righteous men" (2; 727). And God accepts man not as "righteous in himself but because the righteousness of Christ is communicated to him by imputation" (23; 752). Furthermore, Calvin argues, any way of construing the reconciliation of man to God that attaches the slightest importance to what man himself can bring to this relationship in effect makes this reconciliation impossible. For our consciences to be "at peace" we must know "that we are pleasing to God, because we are entirely righteous before him." But such knowledge is destroyed and "the assurance of salvation shaken" when faith pays even the slightest attention to works, "since no one, even of the most holy, will find there anything on which to rely" (11; 739). If we turn in the least degree away from Christ's righteousness and toward our own works, the works of our fallen nature, we lose confidence that God is our father and are driven to despair and rebellion: "God's curse . . . must overwhelm our souls with despair." From this despair "dullness and ingratitude follow"; indeed, "all our senses have become perverted, [and] we wickedly defraud God of his glory" (II.xi.1; 341). The only alternative to complete reliance on God's grace manifest in Christ is continued rebellion against God; if a man is not perfectly assured of being a son of God in Christ, then he can only be God's enemy. Therefore, only by excluding all reference to merit is it possible to "cheer and comfort the hearts of believers" (III.xvi.7; 796).

This teaching is of course directed against the Roman Church, and especially against "the schools of the Sorbonne, mothers of all errors, [which] have taken away from us justification by faith" (xv.7; 794). In various ways, the scholastic theologians "filch something from God and turn it over to man" (7; 795). Although they cannot deny that the principal cause of justification is God's grace, they attempt to secure a place for the independent and meritorious power of free will. They claim to accept justification by faith but reject the addition of the word *alone*, arguing that obedience to the moral law contributes to justification. But Calvin counters that "because the law does not make conscience certain, it cannot confer righteousness either" (xi.19; 748–49).

However, the scholastic theologians are not Calvin's only adversary in his account of justification. Before turning to the Roman doctrine, Calvin devotes eight sections of chapter 11 to an attack on the teaching of a renegade Lutheran by the name of Osiander, who authored two controversial tracts on the doctrine of justification by faith, in 1550 and 1551. Osiander, Calvin explains, "although not intending to abolish freely given righteousness . . . has still enveloped it in such a fog as to darken pious minds" (5; 729). In Calvin's refutation of Osiander's interpretation of "freely given righteousness" he reveals what is most distinctive in his own understanding of this fundamental Protestant teaching.

Osiander's mistake, according to Calvin, consists in claiming that although all our righteousness comes from God, "we are substantially righteous in God by the infusion both of his essence and of his quality" (5; 730). Calvin argues that this doctrine constitutes "some strange monster of 'essential' righteousness" (5; 729). By claiming that the freely given righteousness of God actually infuses the soul of the believer, Osiander in effect preaches a form of works righteousness, thereby undermining the assurance of believers (11; 739); he turns the attention of believers from the righteousness of Christ to the righteousness we are supposed to have received from Christ: "According to Osiander," Calvin explains, "to be justified is not only to be reconciled to God through free pardon but also to be made righteous." Osiander corrupts the pure idea of "free imputation" by referring our righteousness to "the *essence* of God, *dwelling in us*" (6; 731; my emphasis).

This error, Calvin argues, is linked to Osiander's mistake regarding the respective roles of the human and divine natures of Christ in mediating between God and man: "He sharply states that Christ is himself our righteousness, not insofar as he, by expiating sins as Priest, appeased the Father on our behalf, but as he is eternal God and life" (6; 732). Further on, Calvin represents Osiander as holding that since Christ is God and man, he is made righteousness for us with respect to his divine nature, not his human nature" (8; 734). Because Osiander believes that Christ reconciles us to God through his divine nature, he believes that in this reconciliation our natures become intrinsically Godlike. But Calvin objects that human nature in itself always falls far short of God's righteousness; therefore, whoever looks within himself "will hang uncertainly, wavering to this side and to that, for he will not be allowed to assume in himself as much righteousness as he needs for assurance" (11; 740). If man is truly reconciled to God, this can only be because Christ, by his obedience *as man*, mediated between God and man. According to Calvin, although Christ could not have had the power to "cleanse our souls by his blood . . . if he had not been true God"—thus "righteousness comes forth to us from the secret wellspring of his divinity"—yet "it does not follow that Christ . . . is righteousness for us according to his divine nature." Rather, "it is certain that he carried out all these acts according to his human nature" (9, 12; 735, 742). In order for man by obedience to be reconciled to God, human nature had to be strengthened by joining it to divinity in the person of Jesus. But though the two natures are joined, they must remain distinct: if Jesus were not truly man as well as God, then he could not within himself bridge the gap between God and man (II.xii.1–3). If human beings were capable of possessing God's essential righteousness, then we would have no need of a mediator. But true righteousness is accessible to man not in its essence, but only as revealed in Jesus Christ. The work of the mediator accomplishes what appears to natural reason as impossible: that man be righteous without being like God. This is unthinkable except for the revealed fact that God became man.

Calvin does not dispute that when man is justified, he is truly joined to Christ. In fact, he even speaks of "that indwelling of Christ in our hearts . . . that mystical union." Christ "deigns to

make us one with him" (II.xi.10; 737). However, Calvin differs
strongly with Osiander on the nature of this union. He opposes the
"spiritual bond" between Christ and believers to Osiander's
"gross mingling," "essential indwelling" (10; 737), or "mixture of
substances" (5; 731). "For we hold ourselves to be united with
Christ by the secret power of his Spirit" (5; 730). This does not
mean that "man is justified by faith because by Christ's righteousness he shares the Spirit of God, by whom he is rendered righteous." On the contrary, "we are justified before God solely by the
intercession of Christ's righteousness. . . . "Man is not righteous
in himself but . . . by imputation" (23; 752). It is the secret power
of the Spirit to communicate righteousness to man without making it in any degree man's righteousness.

Calvin's constant preoccupation in his treatment of justification is to turn man's attention from his own being to the will of
God. In this he clearly follows Luther's lead. However, a close
examination of what Calvin says here suggests a subtle divergence
from Lutheranism, a divergence with far-reaching implications.

Calvin concedes to Osiander that faith "of itself" or considered
as "some intrinsic power" is always "weak and imperfect" and
thus does not possess the power of justifying, but only in so far as it
receives Christ" (7; 733). Calvin and Osiander thus agree that faith
itself, considered as a human experience, has no power to justify.
However, they respond to this point very differently. Osiander
understands faith as receiving the essence of righteousness, of
being infused with righteousness itself, and therefore of actually
becoming righteous through God's free grace. Calvin quotes Osiander's argument that "faith is Christ": faith as an experience of
fallen man is not righteous in itself; but by union with the essence
of God's righteousness in Christ, the human being becomes, in his
faith, essentially righteous.

Calvin, however, strongly opposes this interpretation of God's
free gift. For him faith is "a kind of vessel; for unless we come
empty and with the mouth of our soul open to seek Christ's grace,
we are not capable of receiving Christ." One must not confuse
faith, which is "only the instrument for receiving righteousness,"
with Christ himself, "who is the material cause and at the same
time the author and minister of this great benefit" (7; 733–34). For

Calvin, faith is an empty vessel, so empty that it is nothing in itself—it is a movement of the pure consciousness of nothingness. And yet, even when the vessel is filled, one must not forget the nothingness that it fills, for to forget this is to confuse the vessel with what fills it—"as if an earthen pot were a treasure because gold is hidden in it." To forget the emptiness of faith is to presume that one truly possesses the essence of righteousness. Thus, although Calvin teaches that justification by faith alone is nothing but justification by the righteousness of Christ, he will not concede to Osiander that "faith is Christ." Faith is not Christ, and yet neither is faith *something* separate from Christ: faith is radically distinct and yet inseparable from Christ. Faith *receives* Christ— the meaning is in the Verb, not in any essence.

Because faith is nothing but the receiving of Christ's righteousness, it is not surprising that Calvin, in his discussion of justification, rarely if ever speaks of "justification by faith." For, "properly speaking, God alone justifies; then we transfer this same function to Christ because he was given to us for righteousness" (7; 733). The word *faith* only reminds us that when we are justified we do not become intrinsically just. "We say that faith justifies, not because it merits righteousness for us by its own worth, but because it is an instrument whereby we obtain free the righteousness of Christ" (xviii.8; 830). Wilhelm Niesel, in *The Theology of Calvin*, thus remarks that although Calvin emphasizes the *sola fide*, "faith does not assume a central position in his description of justification. . . . It is dangerous to speak of faith with too much emphasis" (136).

In this tendency to deemphasize faith, the subjective experience of salvation, and to turn all attention to God, the objective ground of salvation, it is possible to detect in Calvin's thought a subtle but very significant divergence from Luther. In "The Freedom of a Christian" (1520), Luther draws a sharp distinction between man's bodily or external nature and his spiritual or inner nature, "which men refer to as the soul" (53), in order to argue that "no external thing has any influence in producing Christian righteousness or freedom" (54). External works can in no way contribute to the justification of the sinner. By *external works* Luther means not only "any work that can be done by the body and in the body" but even the works of the human soul: "even contemplation, meditation, and all that the soul can do, does not help" (54). Thus even the supposedly highest activities of the natural soul are mere external works: Luther points to an inwardness more inward than contemplation.

This inwardness is of course the inwardness of faith: "Faith alone is the righteousness of a Christian" (55). It is important to notice that in describing the righteousness of faith, Luther dwells much more than Calvin on faith itself as a sort of inward condition of the believer: "Just as the heated iron glows like fire because of the union of fire with it, so the Word imparts its qualities to the soul" (58). The Word in a sense makes the soul good, and "it is always necessary that the substance or person himself be good before there can be any good works, and that good works follow and proceed from the good person" (69). Faith, according to Luther, creates a region in the soul more inward than human reason yet accessible to human experience, an "inner man, who *by faith* is created in the image of God." This inner man is both joyful and happy because of Christ" and serves God "joyfully and without thought of gain, in love that is not constrained" (67). In the inmost soul, the inner man created by God's grace, inward joy and happiness are therefore at one with selfless service to God; in considering "nothing except the approval of God," the inner soul is fulfilled in "spontaneous love" (68).

Thus Luther, despite his attack on speculative mysticism, on the works of the rational or contemplative soul, retains a certain vestige of the mystic's attention to the inward condition of the soul. The inward condition of righteousness is not at all man's doing, but it is still something that man can in a sense experience within himself, because it has some relation to the human experience of love: "God converts whom he converts by giving them the intuition of his love."[1]

It is true that Luther also frequently opposes faith and experience; he argues that faith is in conflict with experience because experience is limited to what natural reason and mind can grasp (Althaus, 62–63). But Luther opposes faith to experience as a different mode of experience. According to Althaus, "it is different from the usual kind of empirical experience; it is experience in a new dimension" (60; see also Strohl, 80 n. 5). Luther posits an experience above experience; faith is the inner organ of this experience.

This view of faith is not identical to Osiander's doctrine of the essential righteousness of faith, but it tends like this doctrine to turn the believer's attention at least in part to his own inward experience or condition. Luther would agree with Calvin—indeed, it is Luther who taught Calvin—that faith is an empty vessel that receives Christ. And yet the emptiness of this vessel tends to play a more positive or substantial role in Luther's thought than in Calvin's; whereas for Calvin emptiness is a sheer nothingness that perpetually drives our attention to the righteousness of Christ, for Luther the exquisite emptiness of the vessel of faith as it receives Christ is itself grasped as the fulfilling activity of a non-natural organ, a kind of joyful experience beyond experience. Although the fruit of this experience is active love toward other men, the experience has its own activity and integrity within itself, which demands the attention of the believer. Ernst Troeltsch, in his classic book *The Social Teaching of the Christian Churches*, draws this conclusion: "Thus the supreme concern of the Lutheran is the preservation of faith and of the state of grace, a constantly renewed effort to maintain intact the purity and stability of faith which is independent of 'works' or 'merit.' Hence all the emphasis is placed upon the cultivation of the emotional life of the individual, on the maintenance of the sense of an unmerited happiness" (II.588).

With this understanding of Lutheran faith in mind, it is possible to see that Calvin in effect takes the final step, radicalizing Luther's attack on works righteousness, on what man can do. Whereas Luther discerned an experience more inward than experience, a spiritual organ deeper in man's consciousness than the rational soul, Calvin tends in effect to turn his attention altogether away from inward experience. The only experience of the believer is his consciousness of worthlessness, which refers him perpetually to the objective source of righteousness. It is true that Calvin also uses the term "the experience of faith," by which he means a sense of God's goodness and one's own worthlessness (III.xi.16; 740); and he often speaks of faith as a "feeling" of the "heart" (ii.8; 552;

14; 559). But Calvin is using these terms in a peculiar sense; he is stretching their ordinary meanings even further than Luther did.

> Faith is so far above sense that man's mind has to go beyond and rise above itself in order to attain it. Even where the mind has attained, it does not comprehend what it feels. But while it is persuaded of what it does not grasp, by the very certainty of its persuasion it understands more than if it perceived anything human by its own capacity. . . . what our mind embraces by faith is in every way infinite . . . the knowledge of faith consists in assurance rather than in comprehension. (14; 559–60)

Like Luther, Calvin locates the experience of faith in a region beyond human capacity. But unlike Luther, he does not interpret this region as a kind of organ that the believer possesses from God. The believer's assurance is not accessible to him in an experience in any way continuous with his human experience. Thus Calvin says of Job that "he did not experience any other righteousness in himself than what at the first moment would wither before God's face" (xiv.16; 783). The righteousness of God is imputed to man, but it is in no way accessible to human experience.

This explains how Calvin can maintain that the human experience of doubt in no way touches the believer's perfect assurance of salvation, or that this perfect assurance is perfectly compatible with the most anxious doubt. The fact that "believers are in perpetual conflict with their own unbelief" or that they enjoy no peaceful repose in no way alters "the certain assurance received from God's mercy" (ii.17; 562). The believer's doubt within his own human experience does not affect the integrity of the assurance of salvation that resides beyond all human experience. "Unbelief does not hold sway within believers' hearts, but assails them from without" (21; 567). By *heart*, then, Calvin clearly means something more inward than emotion; what we usually call the heart is hence located outside the believer. The heart is the locus of our inward union with Christ, but this union is so far inward as to be impervious to the emotion of the human heart. Thus Calvin guarantees the assurance of faith by driving the locus of faith further inward even than Luther, so far inward that this assurance is in no way threatened by the experience of doubt.

Therefore the Calvinist, unlike the Lutheran, is freed from pre-occupation with the inward condition of his soul. He need pay no attention to the perfection of his faith, because faith, since it is Christ's work, can be nothing but perfect, despite the doubts of the believer. It is not doubt that indicates a lack of grace but only the very thought that one's salvation depends upon one's own certainty of salvation and not upon the objective certainty of salvation. The only confirmation of election is the ability not to be distracted by one's inward concern for confirmation of election: "For it is abundantly confirmed when it rests solely upon God's mercy." We must not try to relieve our doubts by attention to our own soul, for this is in effect a reversion to works righteousness; we must rather "be intent upon the promise alone and . . . turn thought away from all worth or merit of man"—even from the human experience of assurance. "Scripture shows that God's promises are not established unless they are grasped with the full assurance of conscience"—and this in spite of the inevitable presence of the human emotion of doubt. It is only the second-order doubt, the temptation to look to human experience for confirmation of election, that indicates the absence of God's mercy. In this special sense, Calvin can say that "wherever there is doubt or uncertainty, [scripture] pronounces [God's promises] void" (xiii.4; 766–67).

Within the realm of human experience, God's promises are not fully present at any given moment but only in the life of the believer considered as a whole, only across a span of time. If one considers human experience, then it is true that "the reprobate are sometimes affected by almost the same feeling as the elect"; they may receive a "confused awareness of grace" (ii.11; 555) or "a fleeting awareness" (12; 556). It is also true that the faith of believers themselves may be "deficient or weak" (12; 357); it may be "tinged with doubt, or . . . assailed by some anxiety" (17; 562). But to attend too closely to these internal states is to invite "the confidence of the flesh [to] creep in and replace assurance of faith" (11; 555). To find true assurance, believers must "transcend all the limits of our senses and direct our perception beyond all things of this world and, in short, surpass ourselves." We must surpass in particular the experience of our natural soul in order to let the

Spirit work in us. We must not let the certainty of God's promise be hindered by the weakness of our own natures: "By being ignorant of certain things, or by rather obscurely discerning what it does discern, the mind is not hindered from enjoying a clear knowledge of the divine will toward itself." We must depend on the irresistibility of God's promise despite the inability of our human nature to grasp it; we take our bearings in this life, as it were, by the sun itself, and let our eyes "dwell on its steadfast brightness," even though we are at present "bound with the filters of an earthly body [and] . . . shadowed on every side with great darkness" (19; 565).

Precisely because the believer does not depend upon his own experience, his certainty of salvation does not vary: "how absurd it is that the certainty of faith be limited to some point in time, when by its very nature it looks to a future immortality after this life is over" (40; 588). Certainty is not a subjective experience in the present but the objective promise of immortality in the future. Thus, "however deficient or weak faith may be in the elect," the mark "engraved by the Spirit of God can never be erased from their hearts." For "the wicked," however, the "common faith"—that is, the common appearance of faith—"may afterward pass away." "Therefore, Paul attributes faith only to the elect" (12; 557, 558).

Only the elect truly have faith, because only the elect "continue" or persevere. When Calvin enjoins believers to "examine their hearts" (12; 557), he is not telling them to interrogate their inward experience in any ordinary sense—for this would be a subtle form of the "confidence of the flesh." The heart they must examine is a heart more inward than the human heart; they must examine themselves to see that they are in no way resting their hopes on any self-examination. This kind of self-examination is therefore directly opposed to the mystical cultivation of inward states; rather, it consists in "forgetting what lies behind and straining forward to what lies before us" (xiv.13; 781). The believer must entirely leave behind any preoccupation with his own works, with his own inward condition, even with his own faith understood as an inward condition, and get on with the business of persevering; he must direct all his energies "forward."[2]

But where is "forward"? If the believer must not be concerned with the inward condition of his soul, then what must he do? Calvin's answer is that his end must be "to serve [the Lord's] will and by every means advance his glory alone" (xiv.9; 776). "The elect are justified by the Lord to the end that they may glory in him and in no other." "The Lord conferred salvation upon us in order to show forth the glory of his name" (xii.2; 764). But how does one glorify God? The believer exhibits God's glory in righteous action; he must show forth "the fruits of repentance" or "holiness and purity . . . in the whole of life." This is not, of course, to say that the elect are holy in themselves; rather "the more earnestly any man measures his life by the standard of God's law, the surer are the signs of repentance that he shows" (iii.16; 609). Calvin thus insists that repentance or "actual holiness of life is not to be separated from free imputation of righteousness" (1; 593). "Christ justifies no one whom he does not at the same time sanctify" (xvi.1; 798).

I have examined what Calvin means by holiness in my section on ethics (chapter 4). Clearly he cannot mean the cultivation of an intrinsically well-ordered soul, for this would represent an attempt to possess part of the glory that rightly belongs only to God. The glory of God is exhibited in the outward actions of men, provided they are done for the glory of God and not in view of any human good. Thus Calvin's absolute rejection of works righteousness yields a new kind of attention to works. Although Calvin denies that human works can in any way be even a partial source of salvation, he teaches that the works God does through us may indeed be considered as signs of salvation. Thus Calvin by no means intends to rule out the believer's reliance on works as "signs of the divine benevolence toward him" for "undergirding and strengthening" his faith (xiv.18; 785). Indeed, he writes that "absence of regeneration . . . shows lack of faith" (7; 774) and calls "the fruits of regeneration" a proof of the indwelling of the Holy Spirit" (19; 786). God's irrevocable election in no way depends upon the inward condition of the believer, but it may be verified in his outward works. These works are indeed the only evidence within human experience of the secret election of the faithful.

Calvin's radicalization of the inwardness of the Lutheran idea of justification by faith alone thus yields a radical outwardness; the

Calvinist learns to leave behind the question of the goodness of his soul and to strain forward in the production of signs of his absolutely certain election. The individual's concern for a good in which he can partake is converted completely into practical activity for the manifest benefit of humanity and the glory of God.

Weber remarks that "the Calvinist, as it is sometimes put, himself creates his own salvation, or, as would be more correct, the conviction of it" (115). My interpretation of Calvin's own thought tends to support Weber's view of later Calvinism. However, it may be that at least in the case of Calvin himself, the more radical and more popular formula, properly understood, is more correct. Calvin attempts to reduce to nothing the distinction between theoretical conviction and practical activity; the believer should have no concern for his own salvation as a problem within his soul but should convert all his spiritual concern into the actual manifestation of works of holiness. By renouncing all hope of creating an absolute inward conviction, the believer allows the Spirit through him to bring forth the salvation decreed by God. Not as a human being but as the locus of the activity of the Spirit, the believer indeed creates his own salvation.

Calvin therefore insists that "the grace of justification is not separated from regeneration" (xi.11; 739). "The sum of the gospel," he writes, consists in "repentance" (that is, sanctification or regeneration) and "forgiveness of sins" (or justification; iii.1; 592). To appreciate fully the distinctiveness of Calvin's teaching, we must now examine more closely the way he connects justification and sanctification, free imputation of righteousness and holiness of life. For Luther also taught, of course, that God's free grace bears fruit in the outward activity of the believer; "a good man does good works" (69). Calvin's innovation consists not so much in joining justification and sanctification as in doing so while insisting on the distinction between them. Although the two cannot be separated, "they are things distinct" (xi.11; 739). There is not one grace with two effects, but a "double grace" (1; 725). This distinction is necessary to complete the detachment of the believer's concern for salvation from the inner life of his soul. By failing to make this distinction with sufficient clarity, Luther tended to refer the works accomplished by the believer to the righteousness he had

received from Christ and therefore to fix attention on this righteousness as an inward possession or quality of the believer: "It is
always necessary that the substance or person himself be good
before there can be any good works." But Calvin insists on referring not only the righteousness of the believer but also the goodness of his works directly to God: "they have their value from
God's approval rather than from their own worth" (20; 750). The
goodness of works is not mediated by any prior and established
righteousness of the soul: just as each discrete work must be
rendered holy by God as the Christian accomplishes it, so "God
does not . . . once for all reckon to us as righteousness [the] forgiveness of sins," but rather "by continual forgiveness he repeatedly
acquits us" (xiv.10; 777). "Accordingly, we can deservedly say that
by faith alone not only we ourselves but our works as well are
justified" (xvii.10; 813). Only by distinguishing the justification of
the believer's works from the justification of the believer is it
possible to prevent a reversion to a subtle form of works righteousness, of inward self-concern. Without this distinction, the attention of the believer will be attracted to the supposed intrinsic
goodness of works, which in turn will refer him to the problem of
his own goodness.

The scholastics, Calvin argues, granted the necessity of grace
but also tormented man by teaching that he can contribute something to salvation by his own efforts. Luther, and in his own way
Osiander, attempted to end this torment by teaching that man is
saved by faith alone. However, from Calvin's point of view, this
tends to threaten assurance by fixing attention on the unstable
inward experience of faith. Calvin perfected Luther's solution by
interpreting God's inward promise as outward activity and by
referring outward activity, not back to the inward promise, but
directly to God. One might say that faith is understood as works
and works as faith; by referring each to the other, Calvin avoids all
reference to the human soul as an inward order. It is true that
Calvin often adopts the language of the mystic, speaking of
"peaceful rest and serene tranquility" (xiii.1; 763), but this peace
is not a stable inward condition; it is an ever-renewed commitment to action. "To have faith is to strengthen the mind with
constant assurance and perfect confidence, to have a place to rest

and plant your foot" (3; 766). Assurance is not possible if it is sought for its own sake: it is only possible as a place to plant the foot. The only stability of the soul is a stability in motion. Calvin's way of joining and distinguishing justification and sanctification solves the problem of assuring the believer by directing his attention to what he can do while suppressing the question of what he is.

Calvin's difference with Luther on the relationship between justification and sanctification has clear analogies in other subtle but important differences between the two reformers. Consider, for example, the fundamental problem of the relationship between the two natures of Christ. Just as Luther sometimes tends to interpret divine righteousness as a goodness human beings could exhibit in their own works, so he extends the traditional doctrine of the "communication of idioms" (the doctrine that the properties of both the divine and human natures can and must be predicated of the one person of Christ) to the point of teaching that the human nature of Christ participates in the ubiquity of the divine nature (Wendel, 224; see also Althaus, 193–98). Calvin, on the other hand, insists that the two natures of Christ are "united but not mingled" (II.xiv.4; 486). Calvin insists on the distinctness of the divine and human natures as much as he does on their union in Christ: "For it is no more permissible to commingle the two natures than to pull them apart" (4; 487). Although "these two natures constitute one Christ," this does not change the fact that "each retains its distinctive nature unimpaired" (1; 482). Christ reconciles man to God without in any way exhibiting anything divine in man or human in God: he mediates without showing a middle ground.[3]

A similar difference between Calvinism and Lutheranism appears in their respective interpretations of the Lord's Supper—a difference that finally forced the rupture between Lutheran and Reformed Protestantism. Lutheran theology employed Luther's own teaching on the ubiquity of the body of Christ to interpret Jesus' words "take, eat, this is my body" quite literally. According to Calvin's account, the Lutherans teach "that the bread of the Supper is truly the substance of an earthly and corruptible element, and suffers no change in itself, but holds the body of Christ enclosed underneath itself." Calvin opposes this view because it assigns to the body of Christ "a ubiquity contrary to its nature" (IV.xvii.16; 1379). But he also opposes the nonliteral and strictly symbolic interpretation of Zwingli, according to which the bread and wine are mere figures that serve to remind the believer of Jesus' promises. Calvin therefore denies both that the bread is really Christ's body and that it is merely a symbol of his promise of salvation. He teaches that this sacrament has two parts: "physical signs, which . . . represent to us, according to our feeble capacity, things invisible; and spiritual truth, which is at the same time represented and displayed through the symbols themselves" (11; 1371). The bread and wine are symbols, but they are not merely symbols or reminders, for they truly indicate the "true and substantial partaking of the body and blood of the Lord," although these things are not enclosed within the earthly element. These benefits are not received "solely by imagination or understanding of mind"; communicants actually "enjoy the thing itself as nourishment of eternal life" (19; 1382).

This actual enjoyment is possible without transforming the material symbol itself, because Christ is not brought down to us, but we are lifted up to him (31; 1403). It is the Holy Spirit that, so to speak, lifts us up. Or, to be more precise, the Spirit is the agent of our union with Christ in the Lord's Supper; our union with Christ must be conceived strictly as a spiritual union: "the Spirit of Christ . . . is like a channel through which all that Christ himself is and has is conveyed to us" (12; 1373). The Spirit accomplishes the union of Christ with the believer without the use of any natural bridge. "Flesh must . . . be flesh; spirit, spirit" (24; 1391)—in the Lord's Supper, as in the two natures of Christ, the two poles are unified without being brought closer together. This doctrine, as Calvin boasts, in no way "depends upon common sense . . . [but], having surmounted the world on the wings of faith, soars up to heaven." "There is nothing more incredible," he continues, "than that things severed and removed from one another by the whole space between heaven and earth should . . . be united" (24; 1390).

In his doctrine of the Last Supper, as in his teaching on the two natures of Christ and on justification and sanctification, Calvin therefore departs significantly from Luther by insisting on the radical distinction between the human or earthly and the divine. Although Luther, no less than Calvin, insists that human efforts are worthless in achieving the salvation that God freely bestows, he tends, unlike Calvin, to interpret God's grace as a goodness having some connection with a good known to human beings—in particular, with the human experience of love. Of course, Calvin too interprets a holy life as a life of love—but by subordinating human love wholly to the idea of the glory of God he drains it of all intrinsic goodness and thus reduces it to "right" or "equity." Thus Ernst Troeltsch (1960) observes that, whereas in Lutheranism "the idea of Love [is] at the center of the conception of God," in Calvinism "God's majestic sovereign will is the supreme cause, the supreme standard." It follows that "the reasons and norms which do exist gain their significance only from God" (II.582).

In order to grasp the significance of Calvin's departure on this key point, it will be useful briefly to consider Paul Althaus's argument that Luther's teaching on the Lord's Supper derives from his rejection of "the concept of flesh and spirit," of "the dualism and the spiritualism of late classical antiquity" (395). According to Althaus, Luther "breaks through [the traditional] idealistic equation of the world of the Holy Spirit with the sphere of inwardness in which there is only 'spirit.'" By casting off this idealistic inwardness Luther is able to show God's relation to man "in the complete concreteness, outwardness, bodiliness of history" (396, 397).

That Luther attempted to discard classical dualism is clear; my analysis suggests, however, that Calvin, in interpreting the opposition between spirit and flesh as absolute, may in practice more effectively destroy this dualism than Luther. One might say that Luther, in attacking mysticism by denying the existence of a "transcendental sphere beyond all earthly history" (Althaus, 397), tended to create a kind of mysticism of this world, a mysticism of the body. He thus interprets the physical world spiritually, as the ubiquitous body of Christ. But mysticism of the body is still mysticism; it still involves an attempt to interpret this world according to some human idea or experience of what the good of the world is. For Luther this experience is disinterested love; the inward experience of spontaneous love continues to serve as a standard for the outward service of the body. Calvin succeeds more fully in removing the inward standard as an obstacle to outward activity; that is, he destroys the vestiges of classical dualism by driving the standard so far inward as to detach it completely from any human experience of the good. By insisting on the absolute distinction between the human and the divine, Calvin is able in practice to join them together much more effectively than Luther. As Strohl remarks, the doctrine of the unity of the church in the body of Christ had to remain for Luther a theoretical ideal, an ideal that could be savored in the individual heart but not made effective in society. Luther's concrete good was not concrete enough; it remained an intention without a program (110). Calvin made the idea of love effective by subordinating it wholly to the glory of God and thereby removing from it any human inwardness which might hinder the activity of God through men in history.

Chapter 7

The Soul and the Image of God

To complete the discussion of Calvin's transformation of Christian inwardness into outward activity, we must consider his thematic treatment of the right condition of the inner man—the
human soul as created by God. For the sanctification or regeneration of the believer is directed toward the recovery of the original
integrity of man's nature in which shone the image of God. The
"sole end" of regeneration, according to Calvin, "is to restore in us
the image of God that had been disfigured and all but obliterated
through Adam's transgression." Through regeneration man increasingly reflects the image of God, which is to say he comes
closer to "the likeness of God" (III.ii.9; 601). To show how this
idea of holiness as the soul's likeness to God is compatible with
the radical distinction and activist joining of the human and the
divine that I have described above, I turn to book 1 of the *Institutes*, "The Knowledge of God the Creator."

Since in the very opening lines of this first book Calvin presents
man's knowledge of God as inseparably bound up with his knowledge of himself, it is appropriate that he should here take up the
question of human nature. He does so most explicitly in chapter
15, which he introduces by explaining that the creation of man "is
the noblest and most remarkable example of [God's] justice, wisdom, and goodness." Furthermore, he argues, "we cannot have a
clear and complete knowledge of God unless it is accompanied by
a corresponding knowledge of ourselves" (I.xv.1; 183). Calvin immediately observes that the phrase *knowledge of ourselves* is

fundamentally ambiguous: "human nature" may refer to "our condition" either before or after the fall of Adam. Here in book 1, Calvin is mainly concerned with "our originally upright nature"—the nature that it is the aim of the gospel to restore.

Calvin describes our original nature as consisting in two principal parts, body and soul, of which soul, which may also be called spirit[1] is the "nobler" part (2; 184). He calls the nobler part an "immortal yet created essence"; in order to establish the immortality of the soul, Calvin must defend its substantiality. Thus Calvin denies that soul is simply the "breath" of the body or the form of the body (as the Aristotelians would have it; v.5; 56–57). It is rather a distinct and independent "substance" (xv.6; 192) that, though created along with the body, is not bound to die with the body. As we have seen (chap. 6), Calvin finds evidence of the transcendence of the human soul in various powers or activities of fallen man.

The third section of book 1, chapter 15, which discusses human nature as the image of God, confirms the subordination of body to soul and also begins to define the internal ordering of the soul itself. Here Calvin teaches that in a general sense the whole of creation, including living creatures other than humans, reflect God's glory and thus may be said to contain his image. But the fact that Genesis ascribes the image of God to humans in particular proves that "man's nature towers over all the kinds of living creatures" (3; 188) or that humans have a closer link to God than animals do. "The proper seat of God's image is the soul," considered as distinct from the "outer man" or body (3; 186). Just what parts or faculties make up the human soul becomes clear as Calvin describes Adam's original integrity as consisting in the "full possession of right understanding . . . , affections kept within the bounds of reason, [and] all his senses tempered in right order." Calvin adds that Adam "truly referred his excellence to exceptional gifts bestowed upon him by his maker" (3; 188). Thus the original imaging of God in human beings seems to have consisted in a healthy cognitive faculty (understanding, reason) that ruled over the affections and the senses and furthermore offered gratitude to God for these gifts. That Calvin has in mind a three-tiered soul is further suggested by the next sentence, in which he names three aspects of the divine image that appear to correspond to understanding, affection, and sense: "And although the primary seat of the divine image was in the mind and heart, or in the soul and its powers, yet there was no part of man, not even the body itself, in which some sparks did not glow" (3; 188).

In section 4 of chapter 15, Calvin, citing Paul's description of regenerated human nature, confirms the argument that the seat of the image of God is principally the intellect and what is ordered by the intellect: "God's image was visible in the light of the mind, in the uprightness of the heart, and in the soundness of all the parts" (4; 189). It is thus primarily by the "light of understanding" that "man excels the remaining living creatures" (190), but the whole soul (and in a weaker sense the whole person) partakes of this image. And since the soul has parts, we must know them in order to know "of what parts this image (of God) consists." Thus Calvin introduces a thematic treatment of the "faculties of the soul" (190).

This treatment, which begins in section 6, is full of surprises. Since the passing references, or apparent references, to the order of the soul that I have just quoted suggest an affinity with the classical notion of a hierarchy ascending from the body to the theoretical faculty, it is puzzling to read at the beginning of section 6 that "it would be foolish to seek a definition of soul from the philosophers" (6; 192). But Calvin's warning here proves to be well-advised, for a careful reading of the final sections (6–8) of this chapter will show that Calvin's understanding of the healthy soul is radically different from the view he ascribes to the philosophers.

The source of the philosophers' errors concerning the soul is, not surprisingly, the present corruption of human nature: "The philosophers," Calvin explains, "ignorant of the corruption of nature that originated from the penalty of man's defection, mistakenly confuse two very diverse states of man" (7; 194). It is critical to understand just how the philosophers are confused. Since Calvin's references to the original integrity of the soul seem to suggest a general agreement with the philosophic understanding of human nature, one might think that the philosophic error consists simply in crediting fallen man with virtues he has lost. But Calvin makes just the opposite argument: the philosophers err by attributing to true, upright human nature characteristics inherent in corrupted human nature. Indeed, how else could they have erred? Having no access to the revealed Word, they must assume that human nature is essentially as it appears in the human beings they observe: "The philosophers were seeking in a ruin for a building, and in scattered fragments for a well-knit structure" (8; 196). The philosophic mistake consists not in attributing to ruins (fallen human nature) the qualities of a building (human beings in their original integrity), but in attributing to a building the qualities of ruins. Philosophers have not so much failed to describe human depravity as to call it depravity—this because they do not know the true nature of human excellence. It is only in comparison with this original excellence that present human nature can be seen as corrupt.

That this is in fact the nature of the error Calvin attributes to philosophers is clearest in his discussion of "those persons who would affirm more than one soul in man, that is, a sensitive and a rational soul." Certain writers, Calvin explains, infer the duality of souls from a disagreement, conflict, or disproportion between the sensitive and rational faculties. Calvin does not dispute that such conflict exists; he argues, rather, that "since this disturbance arises out of depravity of nature, it is wrong to conclude from this that there are two souls" (6; 193).

In what sense other philosophic doctrines concerning the soul reflect a reading of depraved human nature is harder to discern; this question requires a careful comparison of these doctrines as Calvin sketches them with the alternative view of the soul that he proposes. Calvin outlines a view of the soul that he ascribes to Plato. This view divides the soul into three cognitive faculties (understanding, reason, and fantasy) that depend upon the objects of sense as contained in the common sense, and three appetitive faculties (will, capacity for anger, and capacity for inordinate desire). Each of the appetitive faculties is bound to a pair of faculties from the cognitive hierarchy: will to understanding and reason, anger to reason and fantasy, and desire to fantasy and sense.

Calvin seems to prefer this view of the soul over other philosophic accounts, but he is willing to admit other accounts of the powers of the soul, such as one that simply distinguishes the appetitive part from the intellective part, or one that names three principles of action: sense, understanding, and appetite. Those who hold that the soul is divided into intellective and appetitive parts, Calvin observes, find themselves forced to distinguish further between the contemplative and practical in the intellective part and between will and concupiscence in the appetitive part.

Calvin, however, proposes to replace these accounts with a much simpler one: "Let us therefore hold—as indeed is suitable to our present purposes—that the human soul consists of two faculties, understanding and will. Let the office, moreover, of understanding be to distinguish between objects as each seems worthy of approval and disapproval, while that of the will, to choose and follow what the understanding pronounces good, but to reject and flee what it disapproves" (7; 194). Just what is at stake in this revision of the philosopher's account of the soul is not immediately clear. Why does it matter that "no power can be found in the soul that does not duly have reference to one or the other of these members"? (7; 195).

The answer to this question begins to emerge once we see where the argument of chapter 15 as a whole tends. We find Calvin's intention clearly announced at the very beginning of the chapter, where he warns of those who would "blame their depravity on nature, not realizing that they . . . insult God. For if any defect were proved to inhere in nature, this would bring reproach upon him" (1; 183). The conclusion of the chapter will be, then, that all "natural" defects are not the fault of nature or of God, but of man: man "is not excusable, for he received so much that he brought about his own destruction" (8; 196). Thus, according to Calvin, the will as created is *"always* mindful of the bidding of the understanding, and in its own desires awaits the judgment of the understanding" (7; 194). This will is *"completely* amenable to the guidance of reason" (my emphasis). Adam originally possessed "the highest rectitude . . . in his mind and will, and all the organic parts were rightly composed to obedience." It is clear, then, that his "choice of good and evil was free" and that "in destroying himself he corrupted his own blessings" (8; 195).

Still it is not obvious why the inexcusability of Adam requires a doctrine of the soul that assigns all powers either to understanding or to will. The decisive point, I think, lies here: "in this way we include sense under understanding." The conflation of what philosophers have taken to be the lowest and highest parts of the soul seems necessary in order to establish that Adam's will was "completely amenable to the guidance of his reason"; as long as sense is a distinct faculty of the soul, then the deviation of the will from God's ordinance might be explained not, as Calvin wants it, by a sheer lack of perseverance (8; 195) or irreducible unfaithfulness (II.i.4; 245) on Adam's part, but by an inherent tendency in human nature. The philosophers distinguish "sense," which "inclines to pleasure," from "understanding," which "follows the good." It follows that "sensual appetite becomes inordinate desire and lust; the inclinations of the understanding, will" (I.xv.7; 195). By including sense under understanding, on the other hand, Calvin removes the possibility that any sensations might be by nature at odds with the mind or defective with respect to the good of the rational part. Finally, to complete the task of vindicating the perfection of human nature as created by God, Calvin must see to it that sense is not implicitly introduced into the second part of the soul, where it might be thought to oppose the understanding: "Again, for the term "appetite,' which they [the philosophers] prefer, I substitute the word 'will,' which is more common" (7; 195). Calvin repeats his vindication of the goodness or innocence of natural sensual desires in discussing repentance: "We do not condemn those inclinations which God . . . engraved upon the character of man at his first creation, but only those bold and unbridled impulses which contend against God's control" (III.ii.12; 604). Thus, unlike the philosophers, Calvin does not understand the physical appetites as essentially defective with respect to a rational good and in need of a principle of order above them. The senses do not tend by nature to disorder but only become inordinate when corrupted by man's bold unbelief.

Calvin alerts us to another sense in which his account of the soul differs fundamentally from the philosophic account. Setting aside Aristotle's argument that "the mind has no motion in itself, but is moved by choice" as mere "minutiae" involving "useless questions," Calvin asks us to be satisfied with the simpler view "that the understanding is, as it were, the leader and governor of the soul and that the will is always mindful of the bidding of the understanding" (I.xv.7; 194). The Aristotelian minutiae in question can be found in book 6, chapter 2 of the *Nichomachean Ethics.* There the philosopher argues that the "starting point" or "source" of motion—though not its end—is choice, and that choice in turn springs from "desire and reasoning directed toward some end." Pure thought is not in itself the ultimate source of action, but only "thought which is directed to some end and concerned with action." Man may thus be considered "a starting point of action" only as he combines "intelligence" and "desire." That "thought alone moves nothing" clearly did not, however, suggest to Aristotle that thought was in itself idle or worthless. On the contrary, he understood the highest faculty of the soul to be above practical concerns. This faculty, *sophia* or theoretical wisdom, combines intelligence (*nous,* which apprehends fundamental principles) and science (*episteme,* which is concerned with demonstrable, teachable knowledge of what necessarily is; VI.3, 6). Sophia, according to Aristotle, represents "science in its consummation, as it were, the science of things valued most highly" (VI.7; 156). Thus, in book 10 of the *Ethics,* Aristotle concludes that the life of theoretical wisdom is the highest, happiest, and most self-sufficient activity in which humans can engage (x.7).

In putting aside Aristotle's "useless questions," Calvin therefore effectively excludes from his account of the human soul a purely theoretical part, a faculty that seeks knowledge for its own sake. He reduces the understanding to a purely practical faculty necessarily concerned with action, necessarily oriented toward the will: "Let it be enough for us that the understanding is, as it were, the leader and governor of the soul."

Indeed, the conflation of the sensible part of the soul with the cognitive part requires that knowledge be in itself essentially and necessarily practical: if the ends of choice are not in part determined by the subordination of a lower, desiring faculty to a higher, rational faculty, then the rational part must in itself be practical, and the desires must in themselves—that is, without any reference to an end they serve—be good and rational. This much Calvin implies when he disputes the view that "sense inclines to pleasure, while understanding follows the good" (I.xv.7; 195). For

Calvin, the good of reason and the good of the senses are one and the same.

It is clearly necessary, therefore, to correct our earlier impression that Calvin's view of the order of the human soul is similar to the classical, hierarchical account according to which reason must rule irrational desires according to a rational principle. For Calvin the entire creation, including the desires, was unequivocally good; there was no need for human reason to assert a good superior to pleasure.

However, if the intellectual faculty cannot be said to rule over human nature in the usual sense of giving it a shape and perfection it does not receive from nature, then what does Calvin mean by praising the intellect as the special seat of the image of God? This question may be answered on the basis of the fifth chapter of book 1 of the *Institutes,* entitled "The Knowledge of God Shines Forth in the Fashioning of the Universe and the Continuing Government of It" (I.v.1; 51). Section 3 of this chapter treats "man as the loftiest proof of divine wisdom." Here Calvin refers to certain philosophers who "long ago not ineptly called man a microcosm." Although this reference seems to imply a basic agreement with these philosophers, it is not clear that such an agreement is possible for Calvin. For as Calvin's own discussion of the order of the soul suggests, it was characteristic of premodern philosophic conceptions of order or cosmos to differentiate higher, rational kinds of being from lower, irrational kinds. This applied both to the big order, or world, and to the little order, the human soul. On this view, the soul can claim to be a microcosm because it participates intelligently in the order of the cosmos, by virtue of the rule of its rational part. Reason is capable of asserting its rule in order to constitute a hierarchy in the soul analogous to the natural hierarchy.

For Calvin, however, there is no place for reason to assert its rule, since the desires were given all the rule they needed directly from God; the self-assertion of reason is not in accord with the order of creation but is indeed the cause of the fall of the creation into disorder and alienation from God. The very fact that this section on man the microcosm forms part of a chapter in which man is treated as subject (along with the rest of "this most vast and

beautiful system of the universe") to the "continuing government" of a God whose "essence is incomprehensible" (v.1; 51–52)
immediately indicates a departure from the philosophic idea of
order. According to that idea, man's reason gave him a claim to
comprehend the ruling goodness of nature and therefore to rise
above the material system of the universe, to rule a little world in
his own right. But Calvin insists on the total and uniform subordination of the entire creation to its creator: man can in no sense
be his own world, for there is only one God; his essence is incomprehensible to man; and to him alone belongs the government of
the whole universal system.

How then can humanity be the "loftiest proof of divine wisdom"? How can man in any sense distinguish himself from other
created things without robbing God of the glory due him? The
answer can only be that although man cannot *know* God's *essence,* man alone can be *conscious* of the *power* of God; only
humans are capable of acknowledging God and thus of confessing
the absolute dependency they share with the rest of the system.
Thus, in a section on man as "the loftiest proof of divine wisdom,"
Calvin can quote the Psalmist's acknowledgement of man's utter
weakness: "Who is man, that thou art mindful of him?" (I.v.3; 55).
A human being is not his own world but rather a conscious part of
God's world. Man's singularity consists not in some independent
wholeness but in his recognition of "the heavenly grace that
quickens him." For this reason, God's miracle in man can be
equated simultaneously with man as miracle (man's loftiness) and
man as utterly low and dependent (what is man?). Man can be a
perfect miracle only by being nothing in himself. From the philosophic point of view, Calvin's human being does not have a soul:
he finds God within himself precisely because he finds nothing
else.[2] Or, more cautiously, one might say that man finds nothing
"natural" within himself—nothing that *is,* strictly speaking—for
to praise nature by attributing any self-sufficiency, any independent integrity to any part of creation is to "suppress God's name"
(5; 56).

Calvin's refusal to grant any intrinsic goodness to human nature
or to the natural world as it appears to human beings concerned
with their own good necessarily implies a radical depreciation of

human speech, of discursive reason. By forsaking all efforts to order his own life according to a rational idea of his own good, by abjuring any claim to constitute a whole within himself, it is possible to recover direct access—access unobstructed by reasoning about the human good—to the principle of the whole, to God himself: "If there is no need to go outside ourselves to *comprehend* God, what pardon will the indolence of that man deserve who is loath to descend within himself to *find* God" (3; 54; my emphasis). Man rises by descending. He descends to the truth of God's glorious power by renouncing discursive reason, which is only an obstacle to the truth of God's power. By too much thinking, we human beings, "having neglected the true God . . . raise up in his stead dreams and specters of our own brains." If man would simply give up this attempt to raise himself to truth by speech and instead learn to rise by going down, he would find "mute creatures with more than melodious voices to declare" a truth that "eyeless creatures point out to him"; and on which "irrational creatures give instruction" (15; 69). A "clear mirror of God's works is in humankind," but the pride of speech has obscured it: "Infants, while they nurse at their mother's breasts, have tongues so eloquent that there is no need at all of other orators" (3; 55).

The image of God in the mind of man therefore consists not in a human rationality above sense experience but in the sheer consciousness of God's power within man and throughout the creation. This is the link between Calvin's account of man as a microcosm and his treatment of the order of the soul in chapter 15: the glory of the human intellect does not consist in an ability to ascend by discursive reason from the sensible to the intelligible or divine; it consists in the sheer consciousness of the sensible that is already divine, though for no other reason than that it manifests God's power. Reason can in no way claim to be above the senses; the senses are manifestly rational as created by God, and reason knows nothing—no thing—above the senses. Nature is not a hierarchy by which reason can rise to God but a system (*machina*) that as a system implies God; each part of the system is in itself wholly and equally devoid of divinity. Calvin's entire world-system is infinitely holy precisely through the emptiness of each of its parts. Calvin can therefore forbid any praise of nature whatever and, in another sense, admit a certain truth in the saying that nature is God (I.v.5).

The understanding enjoys preeminence in the order of the soul only by virtue of its being the locus of consciousness or conscience of the manifest rationality of God's power, the aperture through which man descends within himself to find God.

It follows from the conflation of sense and understanding, or from the reduction of reason to consciousness of sense, that "we ought not to rack our brains about God, but rather, we should contemplate him in his works." The knowledge of God is no longer confined to the mind: whereas "empty speculation merely flits in the brain," this speechless contemplation "takes root in the heart." Since awareness of God's power is immediately accessible to us, there is no need "to investigate his essence" in the manner of philosophers (9; 61–62). Thus Calvin can write, on the one hand, that "all men are born and live to the end that they may know God" (iii.3; 46) and, on the other, that we ought "willingly to leave to God the knowledge of himself" (xiii.21; 146). Similarly, Calvin teaches both that in order to understand God "he raises us above the world" (1; 121) and that we must forsake all striving to "go forth outside the world" and "willingly remain enclosed within these bounds to which God has willed to confine us" (xiv.1; 161). We know God in immediate consciousness by forsaking the attempt to know God rationally; we are lifted above the world by acknowledging that there is only one world, the world in which we are confined, and that it has no principle of order apart from God's will. We rise by going down, down beneath the pride of reason to the divine power active in the senses.

In rising above the world that reason attempts to order for itself by descending to the power of God within him, man can achieve a knowledge of God at once more certain and more intimate than any rational account. The gods invented by reason, in its "idle speculations" about God's essence, are themselves idle and remote from humanity, like Epicurus's God, "who has cast aside the care of the world only to amuse himself in idleness." "But what help is it," Calvin asks, "to know a God with whom we have nothing to do?" (ii.2; 41). When human nature invents gods according to its own idea of goodness, it alienates itself from its own true good, which the true God abundantly provides. "The pious mind does not dream up for itself any god it pleases, but contemplates the one and only true God . . . [and] is content to hold him to be as he manifests himself." And the pious mind is satisfied that God manifests himself simply as the governor of all things and "the author of every good" (2; 42).

There is no need, of course, to speculate about what is good or what God's goodness consists in, since God plainly manifests his goodness in every good we enjoy. To know God, men must cease to "measure him by the yardstick of their own carnal stupidity," as philosophers do when they concoct the ephemeral "notion of God as the mind of the universe," and be satisfied to "apprehend God as he offers himself" and thus "to know him more intimately" (iv.1; 47; xiv.1; 160). Man can know God intimately; he can know him "in living experience," by being satisfied to know him "not as he is in himself, but as he is towards us" (x.1; 97). There is no need to wonder about what God is when it is obvious what he does. All we need to know about God is his care for our world: "There is nothing less in accord with God's nature than for him to cast off the government of the universe and abandon it to fortune" (iv.2; 48). Thus, although God's glory is far above human reason, before the fall, at least, it was no mystery to human sense. Proofs of the divine majesty "are so very manifest and obvious that they can easily be observed with the eyes and pointed out with the finger." "For the Lord manifests himself by his powers, the force of which we feel within ourselves and the benefits of which we enjoy" (v.9; 61–62). God is beneficial power, and there is no good above the manifest benefits of his power. There is no cause higher than God's will (xiv.1; 161; III.xxii.11; 947), and God's will is wholly present in active care of the universe, in the continuous creation of the visible world: "For unless we pass on to his providence . . . we do not yet properly grasp what it means to say: 'God is creator'" (I.xvi.1.197).[3]

The world is the theater of God's glory (20), and "all things exist to the end that the glory of divine goodness may fully shine forth" (III.xiv.17; 784). But this glory can fully shine forth only when men acknowledge that there is no goodness superior to what shines in the visible creation—benefits manifest to the senses. It can shine forth only when men cease to invent worlds beyond the theater of God's power.

God's glory is therefore nothing *above* his beneficial power; it is simply the consciousness of his beneficial power. This complete orientation of God to his creation corresponds to the conflation of understanding and sense in Calvin's account of human nature: the order of the universe matches the order of the soul. Since God's goodness is identified with sensibly beneficial power, just as human understanding is identified with sense experience, there is nothing distinct from the sensible world but the consciousness that is joined to it. Just as man's knowledge of God consists in his speechless acknowledgement of divine power sensibly active within him, so God's self-glorification consists in consciousness of active power in his creation. " 'So man was created in the image of God'; in him the Creator himself willed that his own glory be seen as in a mirror" (II.xii.6; 471).

The history of the world, according to Calvin, aims at the intensification of this consciousness. In the beginning of this history, man fell from grace when in Adam he asserted himself by failing to believe God's word. Calvin very closely associates faithlessness and pride in his account of the fall: "Unfaithfulness, then, was the root of the Fall. But thereafter ambition and pride, together with ungratefulness, arose" (II.i.4; 245). The essence of sin is the sin of mind, the sheer failure to accept God's will, the attempt to rise to a truth above God's word. From intellectual pride, or the failure simply to believe what is clearly manifest, flowed the other vices: "It was not simple apostasy, but was joined with vile reproaches against God. . . . Lastly, faithlessness opened the door to ambition, and ambition was indeed the mother of obstinate disobedience" (4; 246). Thus the mind's self-assertion entailed the corruption of man's whole nature (9). Even "those inclinations which God . . . engraved upon the character of man at his first creation" participated in man's self-assertion and therefore joined the "unbridled impulses which contend against God's control" (III.ii.12; 604). All that remains of the glory of man as created by God is consciousness of sin and the manifestly rational but largely ineffective instinct of collective self-preservation (see above, chap. 5).

God allowed all this to happen "that from man's Fall he might

gather occasion for his own glory" (I.xv.8; 196). The fall provides
the occasion for the intensification of man's consciousness of
dependence on God. Through a temporary self-assertion, God's
elect learn an enhanced recognition of God's power. The image of
God in Adam was "the light of the mind" or the consciousness of
the activity of God's beneficial power; "the end of regeneration is
that Christ should reform us to God's image," that is, make us
once again the locus of God's glory or power-consciousness. But
this regeneration accomplishes not only the recovery of this consciousness but also its intensification. Thus Paul "commends the
richer measure of grace in regeneration" (4; 189).

This intensification is, of course, accomplished through the
mediation of Jesus Christ. For fallen man, there is no other way to
recover the image of God: "Since we have fallen from life into
death, the whole knowledge of God the Creator . . . would be
useless unless faith also followed, setting forth for us God our
father in Christ" (II.xvi.1; 341). Fallen man is conscious of the
power of God, but due to his own self-assertion he experiences this
power not as beneficial but as a terrible threat.

> For even if God wills to manifest his fatherly favor to us in many
> ways, yet we cannot by contemplating the universe infer that he is
> Father. Rather, conscience presses us within and shows in our sin just
> cause for his disowning us and not regarding or recognizing us as his
> sons. Dullness and ingratitude follow, for our minds, as they have
> been blinded, do not perceive what is true. And as all our senses have
> become perverted, we wickedly defraud God of his glory. (1; 341)

One might say that the proofs of God's power in the universe are
not too difficult for fallen man but too easy. By looking beyond the
clear evidence of his senses, man defrauds God of his glory and
becomes God's enemy. He therefore cannot bear to recognize the
wisdom of God's power in creation but needs another way to God.
Calvin quotes Paul: "Since in the wisdom of God the world did not
know God through wisdom, it pleased God through the folly of
preaching to save those who believe" (1; 341). The preaching of
Christ is foolishness to men, because it contradicts the self-assertion of fallen reason. But only in this foolishness can man overcome the pride of reason and learn to see the beneficence of God's

awesome power and therefore to acknowledge this power with full consciousness.

Christ regenerates the believer, or restores the image of God in him (III.ii.9; 601), by effectuating a union between God and man without violating the vast distinction between divine and human nature—indeed, by exhibiting the utter subjection of humanity to divinity. "Disregarding his own feelings, [Christ] subjected and yielded himself wholly to his Father's will" (II.xvi.5; 508). In taking upon himself the curse of human nature, "he crushed, broke, and scattered its whole force" (6; 510). Christ's obedience thus made it possible for us to overcome sin or self-assertion, to "tear out from our inward parts this most deadly pestilence of love of strife and love of self," this "kingdom in the breast" (III.vii.4; 694). God, by descending to earth joined to a human nature, made it possible again for man to descend deep enough within himself to crush the enemy of God and to find beneath it the active power of God.

Christ's sacrifice is effective, however, only for those who embrace it, only for those who have faith. Faith restores the image of God in man by restoring in intensified form man's consciousness of his dependence on God and of God's continuous beneficence toward him. Faith represents recovery of the "knowledge" of God, but with this difference indicated in the titles of the first two books of the Institutes: the "knowledge of God the Creator" is restored as the "knowledge of God the Redeemer in Christ." Before the fall, man had immediate access to God in his perception of the power of God within him and around him. But even the sense perceptions of fallen man are corrupted by the disobedience of the mind; therefore he must know the benevolent power of God through the obedience of Christ. But this faith-knowledge is no less immediate and certain that the original knowledge of creation. Whereas the mind "does not comprehend what it feels" or attains, faith rises above itself to be "persuaded of what it does not grasp." Thus, "by the very certainty of its persuasion it understands more than if it perceived anything human by its own capacity" (ii.14; 559). Like the knowledge of creation, faith-knowledge is not a speculative knowledge of God's essence but "a firm and certain knowledge of God's benevolence toward us" (7; 551). "For it is not so much our concern to know who he is in himself, as what he wills to be toward us . . . we hold faith to be a knowledge of God's will toward us, perceived from his word" (6; 549). In faith we recover the ability to recognize the benevolent power of God in our own nothingness by embracing Christ, in whom God's power and man's weakness are joined without being confused, that is, in whom divinity and humanity are radically distinct yet intimately unified.

Chapter 8

The Center of Calvin's
Antitheology

From the preceding discussion of the role of Christ in regenerating the image of God in fallen man it appears that the person of
Jesus is the center of Calvin's theology and the ground of his
interpretation of the various manifestations of the relationship
between man and God. Thus, according to Wilhelm Niesel, the
union without fusion of the human and the divine in Jesus is the
deepest source of the many other appearances of the "distinct but
not separate" formula in Calvin's work: "Jesus Christ," Niesel
writes, "controls not only the content but also the form of Cal-
vinistic thought. . . . The structure of Calvin's thought is dependent on the Chalcedonian definition and so on the living fact of
divine self-revelation" (247, 250).

With this argument Niesel addresses a set of problems that have
become classic in the interpretation of Calvin's thought: Does
Calvinism have a central teaching or basic doctrine? And what is
the significance of the *complexio oppositorum,* Calvin's repeated
use of the formula *distincto sed non separatio* and variations
thereon?[1] I have indicated the use of this formula, for example, in
Calvin's accounts of the relationship between spiritual and secular power, between justification and sanctification, and between
the sign and the signified in the Lord's Supper. Niesel enumerates
more than ten examples of the complexio oppositorum (247–50);
Milner's list comes to fifteen (191). According to Niesel's christocentric interpretation, the ultimate explanation of all these cases
of union without confusion, and the final ground of the unity of
Calvin's thought, is simply the "living fact" of Jesus Christ.

This view opposes the interpretation of Troeltsch, who understood Calvinism to be less christocentric than Lutheranism: "To Calvin the chief point is not the self-centered personal salvation of the creature, and the universality of the Divine Will of Love, but it is the Glory of God." Troeltsch argues that although Luther insisted on the distinction "between the hidden and the revealed God," he finally "gave up speculation" and "held to the revealed God of the New Testament." Calvin, on the other hand, pressed speculation on the hidden God further "and in so doing he transformed the whole idea of God" (II.583). Perhaps, in order to suppress completely the self-centeredness of fallen human nature, it is necessary to refer beyond the person of Jesus to the glory or beneficial power of God; that is, perhaps the revealed union of God and man in Christ must be properly grasped or interpreted in order to be effective.

Calvin's introduction to book 3 of the *Institutes*, "The Way We Receive the Grace of Christ . . ." indeed shows a "speculative" tendency in his thought, a tendency to look beyond the revealed fact of the person of Jesus. There he argues that "as long as Christ remains outside us" his suffering "remains useless and of no value for us." To benefit from Christ's suffering "he had to become ours and dwell within us." It is "by faith . . . that we obtain this." But since not all have faith, "reason itself teaches us to climb higher and to examine into the secret energy of the Spirit, by which we come to enjoy Christ and all his benefits" (III.i.1; 537). That is, since the self-revelation of God in the person of Christ is not effective for everyone, it cannot be effective by itself; and surely its effectiveness cannot depend on a human choice either to believe or not to believe—for then salvation would depend in part on human initiative. Therefore reason looks beyond Christ for a cause of salvation: "the secret energy of the Spirit." "The Holy Spirit is the bond by which Christ effectually unites us to himself" (1; 538). "Without the illumination of the Holy Spirit the Word can do nothing" (ii.33; 580). Such arguments as these lead Wendel to observe that "in a good many passages, indeed, the Holy Spirit plays the part of an obligatory mediator between Christ and man, just as the Christ is mediator between God and man" (240).

Benjamin Milner's critique of Niesel's interpretation therefore

seems well founded. He argues that although the complexio oppositorum "is related to the controlling center of [Calvin's]
thought," it does not follow that Jesus Christ is the "unifying
principle." Rather, Milner argues, the "unifying principle in Calvin's theology is . . . the inseparability of the Spirit and the Son"
(3–4). Further on Milner explains that Calvin understands order to
mean the "correlation" of "the work of the Holy Spirit" and the
Word or *ordinatio Dei* (190).

Although Milner's analysis seems formally correct, it is rather
opaque. Just how is it that the sheer ordinations or commands of
God, when "correlated" with the power of the Spirit, can be understood as "order," that is, as right and well-ordered, not arbitrary?
How is it that the will of God has meaning for man? Milner
confronts this question but cannot answer it; he observes that
although Calvin "specifically repudiates" the conception of God
as absolute and arbitrary power, his argument leaves us wondering
"whether Calvin does not, after all, live in a whimsical world,
pervious to the caprice of a tyrannical God whose 'absolute power'
is not bound to any law and order?" (16). Unless Milner can explain how it is that Calvin can understand the will of God as right
or in a sense rational without referring to any goodness above that
will, then his interpretation, by opposing the "christological type"
(e.g., Niesel), must inevitably fall back on the "theological type,"
which stresses "the doctrine of God, and his sovereign predesti-
nating will" (e.g., Troeltsch; Milner, 2).

If God's order is not simply what is revealed in the person of
Christ, then is it nothing but absolute power? In book 3 of the
Institutes Calvin explicitly repudiates the nominalist understanding of God as *potentia absoluta*: "And we do not advocate the
fiction of 'absolute might'; because this is profane, it ought rightly to be hateful to us. We fancy no lawless God who is a law unto
himself" (III.xxiii.2; 950). However, Calvin also refuses to look
beyond God's will for a rule of right: "the will of God . . . is the
highest rule of perfection, and even the law of all laws" (2; 950).
"For his will is, and rightly ought to be, the cause of all things that
are" (2; 949). Calvin agrees with the nominalists that there is no
cause above God's will, but he refuses to conclude from this fact
that from a human point of view God's will is lawless or arbitrary.

Calvin's departure from late medieval voluntarism seems to consist in his insistence on the fact that God's will not only is but *rightly ought to be* the highest rule. Wendel observes that Calvin echoes Duns Scotus's argument concerning the finality of God's will but implies opposition to Scotus's distinction between the "absolute power" and the "ordered power" of God (129). We can make sense of this by viewing Calvin as intending to destroy the residue of resistance to God's power implicit in the Scotist distinction, to eradicate the last impulse of human presumption, by unequivocally identifying order with power.

To understand how this identification is possible and what it means, it is necessary to consider more closely Calvin's teaching on the work of the Spirit. Scripture, according to Calvin, differentiates the three persons of the Godhead in the following way: "To the Father is attributed the beginning of activity, and the fountain and wellspring of all things; to the Son, wisdom, counsel, and the ordered disposition of all things; but to the Spirit is assigned the power and efficacy of that activity" (I.xiii.18; 142–43). The Son or Word is the speakable wisdom of God; the Spirit is his unspeakable power. "For it is the Spirit who, everywhere diffused, sustains all things, causes them to grow, and quickens them in heaven and in earth. Because he is circumscribed by no limits, he is excepted from the category of creatures; but in transfusing into all things his energy, and breathing into them essence, life, and movement, he is indeed plainly divine" (14; 138). The Spirit is diffuse, fluid, formless energy. He is, as we have seen, "the author of regeneration not by borrowing but by his very own energy" (14; 138–39). The fluidity of the Spirit enables him to infuse and regenerate men in a way impossible to articulate speech: "Although the apostles were so taught by his divine mouth, the Spirit of truth must nevertheless be sent to pour into their minds the same doctrine that they had perceived with their ears" (III.ii.34; 582). The active fluid of the Spirit has power to penetrate the self-assertiveness of fallen nature, to dissolve the idols which human nature invents in its attempt to claim some of God's glory for itself; "our souls are cleansed by the secret watering of the Spirit" (i.1; 538). We are "lifted up in mind and heart above our understanding" (ii.34; 582) when the Spirit takes the word that "flits about in the top of the brain" and drives it through the brain to a more effective part of consciousness; in this way, the word "takes root in the depth of the heart" (36; 583).

"Faith is the principal work of the Holy Spirit" (i.4; 54). The Spirit creates faith, or the knowledge of God the Redeemer, by impelling man to descend within himself far enough to rise above his reason. Thus the Spirit progressively restores to man the image of God, or returns him to the relation with God that obtained before the fall; the Spirit restores the right order of creation. But we have seen that the image of God is precisely man's recognition of his own nothingness and acknowledgement of God's power active within him, his consciousness of the continuous energy of the Spirit. Order is not a perfected condition of intelligible being but a consciousness of perpetual becoming. The active and fluid energy of the Spirit is not merely the agent of the process of restoration or order; it is the basis of order itself, for order is a process. That is why the process of regeneration is not only a restoration of order but an enrichment of order: it is an enhancement of consciousness of the power of the Spirit through the Spirit's confrontation with the flesh— that is, with human self-assertion.

The notion of order as consciousness of absolute power is the unifying ground of Calvin's treatment of the order of creation (book 1) and his treatment of the fall and the restoration of order (books 2–4).[2] Furthermore, to examine carefully the work of the Spirit is to see what Calvin means by identifying right order and absolute power, that is, to see how the absolute power of God can have human meaning without being referred to a good in which human beings participate. Man becomes like God when God's Spirit in him shines through the nothingness of his own nature. Man acts as a microcosm of God's whole, not by rising to comprehend within his own soul the essential goodness by which God rules the cosmos, but by descending within himself to feel the power that quickens him and the whole universe. Sheer power can be interpreted as order for human beings because human beings can share in consciousness of power. I suggest that this principle of order is the central teaching or basic doctrine underlying the *Institutes*.

One does not have to look beyond this fundamental conception of order to find the key to the complexio oppositorum, Calvin's repeated use of the "distinct but not separate" formula. Indeed, Calvin provides that key in the very first chapter of the *Institutes*: "The Knowledge of God and That of Ourselves Are Connected" (I.i.1; 35).

The first two sections of this chapter are entitled "without knowledge of self there is no knowledge of God" (35), and "without knowledge of God there is no knowledge of self" (2; 37). These two forms of knowledge are "joined by many bonds" (1; 35); indeed, it is difficult to tell which is prior to the other, for each seems to issue from the other and to refer to the other. And yet the two could not be more radically distinct: knowledge of self is consciousness of utter poverty, of nothingness. The world within us is a "world of miseries" (1; 35–36). The knowledge of God, on the other hand, is knowledge of "infinitude of benefits" (1; 36) and of overpowering majesty (3; 39). The radical distinction between the two kinds of knowledge is precisely what makes their most intimate union possible: nothingness does not know itself without knowing power, and power does not know itself without knowing nothingness. Only by being a world of miseries can man be a microcosm of God's power.

This means that man must always look through the present benefits of God's power to the active power itself; for to consider a benefit as good in itself is to claim something for the creation itself and to defraud God of his glory; it is to posit an "intermediate thing" between nothingness and power and thus to obstruct the active consciousness of power. God's glorious activity does not have an end, for an end would detract from God's glory. It does, however, have a direction: the thriving of the creation, particularly of the rational instincts of innocent human nature, and the laying low of human rivals to his glory. Man must not even attempt to cultivate consciousness of God's power as an inward feeling or secure possession of the mind—for this again is to obstruct God's sheer activity. Consciousness of power is not a benefit of the soul but a spur to action. To be conscious of God's power, to contemplate God's will (III.xiii.11; 711), is continually to enact it.

Man "lives and moves" in God, because the Spirit lives and moves in man (1; 35; cf. *Comm. Acts* xvii.28). The relationship between man and God is the governing instance of union without fusion, to which all the other cases implicitly refer. It is, in particular, the ground on which Calvin radically distinguishes politics and religion in order to unify them in worldly activity for the prosperous preservation of mankind and the glory of God. It is the ground, I suggest, of the historical activism of Calvinism.

Conclusion

Idealism, Materialism, and Legitimacy in the Modern Age

> The only element of Christianity which Machiavelli took over was propaganda. This idea is the only link between his thought and Christianity.
>
> Leo Strauss

> So one must not suppose that at any time, no matter what the political conditions are, the passion for physical pleasures and the conceptions that go therewith can ever satisfy a whole people. The heart of man embraces much more than we suppose.
>
> Alexis de Tocqueville

The foregoing interpretation of Calvin's *Institutes* supports and clarifies Michael Walzer's claim that Calvinist saints were agents of modernization. It suggests, furthermore, that in this matter the question of historical preparation cannot be separated from that of theoretical contribution. The radical activism of Calvinists is rooted in a certain understanding of the divine order and the place of human activity within this order. It is true that this understanding attempts to convert divine order into sheer practical activity; nevertheless, the resulting activity cannot be understood apart from the idea. An antitheology is not the same as an absence of theology. Calvinist activism must be understood as governed by the Calvinist understanding of God.

This does not suffice to show, however, that Calvinism represents a modern viewpoint in the strictest sense, much less that

164

Calvin was the founder of modernity, as Emil Doumergue would have it. It is possible that Calvinism tended to dispose its adherents to ways of life compatible with modern trends in politics and economics but that these trends had sources and foundations distinct from Calvinism or from any religious belief. In Calvinism I detect a religious motive for a certain secular rationalism; but it is possible that this secular rationalism is best understood in some authentic form completely free of nonrational motives. In this case, although Walzer was wrong to sever Calvinist theory from Calvinist practice, he would be right to include Calvinists among the agents and not among the true theoreticians of modernity. Calvinists would have contributed to the progress of a secular rationalism that they did not found, the essence of which they did not knowingly espouse as Calvinists.

Leo Strauss and the Theorists of Secularization

This seems to be the view of the political philosopher Leo Strauss. In *Natural Right and History*, Strauss attacks Max Weber for attributing to Calvinism an influence that at most may be traced to the corruption or degeneration of Calvin's theology, to a "carnal interpretation of a spiritual teaching" (59).[1] R. H. Tawney was right, according to Strauss, to criticize Weber for taking as representative of Calvinism a late Puritanism that "had made its peace with the Capitalist world already in existence." It follows that "the Puritanism in question was not the cause of the capitalist world or of the capitalist spirit" (61n).

If corrupt Calvinism was a modernizing force, then one must attribute its influence not primarily to Calvinism itself but to the agent of corruption. Strauss locates the source of this corruption of Calvinist religion—which corruption, he remarks, might be a good thing, if Calvinism itself is a bad thing (62)—in the "transformation of the philosophic tradition, as distinguished from the transformation of the theological tradition." The cause of modernity is not any religious belief but "a break that took place on the plane of purely philosophic or rational or secular thought."

It does not necessarily follow, however, that religion was irrelevant in the historical implementation of this transformation. Strauss is willing to grant that Calvinism might have been an auxiliary agent or "carrier" of modernity. This is because the religious transformation of the Protestant Reformation had philosophical ramifications: "Puritanism, having broken more radically with the pagan philosophic tradition (i.e., chiefly with Aristotelianism) than Roman Catholicism and Lutheranism had done, was more open to the new philosophy than were the latter." On this view, however, the theological transformation and the philosophical transformation are not entirely separate, as Strauss otherwise suggests, since both involved a repudiation of the Aristotelian account of this world. This implies that the religious tradition embodies an interpretation of this world as much as does the secular tradition; the two traditions do not then constitute wholly independent planes. Calvinism could be a carrier for the new philosophy, it appears, because it agreed at least partially with this philosophy on the non-Aristotelian interpretation of this world.

Indeed, my analysis suggests that Calvinism—in particular the "uncorrupted" Calvinism of its founder—represents not at all a repudiation of this world but an intensification of worldly activity understood as redounding not only to the benefit of God's innocent natural creation but especially to the glory of God. Strauss's claim that Puritan capitalism represented a "carnal interpretation of a spiritual teaching" is therefore quite misleading, for it implies an understanding of flesh and spirit in uncorrupted Calvinism that was not Calvin's. Calvin's hostility to the flesh was not a hostility to the body but a hostility to hierarchy, to human rule according to the purposes of human reason—precisely, one might say, a hostility to Aristotle.

Once one sees that Calvin radically distinguishes the spiritual and the secular in order to join them fast together, it is no longer obvious that Calvinism was only an unwilling carrier of modern secularism or, as Strauss suggests, that "vulgar Calvinism . . . unwittingly destroyed what [it] intended to preserve" (62). If the radically spiritual and the radically secular are not necessarily alien viewpoints, a spiritual doctrine must not necessarily be corrupted or vulgarized to make it effective in secular activity, nor is this-worldly spirituality "an impossible position, a halfway house." But Strauss believes Calvinism was at most an unwilling carrier and not a foundation of secularism because he believes that religion and secularism are mutually exclusive viewpoints resting on opposing foundations.

It would seem that the point of distinguishing carrier from cause in the etiology of modern secularism is to prevent confusion of an incoherent and insubstantial "halfway house" with either of these two genuine alternatives, these opposing but equally intellectually respectable foundations of a way of life. The effect of insisting on the vulgarity of worldly Calvinism is not only to defend the purity of true Calvinism but also, it seems, to establish the integrity of true secularism, of authentically rational rationalism. My interpretation of Calvin's thought suggests that the first defense is misguided. It is certainly true that if Calvin's own intense piety is the standard, Calvinists as a whole have only declined from this standard. But it is inadequate to describe this as a declension from a spiritual to a more secular outlook. Nevertheless, Strauss may be right to defend the integrity of modernity against confusion with Calvinism. It may be that Calvinism does not deserve to be called a true cause of modernity, because modernity has its own foundations that are quite distinct from any religious view. This question is of more than historical interest: does modern rationalism have a rational foundation?

Strauss's answer would seem to be yes: the origins of modernity lie in a break *within* the philosophic tradition. In order to probe more deeply into the rationale behind Strauss's affirmative answer, it is useful to examine Strauss's correspondence with Karl Löwith in 1946, which has recently been published.[2] To understand this correspondence, it is well to be familiar with the thesis of a book that Löwith published in 1949.

Löwith argues in *Meaning in History* that "the modern world is as Christian as it is un-Christian because it is the outcome of an agelong process of secularization." In comparison with the pagan world, "our modern world is worldly and irreligious and yet dependent on the Christian creed from which it is emancipated." Although the modern age rejects Christian "creation and consummation" as "irrelevant myths," its characteristic hopes reflect a residual faith in those very myths. Thus, according to Löwith, the modern idea of progress has no rational foundation but is a secularized faith, an incoherent residue of Christian eschatology. The modern world depends on the Christian God but doesn't know it: "The post-Christian world is a creation without a creator" (201).

There is to my knowledge no letter from Löwith to Strauss extant in which Löwith advances this argument. However, in a letter from Strauss to Löwith, dated August 15, 1946, Strauss clearly seems to be responding to just such a line of reasoning in some earlier communication from Löwith. Strauss argues that it was not part of Condorcet's or Comte's intention, or Descartes's or Hobbes's, to "replace Christianity." Rather, they wanted simply "to replace nonsense with a reasonable order." It was only after the reasonable, secular intention of such authors had been fulfilled that "religion and Christianity [were] brought in." To believe that modernity in some essential way depends upon Christianity is therefore to succumb to the credulousness of the "insufferably sentimental nineteenth century." Modernity, on Strauss's view, is not the offspring, either legitimate (Hegel) or illegitimate (Löwith), of revealed religion. Modern philosophy and the civilization based upon it are just what Descartes and Hobbes wanted them to be: essentially products of human reason.

Strauss returns to this point in a letter to Löwith dated August 20, 1946, where he argues that "modern philosophy is originally the attempt to replace allegedly or really inadequate classical (and that means, at the same time, medieval) philosophy by the correct philosophy." He is willing to concede, here, that "biblical-scholastic motives . . . contributed to modernity, but he insists that "modern science, that is, modern philosophy, is fundamentally to be understood [physically?] and humanly." It was only after "the structure of mechanistic physics and the politics resting on it" had been completed in the Age of Enlightenment that nineteenth-century philosophers found it useful to interpret the Enlightenment itself as motivated by Christianity: "The thus created fable convenue is the basis of the view ruling today." Thus Löwith's secularization theory appears to Strauss as the restatement of a more or less deliberately concocted fable.

There are, however, passages in Strauss's letters which appear to approach Löwith's view. Indeed, Strauss introduces his discussion of the relationship of modernity to Christianity in the August 15 letter by granting part of Löwith's thesis, namely, "that modern philosophy has much that is essential in common with Christian medieval philosophy." For Strauss, however, the important upshot of this commonality is that "the attack of the moderns is directed decisively against ancient philosophy." Löwith might well respond: yes, precisely—modern philosophy is the continuation by new means of the essentially Christian attack on ancient philosophy. But Strauss seems to intend something different; he puts more emphasis on the rational means of attack than on the common ground the modern assailants share with revealed religion. He seems to insist that modern philosophy attacks ancient philosophy *directly*, that is, on purely human and rational grounds. Recall the language of Strauss's discussion of Weber in *Natural Right and History*: In the course of the sixteenth century, a break took place on the plane of purely philosophic or rational or secular thought." From this perspective, any similarities between modern philosophy and medieval Christian philosophy appear quite accidental: "Scholasticism was already disposed of in the sixteenth century, for one turned back from medieval philosophy to its sources, Plato-Aristotle and the Bible." The essential point is to see that "the *new* . . . is the repudiation of *everything* earlier." Thus modernity appears to be completely sui generis; it rejects the Bible and therefore all that is specifically Christian, and from classical philosophy it accepts nothing but the disposition to rely on human reason alone.

This view, however, does not appear consistent with Strauss's concession to Löwith, in the same paragraph as the statement last quoted, that modern philosophy has something essential in common with Christian philosophy.[3] And Strauss immediately confuses matters further by agreeing with Swift's and Lessing's opinion that "the real theme of the quarrel [*des anciens et des modernes*] is antiquity and Christianity." This could serve as an epigraph to Löwith's book—but where does it leave the originality of the moderns, which Strauss seems intent on defending? Swift and Lessing, Strauss continues, "did not doubt that antiquity, that is, genuine philosophy, is an eternal possibility." But if genuine philosophy is identified with antiquity, then the vaunted rationality of the modern attack on antiquity can only be an illusion. The only self-consistent alternative to classical reason would be revealed religion. Strauss says just this toward the end of the letter: "There is only one objection against Plato-Aristotle: and that is the factum brutum of revelation, or of the "personal' God" (108).[4] In this case modern rationalism, like worldly Puritanism, would be an illegitimate halfway house, a blind carrier of inherited motives.

If Strauss believes that no truly rational objection to the essentials of the Socratic school is possible, then it is somewhat disingenuous or ironic of him to refer to "the allegedly or really inadequate classical philosophy." And if we return now to *Natural Right and History* to examine Strauss's discussion of the origins of modern science and politics, it appears indeed that the motives behind modernity are not fully rational—contrary to Strauss's apparent position in his correspondence with Löwith, the founders of modernity did not intend to achieve or discover "the correct philosophy" in the sense of trying "to understand the universe." Whereas true philosophy, as Strauss explains to Löwith, consists in "the attempt to replace opinions about the whole with genuine knowledge of the whole," modern philosophy or "scientific materialism," according to *Natural Right and History*, rests on the belief that the universe is indefinitely subject to man's control precisely because it is unintelligible to him.[5] Since "we understand only what we make," philosophy as Plato and Aristotle knew it is impossible; knowledge is no longer pursued for its own sake but in order to make human beings "masters and owners of nature." Knowledge of the whole is not the end of modern "philosophy," because "all intelligibility or all meaning has its ultimate root in human needs." The purpose or "organizing principle" of modern philosophy is not knowledge of the whole but "the most compelling end posited by human desire" (177). Thus, contrary to Strauss's criticism of Weber's interpretation of Calvinism, *Natural Right and History* seems clearly to argue that modern rationalism has no rational foundation: "Man can be sovereign only because there is no cosmic support for his humanity. He can be sovereign only because he is absolutely a stranger in the universe . . . the vision of the City of Man to be erected on the ruins of

the City of God is an unsupported hope." But what does this "City
of God / City of Man" metaphor suggest but precisely the view
Löwith proposed to Strauss in 1946, namely, that the modern
project consists at bottom in an attempt to replace Christianity?

We have turned to Leo Strauss for help in locating Calvinism in
the history of political thought. Given the profundity and wide
influence of Strauss's unsurpassed studies of the foundations of
modernity, one is compelled to ask whether Strauss's view in any
way allows for the direct and positive influence of the Protestant
Reformation. Both in his correspondence with Löwith and in his
discussion of Weber in *Natural Right and History*, Strauss's answer seems to be a clear no. Furthermore, those familiar with
Strauss's interpretation of modernity will readily see that this
answer extends far beyond a few remarks to Karl Löwith or a few
pages on the subject of Max Weber. For if we compare Strauss's
work on modern political thought with that of such other scholars
as Löwith and Eric Voegelin (who, like Strauss, regret the modern
rejection of classical philosophy and regard modernity largely as a
disease to be diagnosed), a fundamental difference immediately
appears: Both Löwith and Voegelin believe that Christianity, or
Christian heresies, contributed key assumptions to the modern
worldview; accordingly, they offer interpretations of Christian
thinkers and Christian movements. Strauss, on the other hand,
concentrates his attention on a tradition, founded by Machiavelli,
that he believes owes little or nothing to Christianity—yet not, it
appears, because he believes the founders of modernity were philosophers in the full sense.

Eric Voegelin's brilliant and influential contributions to the
study of the relationship between modernity and Christianity
deserve extensive consideration in this connection, but I must
limit myself to a few observations on his *New Science of Politics*.
For Voegelin as for Löwith, the modern mind consists in a defor-
mation of the spirit of Christianity. More specifically, Voegelin
(1952) has described modernity as a Christian heresy: "the essence
of modernity [is] the growth of gnosticism" (126). The gnostic
experience, according to Voegelin, is a temptation that has accompanied Christianity from its very beginning: whereas authentic
Christianity "de-divinizes" the world and reduces man's connec-

tion with God to "the tenuous bond of faith," gnosticism promises relief from the anxiety of Christian pilgrimage through the "re-divinization" of the world. "Uncertainty is the very essence of Christianity" (122), and a specious certainty is the stock-in-trade of gnosticism.

The relief offered by gnosticism does not take the form of a return to the pagan "world full of gods"—this, Voegelin thinks, is lost forever. Rather, it is achieved through the "immanentization" of Christian eschatology: the hope that in the Christian faith attaches to otherworldly "last things" is transferred to the ends of human action. This immanentization may yield a "progressive interpretation of history" or, in more extreme forms, "the active mysticism of a state of perfection, to be achieved through a revolutionary transfiguration of the nature of man, as, for instance, in Marxism" (121). Voegelin summarizes the relationship between Christianity and modern gnosticism:

> Gnostic speculation overcame the uncertainty of faith by receding from transcendence and endowing man and his intramundane range of action with the meaning of eschatological fulfillment. In the measure in which this immanentization progressed experientially, civilizational activity became a mystical work of self-salvation. The spiritual strength of the soul which in Christianity was devoted to the sanctification of life could now be diverted into the more appealing, more tangible, and, above all, so much easier creation of the terrestrial paradise. (126)

By interpreting modern progressivism as a defective religious experience, Voegelin thus turns the progressive interpretation of history on its head: the modern period is now seen to consist in "the evolution from a higher to a lower degree of rationalism" (24).

This assessment seems consonant with Strauss's description of the modern project as an "unsupported hope." Why, then, does Strauss decline to interpret modernity as dependent upon Christianity? Why does Strauss restrict his search for or discussion of the sources of a project he regards as irrational to the self-understanding of men who fancied themselves rationalists? I believe a further look at the Strauss–Löwith correspondence may clarify this question, for there this difficulty in Strauss's view is clearly visible along with its possible motives.

In Strauss's letters to Löwith, the problem of the relationship between Christianity and modernity is discussed against the background of a deeper disagreement concerning the relationship of philosophy to history—a disagreement regarding the very possibility of philosophy in the classical sense. Löwith believes that "Christianity fundamentally modified ancient "naturalness,'" and that "it is not only historical consciousness which has changed, but our historical being" (109). "Even patient, pure learning never escapes its own presuppositions" (110). Similarly, Voegelin believes that the "insight" which "by tradition is called revelation" that "humanity is demonic nothingness" is an irreversible achievement of clarity, the ultimate "differentiating experience" (79).

No return is possible to the relatively dim or confused cosmos of antiquity. It follows, according to Voegelin, that "theory is bound by history in the sense of differentiating experiences." Strauss, on the other hand, in his reply to Löwith admits that "our usual way of feeling is conditioned by the biblical tradition" but insists that this "does not rule out our being able . . . through self-education . . . to correct our feeling" (111). In an earlier letter, Strauss argued that "historical reflection" is not in itself the paradigm of knowledge but only a means by which to recover our abilities as "natural beings with natural understanding" (107). The fundamental difference between Strauss and Löwith, according to Strauss, is that whereas Löwith understands philosophy as "nothing but the self-understanding or self-interpretation of man," Strauss holds to the "simple sense of philosophy," namely, "the attempt to replace opinions about the whole with genuine knowledge of the whole."

Here, again, a kinship can be seen between Löwith and Voegelin. According to Voegelin, "theory . . . is an attempt at formulating the meaning of existence by explicating the content of a definite class of experiences." It is important to note that Voegelin does not necessarily mean by *content* the thing intended or articulated by the subject of these experiences; he means a content identical to the human experience itself, which thus can only be discerned or differentiated after the fact by the historian: "The substance of history is to be found on the level of experiences, not on the level of ideas."[6]

Strauss's treatment of Voegelin, in a reply[7] to Voegelin's review[8] of his *On Tyranny*, is identical in its essentials to his answer to Löwith. Here again, the fundamental question appears to be the relationship between Christianity and the modern age: Voegelin argues that "the "modernity' of Machiavelli's prince has a specific tone through the absorption of such medieval-Christian antecedents as the Joachitic *dux*, Dante's *Veltro*, and the realization of these ideas in the savior tribunate of Rienzo" (243). Strauss, on the other hand, insists on locating Machiavelli in a non-Christian tradition—not that of Joachim of Floris, "but the one which we still call, with pardonable ignorance, the averroistic tradition" (196). This question, however, again arises within the context of a more profound disagreement. In fact, Strauss concludes his discussion of Machiavelli by leaving open the question that seems to be the basis of his opposition to Voegelin: "It is impossible to say how far the epoch-making change that was effected by Machiavelli is due to the indirect influence of the Biblical tradition before that change has been fully understood in itself" (197). On close inspection, therefore, Strauss does not deny that the influence of the Christian tradition on the modern mind is great; he insists only that we understand modernity as far as possible on its own terms before resorting to extraneous or indirect influences, that we concentrate first on the "change itself" as understood by those who deliberately sought change.

Strauss thus attacks Voegelin for "opposing the historical meaning of Xenophon's work to his conscious intention" and for failing to honor the non-Christian intention of Machiavelli's notion of "armed prophets." To refer to indirect or inarticulate influences is to claim that we understand "the historical situation" better than the author in question did, and this is not, according to Strauss, a *historical* but a *philosophical* claim: "we cannot be better judges of that situation if we do not have a clearer grasp than he had of the principles in whose light historical situations reveal their meaning" (195). We must learn from the great authors before we can teach about them. Strauss wants to reserve to philosophers the right to speak of nonphilosophical influences.[9]

In this context we see more clearly the meaning of Strauss's objection to Löwith's interpretation of modernity. Löwith believes that reason or consciousness is necessarily historical; it is inevitable, then, that post-Christian thinkers will carry with them the consciousness of the age of Christianity.[10] Strauss, on the other hand, insists on the eternal possibility of genuine philosophy; and this insistence, I believe, helps to explain the ambivalence of his assessment of the early moderns. In his concern to defend the possibility of philosophy, Strauss is led to defend (rather halfheartedly) the pretensions to philosophy of, for example, Descartes (112). Contemptuous of the "credulous and insufferably sentimental nineteenth century" with its facile merging of reason and revelation, and believing that Löwith has not entirely escaped this credulousness ("You remain bogged down in idealism-historicism"), Strauss insists on the exclusive claims of reason and thus seems to associate himself with the claims of modern rationalists. I can only conclude that, whereas Strauss might have said only that philosophy was in principle accessible to the founders of modernity, he chose instead to say that they were in fact philosophers.

Thus, rather than aligning himself with resignation to history, Strauss defends as far as he can a view of nature he knows to be inadequate; he finds the incomplete self-understanding of the founders of modernity less insidious than the opinion that understanding is always a product of the times. He chooses modern natural right over the modernizing critique of modernity.[11] It is as if, forced to choose between those who believe Christianity does not condition modern thought and those who believe it must, he chooses the former.

The consequence of this confusion or confusing choice for Strauss's work on the foundations of modernity is that, although he often exposes the emptiness of modern rationalism with astonishing insight, he fails or declines to identify and explore the roots of the beliefs or assumptions that filled this emptiness. To see this more clearly, let us return to Strauss's discussion of Hobbes in *Natural Right and History*. There he confesses puzzlement in understanding "how Hobbes could be so hopeful where there was so much cause for despair." Strauss can only offer the suggestion that "somehow the experience, as well as the legitimate anticipation, of unheard-of progress within the sphere which is subject to human control must have made him insensitive to the eternal silence of those infinite spaces" or to the crackings of the *moenia mundi* (175). Notice that Strauss does not question Hobbes's expectation of a new age of unprecedented material progress. What he regards as irrational is that Hobbes finds in this progress more than adequate compensation for the loss of all support of God or nature. The vision of the City of Man is an unsupported hope, not because there are no good grounds for believing man can now more perfectly control the things subject to his control, but because the more important things are not only beyond his control but now totally lost to him. Man may erect a new city, even an incredibly secure and abundant city as human cities go, but it is impossible that such a City of Man should be sufficient to fill the void left by the ruin of the City of God. What good is it to gain the whole world if a man loses his soul? Or, more precisely: What good to master the motion of matter, if the soul of the whole is lost?

It is not Hobbes's materialism that Strauss believes is unsupported, but only the idealism that is joined to this materialism— only the fact that Hobbes's materialism performs an idealistic function. Strauss, in *Thoughts on Machiavelli*, makes essentially the same criticism of the man he believes taught Hobbes the essentials of the project of modernity. "Through an irony beyond Machiavelli's irony," Strauss writes, "his silence about the soul is a perfect expression of the soulless character of his teaching." This soullessness, according to Strauss, is inseparable from an *intellectual* defect; so far from being a paradigm of reason is Strauss's Machiavelli that "philosophy and its status is obfuscated not only in Machiavelli's teaching but in his thought as well." Thus Machiavelli is "unable to give a clear account of his own doing"; his own narrow view of the nature of man "is inadequate to grasp what is greatest in him" (294). The root of this inadequacy is that "the human in man is implicitly understood to reside in an Archimedean point outside of nature." This failure to account explicitly for what is truly human entails a profound theoretical and practical contradiction: "The 'idealistic' philosophy of freedom supplements and ennobles the 'materialistic' philosophy which it presupposes in the very act of negating it" (297).

One is entitled to conclude that, according to Strauss himself, Machiavelli's teaching finally has no rational foundation. Perhaps Strauss intended to leave the door open to this conclusion when, in his discussion of Weber on Calvinism, he located the origins of modernity not exactly within philosophy but in "a break that took place on the plane of purely philosophic *or* rational *or* secular thought" (1950, 61n; my emphasis). The founders of modern rationalism or secularism cannot give rational accounts of themselves. Modernity consists in a materialistic rationalism unknowingly supported by an irrational idealism.

Blumenberg on the Legitimacy of the Modern Age

This formulation of the problem seems to suggest a strategy to anyone choosing to defend reason in modern politics: to salvage the modern age it might suffice to remove rational materialism from its irrational, idealistic foundation. This indeed appears to be the approach taken by Hans Blumenberg in his recent attempt to establish *The Legitimacy of the Modern Age.*

Blumenberg introduces his defense of the modern age with a direct attack on the notion that modernity is a secularized effect of Christianity; still more clearly or openly than Strauss, Blumenberg seizes upon the profound political implications of the theory that the modern world is the offspring of Christianity. Since this theory, according to Blumenberg, plainly contradicts the self-understanding of the offspring itself—modernity's claim to radical innovation—it can only mean that the child is a self-deceived bastard. Furthermore, "secularization" theorists in fact imply that the ongoing self-deception of the modern age, as well as its illegitimate birth, is irreversible. Modern worldliness cannot truly know itself and therefore cannot found itself if its cause is otherworldly; the scheme of secularization thus "involves a premise that is foreign to the modern age's self-understanding." The premise of secularization theory must in fact be regarded as " 'secularized' in its own right" for, "when historical understanding makes use of this category, it enters into religion's self-interpretation as a privileged access to truth." Posing as rational historians, "secularization" theorists in fact make an implicit "claim to have received a revelation," for they posit "a beginning that is not historically explicable, that has no immanent preconditions" (73–74). Their debunking of the modern age, according to Blumenberg, represents at bottom the reaction of the partisans of a new beginning based on revelation against the attempt to make a new beginning based on reason or science. Blumenberg's most fundamental objection to Löwith's argument is thus that "it presupposes as beyond question an absolute and transcendent origin" of what is secularized (29). Modernity remains unintelligible for the theological interpretation of history for the simple reason that the basis of this interpretation is the theological premise of a cause that is absolutely transcendent and thus altogether incommensurable with human reason.[12] The theory that modernity is the illegitimate offspring of Christianity is thus, in the final analysis, nothing but "theological talk" (29).

This is not to say, however, that Blumenberg rejects the secularization theory altogether; he actually objects more to the theological spirit in which the argument is presented than to the substance of the argument itself. Blumenberg in fact agrees with Löwith that the claim of the modern age to make a new beginning is false; he only wants to add that the same is true of the claim of Christianity. Blumenberg grants that the modern age, contrary to its own self-understanding, is "unthinkable without Christianity" (30). What he contests is that this makes modernity illegitimate. Blumenberg's intention is not to *defend* modernity by demonstrating the legitimacy of the new beginning asserted by its founders but to *establish* the legitimacy of the modern age by giving the modern age a new self-understanding that renounces the claim to newness.

Modernity's original claim to newness is false, according to Blumenberg, not because of any defect in the content of the new philosophy but because of the function this philosophy was asked to perform (64). Modern reason is not in itself illegitimate, it is only "overextended"; it "suffers from the appearance of illegitimacy on account of the continuity that derives from its inability to shake off inherited questions." Blumenberg thus agrees with Löwith that modern reason attempted to answer questions or to respond to needs that were inherited from Christianity, but he denies that it must continue to do so: "We are going to have to free ourselves," he argues, "from the idea that there is a firm canon of 'great questions' that throughout history and with an unchanging urgency have occupied human curiosity and motivated the pretension to world and self-interpretation" (65). Elsewhere Blumenberg admits "the possibility that these questions derive from a human interest that lies deeper than the mere persistence of the epochal carry-over." He does not, however, pursue this possibility, and his historical interpretation is guided not by an interest in the deepest questions but by "resignation with respect to the unknowable" (48). Since Blumenberg wants to detach the modest content, the "authentic rationality" (49) of modernity, from the theological function this content was forced to perform, he prefers the term *reoccupation* to *secularization*: modernity is not a perverse form of Christianity but a reasonable project that was perverted by Christianity or its residue. Indeed, Blumenberg is willing to accept the term *secularization* once it is understood who is at fault: "Instead of secularization of eschatology, secularization by eschatology" (37). The point of this distinction is to insist that "no foreign or external factor is at work here employing the authentic substance of eschatological ideas for its own purposes." Thus, nothing but eschatology itself is to blame for secularization: "eschatology historicizes itself." But the key is not so much to assign blame as to know why the process is blameworthy. Eschatology secularizes itself not "by transforming itself and continuing in a false incarnation, but rather by enforcing the reoccupation of its position by heterogeneous material." The fault of religion lies not in its susceptibility to degradation but in its refusal to disappear— or, more precisely, its refusal to take its "position" or "function" in life and civilization with it. It should thus be clear that everything in Blumenberg's argument depends on the "material" of modernity, its content, being "heterogeneous" with respect to the function imposed upon it by eschatology. To establish the detachable heterogeneity of the "authentic rationality" of the modern age corresponds to the strategy suggested by our earlier formula: to sever the rational materialism of modernity from the irrational idealism that has haunted it.

This indeed seems to be Blumenberg's intention. The idea of progress, he argues, arose in a reasonable and relatively modest form long before it was transformed into the comprehensive philosophies of history that Löwith attacks: "the formation of the idea of progress and its taking the place of the historical totality that was bounded by Creation and Judgment are two distinct events" (49). To establish the legitimacy of the modern age, it would seem sufficient to recover the original idea of progress and to reject later totalistic views—to reject, for example, Condorcet and Hegel and to recover Descartes, for whom "the idea of method is not a kind of planning, not a transformation of the divine salvation plan, but rather the establishment of . . . the disposition . . . to take part in a process that generates knowledge in a transubjective manner" (33).

Just what distinguishes "the establishment of a disposition" from "a kind of planning" will be clearer after a closer look at Blumenberg's appraisal of the modern idea of progress in its original form. For Blumenberg's purpose is not at all to recover a modest idea of material progress available in the founding works of the modern age. In the final analysis, even Descartes and Hobbes are not nearly modest or modern enough to supply the foundation of Blumenberg's modernity. The reoccupation of Christian eschatology by totalistic philosophies of history was preceded by a subtler form of the hyperextension of reason, in which nature itself, understood as self-preservation, is elevated to the status of an absolute: "The disintegration of the Middle Ages pulled self-preservation out of its biologically determined normality . . . and turned it into the 'theme' of human self-comprehension" (139). To establish the authenticity of modern reason, it is necessary not only to detach rational materialism from irrational idealism but to detach reason from materialism, to sever the self-assertion of human reason from any and all theoretical claims. Modern reason is resolutely worldly (25), that is, it represents a "new concentration on man's self-interest" (178), but it must not depend on or be limited by any fixed interpretation of the world or of man's self-interest. This is why Blumenberg insists on reducing Descartes's "plan" to a "disposition"; his project consists essentially in dispensing with the obligation to defend the legitimacy of what human beings assert by asserting the legitimacy of pure self-assertion. The self-assertion that Blumenberg defends—no, asserts—is no theoretical proposition about self-preservation or any other aspect of reality; it is an "existential program" (138). "Self-assertion determines the radicalness of reason, not its logic" (97). In order to separate the content of reason from its fundamentally theological function, it is necessary finally to separate reason from its own content, from its own logic—it is necessary to detach reason from rationalism. Only in this way can the "self-assertion of reason" cast off "resignation before the 'laws of nature'" as well as the attitude of "leaving everything to the transcendence of time" (226).

Blumenberg's attack on the residual teleology of self-preservation clearly owes much to Nietzsche, and he acknowledges the debt. In eliminating "the premise that the world has a particular quality for man that in effect prescribes his basic mode of behavior," Blumenberg intends, like Nietzsche, to practice "a kind of thinking that removes problems by specifying the conditions under which they no longer arise" (143). Blumenberg believes, however, that Nietzsche's substitution of "the will to power" for a theory about the world "has only illuminated better what it was meant to destroy." For Nietzsche attempts to use the historical reduction of human problems as a means to "secede from history and throw off its burden"; he attempts through history to be "free of history" and thus ends up endorsing "what is present without putting it in question."

Blumenberg rejects this strategy in favor of a resolute determination not even to attempt to "secede from history." This is the meaning, I think, of his observation that "the legitimacy of the modern age that I intended is a historical category" (97). Blumenberg's modernity requires no authority above or beyond history, beyond the *accident* of history: it consists not in a resignation to "the transcendence of time" but in submission to time conceived without any color of transcendence. Blumenberg asserts the legitimacy of the new age by debunking that age's claim to be new, by showing how the form taken by the absolute self-assertion of the founders of modernity was a response to the provocation of the age of theological absolutism (60). According to Blumenberg, "the concept of the legitimacy of the modern age is not derived from the accomplishments of reason but rather from the necessity of those accomplishments." Human rationalism is legitimate not as radically new or ahistorical but precisely as a necessary response to the erroneous claim to newness of "theological voluntarism" (99).

What is necessary must be legitimate. Blumenberg radicalizes the modern strategy of mastering necessity not by rising above it but by anticipating and thereby appropriating it. If it is true that the "philosophical program for the beginning of the modern age 'failed' because it was unable to analyze away its own preconditions"—that is, because despite itself the new philosophy "is integrable into the declining Middle ages" (74)—then we have only to recognize the necessary dependence of our age on certain theological preconditions in order, in effect, to be free of them. We "analyze away" the historical necessity that binds us by confessing our inability to rise above it. The new age to be founded by Blumenberg's self-assertion will begin when human beings no longer aspire to a legitimacy that is more than a "historical category," when they realize that any appeal to the *whole* of history, or to God or nature, is, like the secularization theory, "an anachronism in the modern age."

The large area of agreement between Löwith, Voegelin, and Blumenberg should now be clear: All believe that the self-understanding of the modern age *necessarily* derives from Christianity. The difference is that, for the secularization theorists this implies the illegitimacy of the modern age, whereas for Blumenberg this consequence can be avoided by a purifying reflection on the necessity of self-assertion. Blumenberg grasps the deepest implication of the secularization theory: secularization implies the impossibility of understanding the modern age, because we are in it (5, 9, 73–74). But he does not so much deny this theory as he transforms its moral and political meaning: to be free to assert ourselves, we have only to understand that we are, necessarily, *in* the modern age. Blumenberg radicalizes the freedom, the idealism of modernity by radicalizing its necessity. He reenacts the modern reaction to the provocation of theological absolutism by a self-assertion that he hopes will be imitated but that will not have to be and cannot be reenacted. He proposes to bring science and technology "back into their human function, to subject them again to man's purposes in relation to the world," with the difference that these purposes must now be understood as having no content but pure self-assertion. The "counterexertion" against the perennial temptation of "objectivization" must itself be taken as representing human self-interest (177–78). To overcome the implication of illegitimacy in the secularization theory, one must simply allow the result of secularization (the modern age) "to secularize the process itself from which it resulted" (18). For Blumenberg, the fact that the modern age is "unthinkable without Christianity" is no longer a reproach; historical indebtedness ceases to be onerous when it is understood to be purely historical. The contingency of existence that oppressed the late Middle Ages becomes liveable for an age that appropriates it—when we make it *our* contingency.

Blumenberg thus does not deny but embraces Löwith's claim that the modern world is a creation without a creator. Modern humanity has, in effect, freed itself from God only by various assertions of a new God; to Blumenberg belongs the glory of revealing that to be finally free of God we have only to concentrate on the human act of assertion itself. Thus, although others call Blumenberg a philosopher,[13] he presents himself as a scholar less interested in "constants" than in "the historian's epistemological situation." However, whether Blumenberg's self-assertion is legitimate seems to me to be more than an historical question. The detachment of content from function that Blumenberg's self-assertion requires would certainly constitute major surgery. If it should succeed, Blumenberg will deserve more credit than his patient for the legitimacy of the modern age.

And what if Blumenberg's project, and that of others like him, should fail? Our interest in political things compels us to consider the condition of the modern age in the event that humanity generally should fail to modernize in accordance with the requirements of Blumenberg's epistemological situation. Whether or not we know or can demonstrate any constants, we find ourselves surrounded by pre-Blumenbergian individuals who defend their interests by asserting something more than the sheer historicity of their own self-assertion—and who act for all the world as if they took the content (whether nature, God, or history) of their assertions quite seriously. Clearly such people present us with a problem that is more than epistemological. But Blumenberg overlooks this problem; he seems to believe that if we succeed in analyzing away our interest in Nature or God, then no fundamental conflicts of interest will remain, and he refuses to offer a theory of history to support this belief, because a theory of history would detract from our "concentration on man's self-interest" (178) pure and simple. "The experiment with absolutes has been played through to its conclusion," Blumenberg reassures us. He is thus confident that "the East/West dualism has only been a short-lived interlude" that can now be analyzed away (91). But it is obvious that, unless human self-interest is understood as defined and limited by human *nature*, then there is nothing to prevent one person's self-assertion from becoming another's "absolute authority" or absolute mastery.

Thus, although Blumenberg agrees with the founders of the modern age in turning our attention resolutely to this world (25), he provides no account of what this world is. He seems to assume that we can all peaceably divide the material benefits of our worldliness without recourse to any standard of justice—consoled, perhaps, by the spiritual delight of a purely formal self-assertion. Blumenberg is a liberal without natural right and an historicist without history. God is dead, and everything innocent is permitted.

The Basis of Legitimacy in the Modern Age

To establish the legitimacy of the modern age will require more and less self-assertion—a different kind of assertiveness—than is implied by Blumenberg's project to establish pure self-assertion as the universal ground of public discourse. Blumenberg fails to take account of the remarkable or unequal character of his own self-assertion and thus appears simply to assume that it will not be opposed by the assertions of ordinary human beings. In other words, Blumenberg does not take the political problem or the problem of justice seriously; his assertions are not fully self-aware (and thus not fully his own) because they are not political—that is, they do not reflect an awareness of the problem of reconciling the extraordinary with the ordinary. By contrast, those writers whom Blumenberg considers the founders of the modern age seem to have known that they were asserting themselves in exceptional ways, and they took care to persuade common people to acquiesce in their uncommon self-assertion. Thus Hobbes in effect claimed the power and therefore the right to imitate God by recreating the political world (at least), but he made it clear to less creative men that their bodies had everything to gain (peace and commodious living) and nothing to lose by submitting to the Leviathan of Leviathans. Similarly, Descartes promised "the fruits of the earth" and especially "the preservation of health" to humankind in general, but he claimed for himself alone the right to develop the method he had authored, accepting only the kind of help that is compensated by money and refusing the assistance of those motivated by love of learning or honor.[14]

However, Leo Strauss has shown (as we have seen) that the political and self-awareness of the founders of modernity was itself defective. Recall Strauss's observation that Machiavelli's teaching is "soulless" because "the human in man is implicitly understood to reside in an Archimedean point outside nature." (In Machiavelli's successors this defect of soul is exhibited, for example, in the incommensurability of Hobbes's "man as maker" with "man as matter" and in the notorious difficulties of Descartes's mind-body dualism.) The founders of the "philosophical or rational or secular" tradition of modernity understood only "implicitly" the idealism that "supplements and ennobles" their own materialism. Thus, according to Strauss, this idealistic materialism is but an "unsupported hope." One might say that, by failing to imitate God's goodness, the would-be founders of the modern age failed fully to imitate his creativity; in harnessing their own creative generosity to the bodies but not the spirits or souls of ordinary men, they failed to create the idealism or virtue needed to sustain their material creations; they lacked precisely the doctrine of an ongoing and pervasive providence or continuous creation that in Calvin's doctrine links divine power with human consciousness or the effectual truth of realism with the spirit of idealism. The secular founders of modern materialism failed to imitate God in the decisive respect of requiring or allowing that the world they created imitate or serve them knowingly or consciously. Thus, rather than identifying the true founders of the modern age, Strauss seems to have shown that it has no founders because it has no foundation.

I do not claim to have described a solid foundation for modernity, and so I cannot claim to have shown that John Calvin made these foundations, that he was the (or a) true founder. However, my interpretation of Calvin does suggest that it may make as much sense to call Machiavelli and Hobbes carriers of a Christian tradition as to call Puritans unknowing carriers of a secular tradition. On Strauss's own interpretation of the meaning of modernity, Calvinism appears to deserve more attention than it has generally received from students of political philosophy, a different kind of attention than that given it by historians of political thought, because this teaching represents a striking case of the distinctively modern combination of materialistic rationalism with irrational or nonrational idealism.

It is true that in Calvin's thought this materialistic rationalism is not so well articulated or so consciously advanced as in the writings of what Strauss calls the philosophic tradition of modernity. Strauss is right to point out that Calvin did not supply the critical "minor premise" essential to the "science of economics" and therefore to the capitalist spirit, namely, that "the unlimited accumulation of capital is most conducive to the common good" (1950, 60–61n). But Strauss infers too much from this very apt observation. Perhaps in the interest of the scientific appearance of capitalism, he proceeds as if the spirit of capitalism were identical to the modern science of economics. This, however, could only be the case if this modern science could give a full, rational account of itself, which Strauss elsewhere implicitly denies. But it is not the case, according to Strauss's interpretation of modernity, that the science of capitalism can account for the spirit of capitalism. Materialism cannot account for its own idealism.[15]

If this is so, then in assessing the relative importance of contributions to modernity by the secular and religious traditions the advantage may not always belong to the secular. If Calvinism cannot fully recognize or account for the residual natural teleology of its own materialism, then even less does the Machiavellian tradition (at least before Rousseau) recognize its own idealism.[16] If one was an unknowing carrier of the science of modernity, the other was as much the unknowing carrier of its spirit. Calvinism is certainly not rational or self-aware through and through, but it has this advantage over Machiavellianism, that it has a name, if not an idea, for its "Archimedean point outside nature": God. In this sense, Calvin's thought can account for itself more fully than Machiavelli's; in this sense, at least, Calvinism exhibits a foundation more clearly than the modern philosophic tradition.

This element of clarity cannot have been without effect in the history of the modern age. Machiavelli and Hobbes, unable to give an account of their own idealism, were bound in effect to keep all the glory of history for themselves (and, secondarily, for the captains of their intellectual armies); all they could offer to the people was security. But Calvin had a name for his idealism, and therefore he could share the glory more readily with his troops.[17] And history has made it painfully clear that the energy of modernity derives less from the security of materialism than from its elusive glory.

This insight may seem in practice to amount to a counsel of despair, to consign us to the role of spectators in the global consumption of the material nature of modernity by its own unnatural and blind idealism. Thus, as Blumenberg argues, despair of this world, or retreat into unknowable absolutes, indeed seems to be the practical meaning of those theological interpretations of the modern age that concentrate on describing or rather evoking the blindness of modern idealism—which concentrate, in particular, on the illegitimate secularization of Christian transcendence or eschatology. And Blumenberg's criticism of Löwith's theological reading of modernity may in fact apply with particular force to Voegelin's account of modernity as the growth of gnosticism. Voegelin blames modern gnosticism for making immanent an eschaton that he understands as absolutely transcendent, as altogether beyond the scope of the world that human beings naturally represent to themselves, or as wholly "differentiated" from any cosmos conceived of as a home for a political order and its virtues. Voegelin does not indicate, however, just what human beings should do with this absolute eschaton: if we do not ignore it altogether, then how can we fail to make it immanent in one way or another—how can we we avoid placing the transcendent in some relation to the world we think we know and in which we must act?[18] How can an eschaton that has meaning for human beings altogether escape implication in the worldly concerns of morality and politics?

Voegelin does not take responsibility for addressing such questions; he seems to believe that the safest political treatment of the eschaton is no treatment at all. He approves of the Christian "de-divinization" of the world that resulted from severing or radically "differentiating" the truth of the soul from the order of the regime and consequently from the cosmos by reference to which the regime justifies itself; but he does not adequately address the problem of the ends of human action in this desacralized or god-less world of politics and morality, nor does he explain how a political cosmos severed from God is to be prevented from becoming its own God. By radically differentiating the two worlds, by denying the commensurability of the truth of the soul and the truth of the cosmos, Voegelin in effect leaves this world to its own devices—and then shudders at the consequences. But the transcendent can limit this world only if it is understood as another world in some sense, only if there is some positive link, some continuity of meaning, between the human and the divine, only if the best of this world in some way participates in the transcendent. What cannot ennoble cannot restrain.

Unrestrained worldliness is of course not the effect Voegelin intends. But if he avoids this outcome, he owes this less to a rational insight into an answer to modern gnosticism—an insight into the connection between the two worlds—than to a disposition to fall back either on the assumptions of a certain Christian orthodoxy (although he does not write as an orthodox Christian) or on a faith in a new science of politics, a science that he concedes does not yet exist but whose "foundations . . . have been laid" (1952, 26). In either case, Blumenberg's critique seems to apply: Voegelin's philosophical analysis of modernity is incomplete because it rests on a premise in some sense theological.

Voegelin's dependence on theological premises is quite clear in his treatment of Calvin. Voegelin suggests that Calvin's *Institutes* "may be called the first deliberately created Gnostic Koran," the first instance of a characteristically modern genre that advances new truth as altogether above criticism and claims to make recourse to all earlier literature useless and eventually to forbid it as dangerous. But in his critique of Calvin, Voegelin simply takes for granted Hooker's "classical and Christian" (137) view that the Puritan and Calvinist "position was not based on Scripture but was a 'cause' of a vastly different origin." It is remarkable that Voegelin fails to offer so much as a single clue into the actual content of the *Institutes*. If he had paused to consider this content, he might have been struck by the fact that Calvin takes the greatest pains to distance himself from the apocalyptic, Joachitic tradition in which Voegelin is eager to place him. On the face of it, indeed, it is hard to imagine any teaching more far removed from the gnostic speculations on a new age than Calvin's characteristic insistence on a radical separation between spiritual and worldly matters.

I have argued, of course, that the distance between the spiritualization of this world and the radical differentiation of world and spirit may not in fact be very great—that is, that the absolute separation and the fusion of divinity and humanity have similar outcomes; but this is my argument, and not Voegelin's. Voegelin tends simply to fall back on what he takes to be an Augustinian dualism of spirit and world (106); he does not take seriously Calvin's claim to the legacy of Augustine. Since Voegelin does not consider Calvin's claim, he is not aware of the ground he shares with Calvin and thus has no answer to Blumenberg's suggestion that Christianity might be the source of its own immanentization or secularization. To be sure, Voegelin's dualism is not so consistent or absolute as Calvin's and may therefore be more stable. But despite his decidedly non-Calvinist solicitude for the "metaphysical" orientation of the "classical and Christian" tradition, Voegelin still puts "experience" above articulate understanding, both in theology and in historical methodology.[19]

The fragility of Voegelin's solicitude for the classical metaphysical tradition is evident in his remark that Machiavelli "recognized the structure of reality" and in his characterization of

Hobbes's political project as "an eminently sensible idea in so far as it put the whole weight on existence that had been so badly neglected by the Gnostics." Voegelin is thus somewhat readier to acknowledge his affinity with the realism of Machiavelli and Hobbes than with the radical dualism of Calvin; he approves of the "Christian" de-divinization of the world and so can hardly disapprove of the realistic or godless interpretation of the structure of the world and of action within it.

Voegelin regrets that "Hobbes countered the Gnostic immanentization of the eschaton which endangered existence by a radical immanence of existence which denied the eschaton" (179). It is not clear, however, that Hobbes's "radical immanence" is much different in practice from Voegelin's own "de-divinization"; furthermore, the distinction between immanentizing the eschaton and denying it will not bear scrutiny. In drawing this latter distinction Voegelin appears to ignore his own account of Hobbes's biblical justification of the politics of immanence. Whether Hobbes's biblical argument deserves to be ignored is a question I shall leave open; it is clear, however, that political realism can start from the premise of absolute transcendence as well as from the denial of transcendence. Thus Hobbes secures his realistic or nonteleogical view of politics by insisting that men cannot "conceive, and imagine, or have any Idea of God"; that "God has no ends," and that God's "Will . . . is not to be understood, as that of Man, for a Rational Appetite; but as Power, by which he effecteth everything." Like Calvin, Hobbes enjoins men not to attribute to God qualities that they can emulate but to fear and love him for his power and his "care of mankind." Hobbes does not have to deny the existence of God in order to secularize the political world; in fact, by destroying the connection between God's nature and human virtues, Hobbes enlists divine "care of mankind" in the very project of secularization. As Voegelin himself observes, Hobbes "denied the existence of a tension between the truth of the soul and the truth of society." One might as well say that for him the truth of society took the place of the truth of the soul, or that he immanentized the eschaton.[20]

This observation casts doubt not only on Voegelin's implicit distinction between religious and nonreligious political realism—

that is, between the denial of the eschaton and the belief that it is beyond and therefore irrelevant to politics—but furthermore on the very distinction between the denial and the immanentization of the eschaton, between realism and modern gnosticism. Is it possible to confine politics radically to this world without attributing to this world the ultimacy formerly belonging to God? Hobbes's materialism does not simply distinguish itself from, or even oppose, a nonmaterialistic tradition; it seeks to replace it. Thus it is not obvious that the Leviathan cannot be "identified with totalitarianism on its own symbolic level of the final realm of perfection" (186). It is true that the evocation of a "final realm of perfection" seems quite foreign to Hobbes's political project, as to Calvin's; but it is useful to consider that Marx, a radical gnostic according to Voegelin, predicts not a realm of perfection but a realm of freedom, and this freedom is identified with the full and effective self-consciousness of material necessity. Voegelin fails to appreciate the continuities between Machiavellian and Hobbesian realism and modern totalitarianism because, in his eagerness to trace the influence of a Christian heresy, he fails to enter into the materialistic and scientific self-understanding of modern idealism. Similarly, Voegelin interprets Calvin as a forerunner of the radical gnosticism of modernity, but he ignores Calvin's political realism and thus fails to see the possibility of fusing radical materialism with radical idealism, a fusion that is characteristic—though only more or less explicitly—of the modern thought of Machiavelli, Hobbes, and Calvin as well as that of Marx.

Just how explicit this fusion is is by no means an otiose question, and Voegelin is certainly right to prefer Machiavelli's implicit reference, as Strauss puts it, to "an Archimedean point outside nature," or Hobbes's implicit restriction to himself of the full right of divine creativity, to the doctrine that all can share equally in the spiritual or ideal as well as in the material benefits of unrestrained freedom or creativity. The Machiavellian germ of gnosticism is certainly preferable to the disease in full fever. Still, to diagnose the disease, it is important to examine the germ.

The limitations of Voegelin's approach to modernity can be seen in the term gnosticism itself, which, as Hans Jonas has pointed out, fails to take account of the radical nature of the modern rejection of teleology. This difference is apparent, Jonas explains, in the fact that "gnostic man is thrown into an antagonistic, anti-divine, and therefore anti-human nature, modern man into an indifferent one." The former conception, though "hostile" and "demonic," is still in a way "anthropomorphic." Thus "only the latter case represents the absolute vacuum, the really bottomless pit." Whereas the gnostic view of reality imparts at least a "negative direction," a "negative transcendence," to humanity, "modern science" gives "no direction at all." Jonas concludes that "this makes modern nihilism infinitely more radical and more desperate than gnostic nihilism ever could be." The predicament of modern humanity is "a truly unprecedented situation" (338–39).

Gnosticism is practically more self-consistent than modern nihilism because it is less radical or thoroughgoing in its rejection of this world; what is rejected remains commensurable with the soul in at least a negative way; ancient gnosticism thus retains what one might call a negative natural theology or teleology. The modern doctrine of freedom rejects this negative teleology no less than the positive teleology of the classical or "classical and Christian" tradition; the only meaning accessible to humanity is thus that which we make for ourselves—a meaning only tangible in the activity of destroying "natural" meanings. Thus ancient gnosticism may have more in common with the "classical Christian tradition" than with the modern age Voegelin describes as gnostic. It is indeed a wonder if not a miracle that this "unsupported hope" (Strauss) of absolute freedom lasted as long as it did, or that the nihilism of modernity became known by that name only in the twentieth century.

Voegelin fails fully to address the challenge of legitimate order in the modern age because he fails to understand modernity on its own terms and thus fails to see clearly what an alternative to modernity would consist in. Voegelin finds hope in the fact that "the American and English democracies which most solidly in their institutions represent the truth of the soul are, at the same time, existentially the strongest powers," and he summons us to repress "Gnostic corruption" and to restore "the forces of civilization." But Voegelin's treatment of the problem of modernity names but does not articulate or represent the forces of civilization. It is at once too theological and too scientific and therefore risks radically distinguishing and thus practically fusing the truth of the soul and existential power. Voegelin's work suggests that unless we understand the unity of modern idealism and modern realism, we risk experiencing this unity.

Leo Strauss, on the other hand, takes us further into the self-understanding of modernity and indeed often seems to proceed as if this self-understanding were an adequate basis of civilization. But once we see that modernity approaches practical self-destruction as it approaches theoretical consistency, or that the theoretically most consistent or self-aware version of modernity is also in a sense the blindest and the least apt to supply a foundation for morality and politics, then clearly the time for disparaging the halfway houses or carriers of modernity has passed. Strauss wrote in "Jerusalem and Athens," "We wonder whether the two ingredients of modern culture, of the modern synthesis, are not more solid than that synthesis" (23). The two ingredients are reason and revelation, and Strauss here seems to accept Herman Cohen's view that the modern faith in science represents their synthesis. However, he is "less certain than Cohen that the synthesis is superior to its ingredients"; either true philosophy or unmitigated piety is superior to the attempt to combine them. Perhaps Strauss's unenthusiastic defense of early modern rationalism indicates that a partial or unconscious attempt to synthesize faith and reason—an attempt that considers itself rational—is superior to a full attempt. But if this halfway house of modern rationalism is worth defending, then the same might be said for the progressive Christianity, the modernizing piety that has "made its peace with the world," that Strauss condemns. The theoretical defect in each of these carriers may be a sign of a practical virtue, of a vestige of one or the other of the two fully self-consistent ingredients of Western civilization; the residue of reason in rationalism and the survival of piety in progressive Christianity may prevent each from knowing the other as an aspect of itself—may forestall, that is to say, the self-consuming self-consciousness of modernity. Thus the tension between these two imperfect syntheses of faith and reason might provide a firmer foundation for modern civilization than either of these halfway houses taken singly.

The opposition between these two forms of modernity, an opposition that still possesses some vigor, at least in the United States, might preserve a space in which those acquainted with the higher tension can assert themselves. Thus Tocqueville praises the "marvelous combination" in America of *the spirit of religion and the spirit of freedom*" (47), but he loves neither spirit as he does the opportunity for "man's true greatness" that this combination allows. The unequal asserts itself in the space created by the tension between material and spiritual equality.

Whether such an assertion of greatness is just—that is, whether this inequality is of such a nature as to allow or comprehend the participation of the equal—would seem to depend on whether the superiority of the ultimate tension Strauss refers to, the tension between reason and revelation, is itself grounded in a higher good or God. For the greatest men to be truly just, and for a regime to bear the stamp of their greatness as well as their power, it must be possible for human beings to take their bearings from God's goodness as well as from his creativity.

Notes

Introduction

1. Benjamin Constant, "The Progressive Development of Religious Ideas," quoted in Arieli, p. 216.

2. See Butterfield, pp. 40–47.

3. For an account of the historiography of the Reformation, see Bainton, Hillerbrand, and especially Grimm (1964).

4. One might argue that Allen aims to give us not *reasons* but *causes* for the emergence of modern politics, that we must look not to ideas but to material conditions for an explanation of modernity. This more materialistic approach would seem right if, as Allen believes, it is generally true that a man's "activities determine his theory . . . The theory is an after thought, a by-product, an apology, even a pretext" (515). Elsewhere, however, Allen indicates that "it is perhaps its assumptions that most profoundly distinguish the thought of one age from that of another" (xvii). It appears that, if "activities determine . . . theory," then activities themselves are determined by assumptions, assumptions that can shape the activity and theory of entire ages, however "radically changing" the circumstances at another level. But if the most fundamental circumstances are assumptions, then it remains to account for changes in assumptions or for the replacement of one set of assumptions by another.

5. Here Skinner quotes from Calvin's *Three Sermons on the Story of Melchezidek.*

6. Note, however, that the radically populist formulae of Marsiglio have "to be applied in the case of a *regnum* as well as a *civitas*" (I.65) to be considered truly modern. And once we consider that, according to Skinner, modern politics is essentially the politics of "omnipotent yet impersonal" powers we call "states" (II.358, I.9–10), it appears that the application of Marsiglio's populism to larger bodies is a step of considerable importance. But Skinner never explains how populism and statism were

fused to produce the modern theory. Indeed, it is only in the liberalism of John Locke that the omnipotent, impersonal state is stripped of its absolutist implications and made fully compatible with the doctrine of popular sovereignty (II.347). Only with Locke, it appears, is the sixteenth-century "confusion" regarding the "relationship between the powers of the State and those of the ruler" dissipated; only with him does it become clear "what it might mean to be the citizen of a State as well as the subject of a prince" (II.358). The theory of modern politics is "founded" in the sixteenth century—but not until the seventeenth are the foundations clear.

7. Skinner's criticism of the argument of another defender of the contribution of Calvinism, Hans Baron, seems also to miss the mark. (See Baron, "Calvinist Republicanism and Its Historical Roots.") Baron concedes that as early as the fourteenth century, scholastic political theory had articulated democratic views that "foreshadow conceptions dominating the eighteenth century." But he thinks these ideas were practically ineffective in the absolutist sixteenth century; the real source of resistance to absolutism lay in the fusion (in Butzer's Strassbourg) of humanism with Calvinism, a fusion that seems to have been grounded in a common recourse to a "philosophy of history" (33; see also 36).

Baron concedes that the humanist-Calvinist view is not "identical with the democratic modern conceptions of the sovereignty of the people" (40n. 23), conceptions already foreshadowed in scholastic doctrines. But he also points to "the historic impulse which was to radiate from Calvinism to the political thought of modern times."

Skinner might well ask Baron to explain just what it is that Calvinist republicanism and modern theories have in common and wherein the modern differs from the scholastic teaching. Baron offers this hint: "In the seventeenth and eighteenth centuries Calvinist countries were best prepared to accept and develop the principle of natural law. But by that time, natural law was no longer simply that of the middle ages. It had absorbed the vigorous anti-monarchic spirit of political Calvinism" (41–42). Since the doctrinal basis of this "spirit" was a certain understanding of providence, it seems that the vigor of the new natural law sprang from its power to combine the doctrine of popular sovereignty with a sense of the sovereignty of God in History.

8. Cf. Walzer, 308: "Now it is probably not true that Calvinism induced anxiety; more likely its effect was to confirm and explain in theological terms perceptions men already had of the dangers of the world and the self." For Walzer, the "theological" explanation is apparently not to be taken seriously on its own terms; the real meaning of these "perceptions" is to be sought in the fact that Calvinists lived in "an age of social transformation" (310). This transformation, Walzer explains, became necessary after "some point in the later Middle Ages, [when] the complex institutional structure of European traditionalism began to weaken and

erode . . . [and] its philosophical rationalizations were called into question" (311).

But if, let us suppose, the philosophy and theology of the Middle Ages represent not mere rationalizations of a certain traditionalism but the very self-understanding of the age, a self-understanding underlying political and social institutions, then the weakness of political structures would be inseparable from the failure of a philosophy and a theology. In this case it would be wrong to explain Calvinist theology as a response to nontheological anxiety. It would be nearer the truth, indeed, to say that Calvinism gave vigorous expression to a distinctive feature of the late-medieval understanding of order (the radical transcendence of God with respect to human reason) that was proving impossible to live with; it also transformed this feature in showing how one could live by it. Or, more concretely: human activity was becoming meaningless—Calvin showed that divine activity in human beings was all the more possible.

9. Walzer's basic confusion stems from his hesitation between two approaches. On one hand, he seems to argue that modernity becomes more intelligible in the light of Calvinism. On the other, he attempts to explain Calvinism in distinctly modern terms as an ideology, an effort to "cope" with the anxieties of a social transformation. Walzer is not sure whether modernity is a kind of Calvinism forgetful of its basis or whether Calvinism is just another form of self-interest that has not learned to be frank. In the last analysis, the point of view of *Revolution of the Saints* seems to be that Calvinists and liberals each possessed half the self-awareness that is now possible: Calvinists, unlike Locke, "knew about human sinfulness," but only because they understood themselves to be fallen from the grace of "God." Liberals were frank about being motivated by self-interest, but they were ignorant of sin. The true heroes of Walzer's story are those later revolutionaries who "knew about sin" without being deluded by religion, who could carry on the warfare against human nature without the help of "God." Thus, although when Walzer began his research he considered Puritanism "strange and disturbing," he later found striking similarities between Puritans and later "agents of social and political reconstruction" (vii). It is because of his obvious sympathy with these later "radicals" that Walzer is able to forgive the Puritans for believing in God and to justify them before the bar of modern scholarship. "My only object," he writes in his preface, "is to make Puritan radicalism . . . humanly comprehensible" (ix). But one must ask whether it is not the assumption that a doctrine's power to "activate adherents" is something distinct from its account of God or of the world that is most "strange" and perhaps even "disturbing."

10. By not taking Calvinist antitheology seriously enough, Walzer may owe more to Calvin than he allows himself to discover—namely, the assumption that history is more to be trusted than theory. Walzer recog-

nizes that "a destroyer of an old order" will be the "builder of a repressive system"; but he is confident that this destruction deserves the name of "reconstruction"; that the destroyer is a man of "great works"; and that after a period of endurance the repressive system will be "escaped" if not "transcended."

Thus, although he has described radical activists as a "band of the chosen [that] confronts the existing world as if in war" (317), whose aim is to "universalize sainthood . . . without any regard for established forms" (318), he considers the "equation of radicalism and totalitarianism" false and defers any "critique of the increasingly total forms [radical politics] has taken in our own time" (viii). Walzer never asks whether Calvin might have been a "cause" of modernity rather than its "agent" because he never considers the possibility of choosing against modernity.

11. Walzer does not deny that Calvinist theory along with Calvinist habits retained some importance in modern societies. He grants that certain "elements in Calvinist theory and practice [were] later incorporated into the modern world" (300), that "particular elements of the Puritan system were transformed to fit the new routine" (316). But he never explains what was essentially *new* about the new routine and thus neglects to ask how it was that Calvinism was an "ideology of transition" which made possible a new kind of transition—modern revolution.

12. Walzer goes on, however, to add that modernity "represents a routinization of . . . frenetic mobility" (311). But surely this is quite different from a return to stability. Indeed, in comparison with the traditional view of politics, the modern conception of order appears as the routinization of revolution, as the attempt to grasp motion as the principle of order. Surely one fails to understand the meaning of this attempt by classifying it among other "routines."

13. Thus Skinner devotes no space to Calvinist theology, and although he does include a chapter on "the principles of Lutheranism," even there he does his best to make Luther a Catholic.

14. Whereas Skinner finds the Huguenot defense of a secular right to resist clearly more modern than the Puritan belief in a duty to resist (II.239–240), Walzer finds the Puritans more modern or more nearly modern than the Huguenots because the Puritan idea of eternal warfare broke more radically with the traditional view than did the Huguenot understanding of constitutional history as secular revelation (77, 96). This basic difference between Skinner's and Walzer's interpretations also appears in their estimation of the two strains within the Huguenot argument. For Skinner the modern element in the Huguenot argument is the "secularized thesis about the natural rights and original sovereignty of the people" (II.338). For Walzer, all such arguments are "supplementary" to the distinctively Calvinist conception of resistance as the "disciplined acting out of constitutional and moral obligations" (87–88).

15. Aristotle of course also argues the self-sufficiency of the polis. What this apparent contradiction means is not our subject; my point is simply that Skinner seems completely unaware of it. He is also unaware that the Aristotelian argument for the self-sufficiency of the polis implies more than independence—it implies rule. Aristotelian political science is not, as Skinner thinks, a "distinct branch of moral philosophy" or of any other discipline; it claims rather to be the architectonic science (*Nichomachean Ethics* I.2).

16. Skinner's non-Aristotelian estimate of this world clearly has affinities with the Christian view that results from a radical disjunction between the natural and supernatural realms.

17. See I.340, where Skinner mistakenly calls the idea of a natural human condition which is social but not political an "Aristotelian" account. Cf. I.239 on Locke.

18. Curiously, this promised clarity was never achieved, according to Skinner himself, in the period he studies (II.352–358). The full vision of modernity came later. But Skinner's scanty suggestions as to the form this clarity took once medieval confusion was finally vanquished seem to indicate that the human will rids itself of the authority of nature only to embrace the absolute power of the abstract state. Whereas the classical regime, however controversial, was the product of human choice, the state is an "omnipotent yet impersonal power" (II.358), a "locus of power distinct from either the ruler of the body of the people" (II.355), a concept conceived by no one and only understood in the sense that it is used. How humble the freedom subject to such omnipotence. How marvelous the concept immaculately conceived. How steadfast the will that, to know itself, confesses such mystery.

19. There is reason to worry, however, that "change," or human creation itself, can become at least as impersonal, omnipotent, and alien a force over the will as the modern state. Walzer's modern revolutionaries are radically free from tradition, but only through radical obedience to some abstract "historical process."

20. François Wendel, in *Calvin: The Origins and Development of his Religious Thought*, offers this assessment of the importance of the *Institutes* in Calvin's work: "Not only do the *Institutes* occupy the central place in Calvin's literary production, so abundant in other directions; this is also a work in which, during his whole career as a reformer, he methodically set down all the problems that were presented to his reflection, or that a deepening of his own thought led him to examine more closely. Whatever interest and value may attach to his other theological writings, the *Institutes* are the faithful summary of the ideas he expounded in them. Moreover, the *Institutes*—at least in their final form—purport to give a complete account of Christian teaching. They therefore present a synthesis of Calvinist thought, and one that is sufficient in itself" (111).

1   The Separation and Union of Religion and Politics

1. Both quotations are from the preface to the French edition of 1560, "Subject Matter of the Present Work," 7, 8.

2. This brief discussion of Augustine is of course a gross simplification of his complex and possibly equivocal view of the status of government. Note, in this connection, that Thomas Aquinas's interpretation of this passage from Augustine differs from mine: *Summa Theologiae* I–II.96.4.

3. "If scripture did not teach that [the duty of magistrates] extends to both Tables of the Law, we could learn this from secular writers: for no one has discussed the office of magistrates, the making of laws, and public welfare, without beginning at religion and divine worship. And thus, all have confessed that no government can be happily established unless piety is the first concern; and that those laws are preposterous which neglect God's right and provide only for men. Since, therefore, among all philosophers religion takes first place, and since this fact has always been observed by universal consent of all nations, let Christian princes and magistrates be ashamed of their negligence if they do not apply themselves to this concern" (IV.xx.9; 1495).

4. Similarly, Walzer observes that in apparent contradiction to his defense of "the most brutal repression, Calvin . . . sought to establish . . . a qualitatively different tranquility." He notes, "Calvinism brought conscience and coercion together—in much the same way as they were later brought together in Rousseau's General Will. . . . As with the later French writer, Calvin was acutely aware of the vast increase in social control that would result if human beings could be made to will that control themselves and to consent to it in their hearts" (47).

However, Walzer does not adequately investigate how it is possible to regard this consenting consciousness of coercion not only as "qualitatively different" from "the most brutal repression" but as positively manifesting the goodness or glory of God himself. And thus he cannot explain why, in Calvin's writings, despite this "qualitative difference" between the political and the spiritual, "the defense of secular repression and the assertion of the 'claims of God' are so closely woven together that it is extremely difficult to disentangle them" (48).

It may be useful here to summarize the arguments of two eminent French interpreters of Calvin, Emil Doumergue and Marc-Edouard Chenevière. A comparison of these two authors vividly illustrates the difficulty of defining Calvin's position on the status of politics. Emil Doumergue's interpretation of Calvin's politics (*Jean Calvin*, V) reveals but again fails to address the puzzle noted above. For Calvin, as for the Middle Ages, earthly justice is a remedy for sin. But Doumergue argues that Calvin departs from the medieval view in teaching that the remedy is one provided by God himself: "The state is a divine institution . . . the occasion of the state was human wickedness; the cause of the state was divine goodness" (V.400). Doumergue believes that this teaching underlies the modern idea of the state. "Here we have the modern idea of the state established, affirmed, and specified against all attacks . . . the state has a positive and moral content; it has a substantial, immanent morality. The state has a vocation" (V.402).

From this it follows that a state, to be true to its vocation, must be a "Christian state." But these points raise the question how it is possible for the goodness of a revealed God to endow a state that serves as a remedy for sin with a "positive" and "immanent" morality. How can the state be both divine and natural?

Marc-Edouard Chenevière, in *La pensée politique de Calvin*, argues that for Calvin "there is no Christian state." He explains thus:

> The goal of laws is not . . . to make us Christians . . . but simply to allow mankind to subsist . . . they are thus a part of the apparatus of constraint created by God in order to contain the sin of men. (105)

> [The political order] is designed to make of the world which human sin has led into chaos, not an ideal world, not even the beginning of an ideal world, but a provisional order [*ordre d'attente*] which simply permits man to live on this earth before acceding to the Kingdom of God. (111)

Chenevière's view thus appears to be directly opposed to Doumergue's argument that Calvin's state has a positive, immanent moral content. Furthermore, Chenevière denies emphatically that Calvin was a founder of modernity (10). Paradoxically, the author who makes Calvin the proponent of the Christian state also makes him a founder of modernity, and the author who reads Calvin as denying the possibility of a Christian state also denies that Calvin has any connection with the modern secular state.

However, on closer inspection the differences between Doumergue's and Chenevière's interpretations are not so clear. Chenevière's Calvin agrees with Doumergue's that although the state was provided in response to the needs of fallen human nature, it is founded not on those needs but on the will of God (127). And he agrees that Calvin "insists much on the great value of the state" (141). "In opposition to Luther, who assigned to the state the rather negative role of a brake barely tolerated by God, Calvin conceives of the state not only as a brake, but also as a positive organ created by God in order to organize the harmonious life of human societies" (143). Still, Chenevière denies that the state is master of a distinct temporal domain; he thus seems directly to oppose Doumergue's view that the political order has a substantial, immanent morality: "The ends pursued by the state are as much religious as civil" (270). But when one notices that, for Doumergue, a "substantial, immanent morality" is at the same time a "vocation," then it is not so easy to differentiate his interpretation from Chenevière's. Both argue, it seems, that the state is divine; and both say that it serves natural ends—or, rather, natural needs.

The difference between Doumergue and Chenevière on the meaning of modernity is somewhat clearer. Doumergue believes that modern democracies were founded on the doctrine of the sovereignty of God understood as the cause of the (conditional) sovereignty of the people (V.388, 507–8). He understands this modern view of political authority to be opposed both to the view characteristic of the early middle ages that "the state is a work of the devil and of sin," a work which receives its only legitimacy from the church; and to the view, represented by the work of Thomas Aquinas and his followers, that the state is founded immediately on human nature or human will and only remotely on the will of God (V.456).

Chenevière also understands Calvin's thought as fundamentally opposed to that of Aquinas. This opposition appears most clearly in the fact that whereas Aquinas believed reason was competent to know man's temporal end and therefore to serve man as a moral guide (41), Calvin believed that reason was "simply an organ of experiential knowledge of the external world rather than an organ expressing a moral rule" (46). But Chenevière, somewhat like Skinner, understands modernity as a continuous liberation of reason extending from the middle ages through the enlightenment: "The notion of reason undergoes a perfectly logical development in passing from the hands of Saint Thomas to those of Grotius or of Locke" (45). According to Chenevière, Calvin was liberated by his theology from this logical historical development (49); his teaching thus stands "outside time" (13). Therefore it is obvious to him that "there is no spiritual kinship between the Reformation and modern democracy" (9). Since Chenevière assumes a dichotomy between knowledge of nature and knowledge of ends, he does not see that a denial of the possibility of the natural knowledge of ends might be understood as the basis of the liberation of reason.

5. Charles Mercier ("L'esprit de Calvin et la démocratie"), like Wolin, emphasizes similarities between Calvin's political thought and the ideas of Aristotle and Aquinas. Mercier believes that Calvin's political thought is totally alien to that of modern democracies (40). He points out that for Calvin, the civil order as much as the religious order is necessary for man and willed by God. Mercier quotes a passage from the eleventh chapter of the 1539 *Institutes* that to him indicates Calvin's fundamental agreement with Aristotle: "Homo animal est natura sociale." Submission to political authority is necessary for man "to realize the ends which oblige him to live in society" (35). But Mercier also observes that Calvin understands the state as a remedy for the corruption of human nature, a universal corruption that makes perfection impossible and that makes politics as necessary as bread, water, sun, and air. And he fails to notice the distinc-

tion between what is necessary to human life and what contributes to the realization of the ends of human nature; his quotations in fact show no more than that man is a social animal in the sense that man cannot survive without the help of other men: "les hommes . . . ne peuvent vivre sans s'aider les uns les autres." Mercier, like Wolin, fails to show that Calvin agreed with Aristotle and Aquinas that political society aims at the perfection of man's nature or soul.

2 Providence, Christian Freedom, and Spiritual Government

1. Benjamin Milner thus refers to Calvin's doctrine of creation as that of a *Creatio Continua* (17).
2. Calvin might have cited Aquinas as an example here. See *Summa Contra Gentiles* III.63.
3. Cf. Strauss, *Natural Right and History*, 317: "The theological tradition asserted . . . that man cannot take his bearings by God's providence but only by God's law, which simply forbids man to do evil."

3 Government and the People

1. Chenevière introduces part 4 of his book on Calvin's teaching, entitled "The Forms of Government," with a chapter called "Calvin's Indifference Concerning This Problem" (181; cf. Skinner, II.193). And Harro Höpfl, in his recent *Christian Polity of John Calvin* (1982), refers to this section of the first edition of the *Institutes* when he remarks that "Calvin's brief survey of the topic [is] notable chiefly for its derivativeness and superficiality" (51).
2. Chenevière insists that for Calvin, since God is the author of all forms of government, "all forms of government are . . . equally pleasing in the eyes of God" (184). But then he has to admit that Calvin indeed seems to see aristocracy as the ideal political regime (189). However, Chenevière overcomes the opposition between these two propositions by noting that Calvin's aristocratic preference is based not on "abstract reasoning" but on "experience," on "empirical reason" which takes account of "history" and "circumstances" (181). He observes that Calvin does not prefer aristocracy "of itself" but because experience has shown that kings rarely exercise self-restraint (180, 189). Note, however, that Calvin first argues the excellence of aristocracy when considering the three forms of government "in themselves" (IV.xx.8; 1493). Chenevière seems to assume that the tension between the exhaustive providence of God and the prudent deliberation of men is resolved by making this prudence dependent on history and circumstances, that it is only "abstract reason" which tends to be at odds with the will of God as manifest in history.
By "abstract reason" Chenevière clearly understands mainly the ra-

tionalism of modern democracy. He insists that Calvin is "absolutely remote from the dogmas of modern democracy . . . he believes neither in popular sovereignty nor in individual rights" (190). And Chenevière denies that Calvin was in any way opposed to the *principle* of monarchy. He believes that all texts cited by other interpreters to show Calvin's opposition to monarchy in fact demonstrate that he attacked only the *abuses* of this form of government, not the form itself (226–27). In particular, Chenevière suggests that Calvin's frequent antimonarchic bent may be attributed to his individual experience with the French monarchy. If the French government had not opposed the Reformation, then Calvin would not have opposed kingship (228).

3. Doumergue quotes at length first from the various editions of the *Institutes* (1536–59) and then from various commentaries and sermons, dating from 1551 to 1563, to demonstrate that Calvin authored "an extremely sharp criticism of kings." From the first (1536) edition of the *Institutes*, Doumergue quotes Calvin's remarks (retained in the 1559 editions; see IV.xx.7; 1492) that, of all forms of government, kingship is "the least pleasant to men . . . it has always been displeasing to all men of excellent and noble spirit" (V.432). From the edition of 1543 (retained in 1559), Doumergue quotes Calvin's preference for aristocracy. The 1559 edition added the argument (IV.xx.8) that kings rarely control themselves and that "men's fault or failing causes it to be safer and more bearable for a number to exercise government" (8; 1493; Doumergue, V.434). Marshalling four folio pages of excerpts from commentaries and sermons, Doumergue amply illustrates Calvin's antipathy for kings:

> *Commentary on Isaiah* (1551): The more powerful kings are, the more they oppress their people (V.436).

> *Commentary on the Psalms* (1557): We know and we see by experience, that all kings are drunk with their own greatness (V.436–37).

> *Sermons on Deuteronomy* (1562): Princes almost think they are not mortal creatures, having risen so high, they think they are demi-gods. They will no longer be subject to reason or rectitude (V.437).

> *Homilies on the First Book of Samuel* (1561): Princes tend to violate every right, all equity, under the pretext of power and authority (V.439).

> *Commentary on Jeremiah* (1563): They want to be exempted from all law, freed from every yoke . . . they think the whole world was created for them (V.439).

Doumergue summarizes these and many other quotations: "Calvin, from the beginning to the end, before 1560 as after, showed himself to be as

little favorable as possible to the monarchical form of government"
(V.439).

Chenevière, as we have seen, dismisses Doumergue evidence as beside
the point, since it shows Calvin's hostility toward the abuses of monarchy, not toward monarchy itself. But here I must agree with John T.
McNeill (1949) that it is misleading to insist on this distinction in the
way Chenevière does. "It is fair to say that a writer who habitually and
emotionally harps on the abuses of an institution while rarely calling
attention to its excellences, cannot be regarded as either a partisan of the
institution or quite neutral toward it. One who persistently represents
kings as abusers of their power, even though for scriptural reasons he
opposes acts of rebellion against them, can hardly be regarded as indifferent to kingship itself" (161).

There is, then, no denying a strong antimonarchic element in Calvin's
teaching (although it is also true that Calvin never ceased to insist that
kings, even wicked kings, are authorities ordained of God).

4. Chenevière cites the following text (not from the *Institutes*): "And
even though they [princes] be enemies of God and his Church, where civil
order [*la police*] is concerned, we must grant them honor, and repute; we
must subject ourselves to them, in order to observe their laws and edicts"
(354).

5. Doumergue, on the other hand, will not concede that Calvin contradicts himself. Specifically, he does not concede that certain passages
suggest a *private* right of active resistance to authority (V.500). And it is
true that, even in the strongest passage quoted by Skinner, Calvin says "it
is necessary that they [impious princes] should be laid low"—but he does
not say that anyone who can has the right to lay them low. Doumergue
will admit no more than that "between the *Institutes* and the *Sermons*, a
considerable difference of tone was required by the nature of things"
(V.433). I would say that a difference in tone can become so great as to
amount to a difference in substance. Doumergue himself shows that
Calvin exalts political authorities but then says we should "spit in their
face" (V.498). And this is addressed to all believers, public and private.

By the "nature of things," I believe Doumergue refers mainly to the fact
that the *Institutes* was Calvin's most public and therefore most cautious
statement.

6. Here I agree to a point with J. W. Allen, who notes that "the attitude
of Protestants towards civil authority was determined by their particular
circumstances" (9; see also Höpfl, 210–17). This is not to say that Protestantism itself had no significance for political thought (cf. Sabine, 345,
358, 362, 367), but only that the fundamental idea or spirit that motivated
the reformer revealed different aspects according to different circumstances.

7. Neither Chenevière (300–331) nor Doumergue (V.499–500) attempts to link the "lawful calling" of the providential avenger with that

of the inferior magistrates. In fact, both of these authors are at pains to minimize the significance of this section—Chenevière, because he emphasizes the duty of passive resistance, and Doumergue, because he insists on limiting active resistance to inferior magistrates.

Chenevière notes that "God . . . may raise up men to save or deliver peoples who live under tyranny; but the people themselves must wait and suffer, if necessary, without revolting" (331). This is true in that the people who must wait, the "private persons," are simply the people who have not been called. And God calls whom he will.

Doumergue, who finds in the constitutional theory of inferior magistrates the only mean between absolutism and anarchy (V.503), can only note that the theory of providential deliverance was not Calvin's invention and that subsequent Calvinists, recognizing its dangerous potential, hastened to abandon it (V.500). Like Chenevière, he also quotes Calvin's own attempts to limit the application of this theory; but these only give the reader a stronger sense of the radical potential of the theory itself. "If God gives some special privileges to his own and drives them to such and such a work, nevertheless, he does not at all want us to make of this a rule or example" (V.494; cf. Chenevière, 331).

4 Law and Ethics

1. See also II.viii.7; 374, and see Troeltsch, II.614, 898n. 351.

2. See *Comm. I Corinthians* 13:13, 432–33. This interpretation of Calvin's thought lends support to Weber's interpretation of Calvinism: "Brotherly love, since it may only be practiced for the glory of God and not in the service of the flesh, is expressed in the first place in the fulfillment of the daily task given by the *lex naturae*; and in the process this fulfillment assumes a peculiarly objective and impersonal character, that of service in the interest of the rational organization of our social environment . . . the source of the utilitarian character of Calvinist ethics lies here" (108–9).

David Little's account (57–60) of the utilitarian character of Calvin's order is very useful. His fundamental agreement with Calvin is evident, however, in his contrasting the utilitarian or "functionalist" view not with another idea of what the good is but with "a preferential or hierarchical view, which organizes the economy *in favor of special groups*" (60; my emphasis).

3. Calvin amplifies this point in a sort of poem:

We are not our own: let not our reason nor our will, therefore, sway our plans and deeds.

We are not our own: let us therefore not set it as our goal to seek what is expedient for us according to the flesh.

We are not our own: in so far as we can, let us therefore forget ourselves and all that is ours.

Conversely, we are God's: let us therefore live for him and die for him.

We are God's: let all the parts of our life accordingly strive toward him as our only lawful goal . . . (III.vii.1; 690)

5 Reason, Rationalism, and History

1. August Lang, *Die Reformation und das Naturrecht*, 20; *Göttingesche Gelehrte Anzeigen* (1912), 272. Quoted in Doumergue, V.465.

2. Chenevière grants that the Decalogue represents not a fully detailed practical guide but only a general scheme (86). He believes, however, that the Bible as a whole is by itself sufficient to fill any gaps in this scheme. He therefore concludes (in agreement with Lang) that "Calvin proclaims that the Decalogue, interpreted by means of the Holy Scriptures, constitutes for the Christian the unique standard of political morality" (88).

3. The meaning of this "in a sense" will become clearer below.

4. See Little, 61.

5. "Furthermore, we see, when tyrants rule, that there are great corruptions; nevertheless, this is more tolerable than if there were no order. Let us place on a scale one tyrant or many who commit every cruelty . . . on the other side, let us place a people who have no head, who have neither magistrate nor authority among them, but are all equal: it is certain that there will be a greater and more horrible confusion when there is no preeminence than there would be under the most exorbitant tyranny in the world. Why? Because even if there are incarnate devils occupying the seat of justice, no matter how much they strive to do harm, still God does not permit them to go so far as to overthrow all justice: there must remain a few traces of good" (Chenevière, 315–16).

6. Cf. Höpfl, 181: "Natural law was systematically being ground into insignificance between the upper millstone of divine law and the nether millstone of positive law."

7. For Hans Baron, see above, Introduction, n. 7.

8. David Little's excellent survey "The New Order of John Calvin" in *Religion, Order, and Law* points toward this conclusion but does not reach it. Little observes a tension between what he calls the "coercive element endemic to political order" and the "voluntaristic, free-willing characteristics of the Christian life" (56); he believes that such "contradictory elements will fall into place" when seen as springing from "the inner dynamics of Calvin's pattern of order" (79). He even notices that "Calvin believed the law and the political ruler must drive men toward

spontaneous, cooperative economic action" (75) and that "the use of earthly power to stimulate righteousness was, wherever feasible, a simple necessity" (77). However, because Little does not see the underlying dynamic unity of necessity and spontaneity in Calvin's thought—because he does not see that spontaneity has nothing to do with "free will," he fails finally to grasp these "contradictory elements" in one "inner dynamic." See below, chap. 8.

6   Justification and Sanctification

1. Quoted in Strohl, 85. Strohl emphasizes the importance of inward experience for Luther. "Regeneration is a fact of experience. Luther speaks continually of his religious experiences. . . . Only he who possesses faith, love, or hope knows what these terms mean. The reality of these conditions of the soul is beyond doubt. . . . Faith is an organ for the direct apprehension of the transcendent realities" (80). Althaus also insists upon the experiential quality of faith for Luther: "There is such a thing as experience wrought by faith itself. . . . True faith is . . . created by the Holy Spirit through the word. And faith knows this too; it "feels" this much about itself" (60). Because of Luther's emphasis on the inward experience of faith, he cannot affirm with Calvin the possibility of a perfect and ongoing certainty of salvation (Strohl, 82–83); he therefore insists much less than Calvin on the doctrine of predestination.

2. Cf. Troeltsch (1960), II.588–89; Weber, 112–15.

3. To be sure, Calvin's understanding of the two natures of Christ is perfectly orthodox in the sense of conforming to the affirmation of the Council of Chalcedon (A.D. 451). But understanding this does not prevent Francois Wendel from arguing that this christology "is a very important aspect of Calvin's theological thought, and perhaps what is most original in it" (219).

Indeed, there is nothing in my interpretation of Calvinism as constituting a radical intellectual innovation that necessarily contradicts the claim that Calvin offers nothing more than a purified and clarified statement of orthodox Christianity or of Holy Scripture itself. One may, in fact, view Calvin as following certain orthodox dogmas more faithfully or ruthlessly to their extreme conclusions than any of his predecessors.

7   The Soul and the Image of God

1. Elsewhere Calvin considers spirit as distinct from soul, the "life-giving spirit" from the "living soul" (I.xv.4; 189).

2. Cf. Torrance (1957), 26: the Soul has "no durability in itself"; 25: "if God was for one instant to withdraw his spirit we would drop into nothingness."

3. Cf. above, chap. 2 n. 1 and accompanying text.

8   The Center of Calvin's Antitheology

1. The quoted terms are from Hermann Bauke, *Die Probleme der Theologie Calvins*, quoted in Milner, 2–3. Milner's introduction contains a brief account of the emergence of these classic problems in Calvin scholarship.

2. Edward Dowey is wrong, therefore, to argue that "there is . . . no [observable or theologically formulable continuum] in Calvin's theology between the two orders of knowing and their parallel parts" (241).

Conclusion

1. Strauss (1961), restates, somewhat less tentatively, his critique of Weber's thesis regarding Calvinism, repeating verbatim many of the arguments from *Natural Right and History*.

2. It is generally preferable to regard as most authoritative those works an author intends for publication. However, Strauss's various published statements on the very fundamental problem of the relationship between Christianity and modernity are sufficiently perplexing that one must be grateful to find any clues one can in another source. My aim is not to use private statements to contradict public ones, but rather to illuminate and attempt to reconcile or make sense of apparent contradictions in the public arguments.

3. Cf. Strauss (1946, 328): "Generally speaking, medieval philosophy has in common with modern philosophy the fact that both are influenced, if in different ways, by the teaching of the Bible."

4. The reference to two fundamental alternatives, revealed religion and philosophy, seems to be central to Strauss's work. See especially "Jerusalem and Athens." However, compare on this point *Thoughts on Machiavelli*, 298–99, on "the essential defect of classical political philosophy."

5. *Natural Right and History*, pp. 174–75. Strauss is here discussing Hobbes in particular, but he observes that "his philosophy as a whole may be said to be the classic example of the typically modern combination of political idealism with a materialistic and atheistic view of the whole."

6. It is not clear how this reduction of history to inarticulate experience accords with Voegelin's argument that "articulation is the condition of representation" (41) and his keen analysis of the connection between political and metaphysical "representation" (58–59). Voegelin seems to agree with Aristotle that it is as speaking beings that men constitute political society; articulate representation would thus be the most important and most knowable reality of history. But Voegelin immediately adopts another viewpoint: "Behind the symbol articulation there hides nothing less than the historical process" (41). The bond between political representation and truth about the whole seems only to hold for certain

ages of humankind, namely, the cosmological and, in a perverse sense, the modern gnostic age. Apparently the Christian differentiation of "insight" from world-articulation makes possible the modern historian's differentiation of process from representation. History, according to Voegelin, has no *eidos* (120); it does not need one, because it is a "substance" (125).

7. Strauss, "Restatement on Xenophon's Hiero," in *On Tyranny*, 189–226.

8. Voegelin (1949), 241–44.

9. Strauss introduces Voegelin as one of the leading contemporary historians of political thought. In the same essay, he presents Alexander Kojève as "a philosopher and not an intellectual." Strauss recommends to Voegelin a "change of orientation" or "second education." See Strauss's account of his own "self-education" with regard to Aristotle's concept of magnanimity ("Correspondence," 111).

10. However, in *Meaning in History*, Löwith writes: "It is not the historical world but rather human nature which persists through all historical changes." It is not clear whether he believes human nature can be known through the layers of historical consciousness.

11. Cf. *Natural Right and History*, "Preface to the 7th Impression (1971)": "Nothing that I have learned has shaken my inclination to prefer 'natural right,' especially in its classic form, to the reigning relativism, positivist or historicist." Note that Strauss prefers especially, and not only, classic natural right.

12. Blumenberg, in this context, writes that he regards "the secularization theorem as a special case of historical substantialism," that is, of the unsupported belief in constants in history. But if a constant could be known, then the theological reference to absolute transcendence would not be necessary. Like his antagonists, Blumenberg confuses philosophy and theology.

13. See, for example, the remarks by Stephen Holmes and Karsten Harries on the dust jacket of *The Legitimacy of the Modern Age*.

14. *Discourse on the Method*, pt. 4. For Hobbes, consider *Leviathan*, "Introduction," I.5, and II.31, "Conclusion of the Second Part"; see also *Concerning Body*, "Author's Epistle to the Reader."

15. I agree with Strauss that Weber was wrong to sever "the connection . . . between the emergence of the capitalist spirit and the emergence of the science of economics." However, in his "Comment" on Hudson's "The Weber Thesis Reexamined," Strauss goes so far as to argue that "the science of economics is the authentic interpretation of 'the Calvinist Spirit.'" But Strauss himself gives us every reason for resisting the identification of that science with that spirit, which would be analogous to regarding modern science as an adequate articulation, all by itself, of the spirit of modern civilization. In fact, in this very "Comment," Strauss refers approvingly to Nietzsche's insight into the ascetic or non-natural quality of modern life, a quality that cannot be accounted for by the

science of economics or any modern science. Strauss does not mention that, for Nietzsche, this modern asceticism is clearly derivative of Christianity.

It seems to me that Strauss comes closer to the mark in locating the source of the capitalist spirit when he observes that "its sufficient condition is the attempt at a new understanding of social reality—an understanding which is 'realistic' in the sense that it conceives of the social order as based not on piety and virtue but on socially useful passions or vices" ("Comment," 102). What Strauss apparently fails to see, however, is that piety might divorce itself from virtue in the traditional sense and ally itself rather with the "socially useful passions." Such an alliance could provide a foundation at once for the asceticism and the realism of modern civilization, including modern capitalism.

16. When modern materialism becomes conscious of its own idealism (most notably in the thought of Hegel), then it will, like Calvin, tend to overlook its dependence on a residual natural or nonhistorical teleology, or else it will finally disappear into the formless creativity of the absurd.

17. This might illuminate Sheldon Wolin's opinion that the Reformers were more able ideologists and thus more modern than Machiavelli or Hobbes (194).

18. Voegelin, of course, shares this problem, not only with Calvin but with the whole Christian tradition. Let it suffice to note here that Augustine at once deplores the human pride expressed in the Platonic idea of the natural (however rare) perfection of the human soul and relies upon essentially Platonic notions to describe the order of the soul which is the end of political order (see *City of God* x.29, xix.13–14). Calvin certainly must be preferred to Augustine for consistency. This is a view that Strauss seems to share. Strauss, however, seems not to see that the religious pilgrim, so long as he lives in this world, must interpret this world along the lines either (speaking very broadly) of classical teleology or of modern historicism.

19. One might mark the obvious differences between Calvinism and Voegelinianism by pointing to the contrast between the fanatical certainty of the Puritan and Voegelin's view that "uncertainty is the very essence of Christianity" (122). Uncertainty, however, makes a peculiar kind of essence (as may be gathered from chapter 6, above), and Voegelin's case by no means refutes Calvin's view that perfect assurance is perfectly compatible with the most anxious doubt.

20. Descartes's theology plays a similar role in relation to his practical intention: by raising God far above the limits of purposes intelligible to human beings, Descartes frees human beings to undertake the "mastery and possession of nature" unencumbered.

Bibliography

Allen, J. W. *A History of Political Thought in the Sixteenth Century*. New York, 1928.

Althaus, Paul. *The Theology of Martin Luther*. Trans. Robert C. Schultz. Philadelphia, 1966.

Arieli, Yehoshua. *Individualism and Nationalism in American Ideology*. Cambridge, Mass., 1964.

Aristotle. *Nichomachean Ethics*. Trans. Ostwald. Indianapolis, Ind., 1962.

——. *Politics*. Trans. Lord. Chicago, 1984.

Augustine. *The City of God*. Trans. M. Dods, assisted by G. Wilson and J. T. Smith. In Whitney J. Oates, ed., *Basic Writings of St. Augustine*. Grand Rapids, Mich., 1980.

——. *Concerning the City of God against the Pagans*. Trans. H. Bettenson. New York, 1972.

Bainton, Roland H. "Interpretations of the Reformation." In Lewis Spitz, ed., *The Reformation: Basic Interpretations*. 2d ed. Lexington, Mass., 1972.

Baron, Hans. "Calvinist Republicanism and Its Historical Roots." *Church History* 7 (1939), 30–42.

Battenhouse, Roy W. "The Doctrine of Man in Calvin and in Renaissance Platonism." *Journal of the History of Ideas* 9 (October 1948), 447–71.

Blumenberg, Hans. *The Legitimacy of the Modern Age*. Trans. R. M. Wallace. Cambridge, Mass., 1983.

Bohatec, Joseph. *Bude und Calvin: Studien zur Gedankenwelt des Französischen Frühhumanismus*. Graz, 1950.

Butterfield, Herbert. *The Whig Interpretation of History*. New York, 1965.

Cadier, Jean. "Calvin et Saint Augustin." Pp. 1039–56 in *Austinus Magister*. Paris, 1954.

Calvin, John. *Commentaries*. 22 vols. Various translators. Grand Rapids, Mich., 1981.

——. *Institutes of the Christian Religion*. Ed. John T. McNeill, trans. Ford Lewis Battles. 2 vols. Library of Christian Classics. Philadelphia, 1960.

——. *Institutes of the Christian Religion*. Trans. John Allen. Philadelphia, 1930.

——. *Institution de la Religion chrestienne*. 5 vols. Ed. J. D. Benoit. Paris, 1957–1963.

——. *Theological Treatises*. Trans. J. K. S. Reid. Library of Christian Classics. Philadelphia, 1954.

Chenevière, Marc-Edouard. *La pensée politique de Calvin*. Paris, 1937.

Cicero. *De Re Publica and De Legibus*. Trans. C. W. Keyes. Loeb Classical Library. Cambridge, Mass., 1928.

Descartes. *Discourse on the Method*. In *The Philosophical Works of Descartes*, Vol. I. Cambridge, 1911.

Doumergue, Emil. *Jean Calvin: Les hommes et les choses de son temps*. 7 vols. Lausanne, 1899–1927.

Dowey, Edward A., Jr. *The Knowledge of God in Calvin's Theology*. New York, 1952.

Dunning, William Archibald. *A History of Political Theories from Luther to Montesquieu*. New York, 1913.

Eisenstadt, S. N., ed. *The Protestant Ethic and Modernization: A Comparative View*. New York, 1938.

Frischoff, Ephrahim. "The Protestant Ethic and the Spirit of Capitalism: The History of a Controversy." Pp. 67–86 in S. N. Eisendstadt, ed. *The Protestant Ethic and Modernization: A Comparative View*. New York, 1938.

Froehlich, Karlfried. *Gottesreich, Welt, und Kirche bei Calvin*. Munich, 1930.

Gilson, Etienne. *The Spirit of Medieval Philosophy*. Trans. A. H. C. Downs. New York, 1936.

Graham, W. Fred. *The Constructive Revolutionary, John Calvin and His Socio-Economic Impact*. Atlanta, 1971.

Grimm, Harold J. *The Reformation Era, 1500–1650*. 2d ed. New York, 1973.

——. *The Reformation in Recent Historical Thought*. New York, 1964.

Hegel, G. W. F. *The Philosophy of History*. Trans. J. Sibree. New York, 1956.

Hillerbrand, Hans J. "The History of Reformation History." In his *Men and Ideas in the Sixteenth Century*. Chicago, 1969.

Hobbes, Thomas. *Leviathan*. Harmondsworth, Middlesex, 1968.

Höpfl, Harro. *The Christian Polity of John Calvin*. New York, 1982.

Jonas, Hans. *The Gnostic Religion: The Message of the Alien God and the Beginnings of Christianity*. Boston, 1958.

Lagarde, Georges de. *Recherches sur l'esprit politique de la réforme.* Paris, 1926.

Little, David. *Religion, Order, and Law.* New York, 1969.

Locke, John. *Two Treatises of Government.* Rev. ed. Ed. Peter Laslett. Cambridge, 1963.

Löwith, Karl. *Meaning in History.* Chicago, 1949.

Luther, Martin, "The Freedom of a Christian." Pp. 42–85 in J. Dillenberger, ed., *Martin Luther: Selections from his Writings.* New York, 1961.

Luthy, Herbert. "Once Again: Calvinism and Capitalism." Pp. 87–108 in S. N. Eisenstadt, ed., *The Protestant Ethic and Modernization: A Comparative View.* New York, 1938.

McNeill, John T. "The Democratic Element in Calvin's Thought." *Church History* 18 (1949), 153–71.

——. *The History and Character of Calvinism.* London, 1954.

——. "Natural Law in the Teaching of the Reformers." *Church History* 26 (July 1946), 168–82.

——. "Thirty Years of Calvin Study." *Church History* 17 (1948), 207–40.

Mercier, Charles. "L'esprit de Calvin et la démocratie." *Revue d'Histoire Ecclesiastique* 30 (January 1934), 5–53.

Mesnard, Pierre. *L'essor de la philosophie politique au XVIe siècle.* Paris, 1951.

Milner, Benjamin Charles, Jr. *Calvin's Doctrine of the Church.* Leiden, 1970.

Niesel, Wilhelm. *The Theology of Calvin.* Trans. Harold Knight. London, 1956.

Ozment, Stephen. *The Age of Reform, 1250–1550.* New Haven, Conn., 1980.

Plato. *The Republic.* Trans. Alan Bloom. New York, 1968.

Sabine, George H. *A History of Political Theory.* New York, 1937.

Skinner, Quentin. *The Foundations of Modern Political Thought.* 2 vols. Cambridge, 1978.

Spitz, Lewis A., ed. *The Reformation: Basic Interpretations.* 2d ed. Lexington, Mass., 1972.

Strauss, Leo. "Jerusalem and Athens." *City College Papers,* no. 6 (1967).

——. "Comment on W. S. Hudson, 'The Weber Thesis Re-examined.'" *Church History* 30 (1961), 100–102.

——. *Natural Right and History.* Chicago, 1950.

——. "On a New Interpretation of Plato's Political Philosophy." *Social Research* 13 (1946), 326–67.

——. *On Tyranny.* Ithaca, N.Y., 1968.

——. *Thoughts on Machiavelli.* Chicago, 1958.

Strauss, Leo, and Karl Löwith. "Correspondence concerning Modernity." *Independent Journal of Philosophy* 4 (1983), 105–19.

Strohl, Henri. *L'épanouissement de la pensée religieuse de Luther de 1515 à 1520.* Strasbourg, 1921.

Tawney, R. H. *Religion and the Rise of Capitalism*. London, 1926.

Thomas Aquinas. *Summa Theologica*. In A. C. Pegis, ed., *Basic Writings of Saint Thomas Aquinas*. 2 vols. New York, 1945.

——. *Summa Theologica*. 2 vols. Trans. Fathers of English Dominican Province. Rev. Daniel J. Sullivan. Great Books of the Western World. Chicago, 1952.

Tocqueville, Alexis de. *Democracy in America*. Garden City, N.Y., 1969.

Torrance, T. F. *Calvin's Doctrine of Man*. Grand Rapids, Mich., 1957.

——. "Knowledge of God and Speech about Him according to John Calvin." Pp. 140–60 in *Regards contemporains sur Jean Calvin*. Paris, 1965.

——. *Les réformateurs et la fin des temps*. Trans. R. Brandt. Neuchatel, 1955.

Troeltsch, Ernst. *Protestantism and Progress: A Historical Study of the Relation of Protestantism to the Modern World*. Boston, 1958.

——. *The Social Teachings of the Christian Churches*. 2 vols. Trans. Olive Wyon. New York, 1960.

Voegelin, Eric. *The New Science of Politics*. Chicago, 1952.

——. "Review of Leo Strauss, *On Tyranny*." *Review of Politics* 11 (1949), 241–44.

Wallace, Ronald S. *Calvin's Doctrine of the Christian Life*. Edinburgh, 1959.

Walzer, Michael. *The Revolution of the Saints: A Study in the Origins of Radical Politics*. London, 1966.

Warfield, Benjamin Breckinridge. *Calvin and Augustine*. Philadelphia, 1956.

Weber, Max. *The Protestant Ethic and the Spirit of Capitalism*. Trans. Talcott Parsons. New York, 1958.

Wendel, François. *Calvin: The Origins and Development of His Religious Thought*. Trans. P. Mairet. London, 1963.

Wolin, Sheldon. "Calvin: The Political Education of Protestantism." Chap. 6 of *Politics and Vision: Continuity and Innovation in Western Political Thought*. London, 1969.

Index

absolute power, 159–60, 61
activism, 21, 88–89, 91–92, 94–95, 98–99, 109, 115, 118–19, 134–35, 163, 164, 166, 197–99; Walzer on, 10, 15, 17–18
Allen, J. W., 3, 4–7, 19, 32, 56–57, 205; methodology of, 195–96; and Skinner, 10, 15
Althaus, Paul, 129, 139
Anabaptists, 74
appetites, 43, 145–46
Aquinas, Thomas, 32, 33, 85, 89–91, 200, 202, 203
aristocracy, 65–68, 203–4
Aristotelianism, 16, 142, 166
Aristotle: and aristocracy, 67–68; and highest good, 109, 146–47; Mercier on, 202; Skinner on, 16–17, 19, 32–33, 118, 199; status of politics, 199; Strauss, 210; Voegelin on, 209. *See also* Aristotelianism
assurance. *See* certainty of salvation
Augustine, 200; on status of politics, 28, 29, 31–32; and Voegelin, 189, 211
authority: and resistance, 70–81; of history, 76–79

Baron, Hans, 118, 196
Barth, Karl, 2
Bartolus, 10
being and becoming, 161
Bible (or Scripture), 25, 47, 65, 92, 100, 208; Allen on, 5; Chenevière on, 207; Strauss on, 169, 209; Voegelin on, 189

Blumenberg, Hans, 21, 177–84; on creation, 183; on eschatology, 179; on history, 181–82, 183–84, 210; on necessity, 182; on Nietzsche, 181; and politics, 183, 184–85; on progress, 180; on science, 182–83; on self-assertion, 180–81, 182–83; on transcendence, 178, 181; on voluntarism, 182
Bodin, Jean, 17

calling, 30, 62, 95, 98–99, 206; political, 68, 70; of providential avenger, 77; public and private, 58, 71–73, 99
capitalism, 165, 166; and Strauss, 165, 166, 186, 211; Weber on, 3, 21
certainty of salvation, 131–133, 135, 137, 155; and church, 49; Luther on, 208; Voegelin on, 171–172, 211
Chalcedon, Council of, 157, 208
Chenevière, Marc-Edouard, 57, 65, 70, 79–80; on Calvin and modernity, 3; on democracy 203–4; on natural law, 101, 112, 113, 118; and right of resistance, 72–74, 77, 203–4; status of politics, 200–202
Christ, Jesus, 40, 44, 47, 48, 61, 82, 208; center of Calvin's theology, 157; mediator, 126–27, 137, 154–55; saving doctrine, 80
Christian freedom, 39–44, 45, 46, 52
church government, 44–62; and civil government, 26–28, 30, 32, 55–62, 88
Cicero, 67, 82–83

individualism, 4, 5, 73
inequality, 184, 194
Institutes of the Christian Religion, 8,
72–75, 78–80, 108, 189, 205; editions of, 38, 64–65, 202, 204; status
of, 20, 24, 199
inwardness and outwardness, 134, 136
Israel, 47, 66, 78, 79, 87, 117

Jonas, Hans, 191–92

knowledge: of God, 151, 152; as faith,
155–56; and self, 107, 141, 162
Knox, John, 17

Lang, August, 100
law: equality before, 66, 69–70, 92;
freedom from, 40, 44; natural,
moral, or divine law, 82–92, 100–
102, 106–14; spiritual, 42, 92
Lenin, Vladimir, 17
liberalism, 11–12, 14, 70, 98; and
Blumenberg, 184, 196–97
Little, David, 80, 206, 207–8
Locke, John, 17, 20, 114–115, 117,
196, 197, 202
Lord's Supper, sacrament of, 137–38
love, 40; and faith 91–92; Hobbes on,
190; Luther on, 129, 139, 208; of
neighbor, 89; rule of, 86–88, 91, 92,
100, 110, 114; of self, 89 93, 98, 155;
subordinated to God's glory, 139–
40; of truth 104–5; Weber on, 206;
Walzer on, 18
Löwith, Karl, 21–22, 167–70, 173–75,
178, 187; and Blumenberg, 182–83,
on history, 210
Luther, Martin, 2, 33, 60, 166, 198;
Chenevière on, 201; Christology,
137; and church, 140; experience,
127–28, 130, 208; and justification
by faith, 124; on Lord's Supper, 137;
and love, 139; and mysticism, 129–
30, 139; and sanctification, 135–36;
Quentin Skinner on, 8; Troeltsch
on, 158

magistrate, 30, 62, 63, 76, 77; coercive
character, 62, 63; and laws, 82–84;
mandate from God, 32, 67, 84; resistance to, 70–81
Marsiglio of Padua, 10, 16, 195
Marx, Karl, 117, 172, 191

materialism, 22, 99; and idealism, 20–
21, 25, 176–77, 179, 180, 185–87,
191, 209, 211
McNeill, John T., 72, 81, 83, 205
medieval thought, 4, 7, 19, 160, 197;
Allen on, 5–6, 32; Blumenberg on,
180, 182, 183; Doumergue on, 200–
201; Skinner on, 10, 15–16; Strauss
on, 168–69, 209; Voegelin on, 174;
Walzer on, 15, 196; Wolin on, 57
Mercier, Charles, 57, 67, 70, 79, 202–3
Mesnard, Pierre, 75
microcosm, 148, 161
Middle Ages. *See* medieval thought
Milner, Benjamin, 157, 159, 203, 209;
on Niesel, 158–59
minister, role of, 46–8, 69
Moses, 84–85
mysticism, 129–30, 133, 136

Niesel, Wilhelm, 128, 157, 159
nihilism, 192; J. W. Allen on, 6
nominalism, 159

obedience: duty of, 73, 75, 77; and
love, 88. *See also* resistance
Osiander, 125–28, 130, 136

pastor. *See* minister
perfection, 28, 48–49, 52, 54, 58, 60,
88–89, 105, 118, 159, 161, 202–3;
Augustine on, 211; Cicero on, 49;
Skinner on, 17; and Voegelin, 172,
191
philosophy, 48, 109, 144, 165–77, 204;
and Blumenberg, 183, 210; and
ethics, 92–93, 95; and ideology, 13;
and outward worship, 30; political,
and study of Calvinism, 187; and
soul, 101–5, 143–49, 151–52; and
Voegelin, 188, 210
Plato, 33, 82, 109, 144; Strauss on,
170; and Voegelin, 211; Wolin on,
33
political order. *See* civil government
Ponet, John, 9
preaching, 46–49; and discipline, 50,
55
predestination, 132–35
preservation, 39, 110–15, 117, 153;
Blumenberg on, 180–81
priests, 41–42, 46–47, 58
Protestantism, 26, 33, 34, 75, 78, 171
providence, 35–39; and creation, 152

Library of Congress Cataloging-in Publication Data

Hancock, Ralph Cornel.
  Calvin and the foundations of modern politics.

  Bibliography: p.
  Includes index.
  1. Calvin, Jean, 1509–1564. 2. Christianity and politics—History. 3. Political
science—History. I. Title.
BX9418.H28   1989   230′.42′0924   88–47931
ISBN 0–8014–2118–7 (alk. paper)